Open-hearted and hard-headed in equal measure—and with a delicious sense of humor—Diana Leafe Christian takes the reader on a comprehensive tour of the world of ecovillages and intentional communities. This is the volume for those exploring the options and willing to learn from those who have already trodden the path. There could be no better guide on the path of exploring this lifestyle.

— Jonathan Dawson, president, Global Ecovillage Network;
author, *Ecovillages: New Frontiers for Sustainability*

When you combine encyclopedic knowledge plus wry humor plus a realistic assessment of what the future holds for all of us, you get the wise advice in *Finding Community*. In a world after fossil fuels, it can extend the keys to your next car, your next house, and the rest of your life. If there is a silver lining to the clouds on the horizon, it will be found in the redesign of human communities. No one knows this subject better than Diana Leafe Christian. To a troubled world, here is the core of the solution.

— Albert Bates, co-founder, Global Ecovillage Network;
author, *The Post-Petroleum Survival Guide and Cookbook*

Through long experience and sheer social honesty, Diana Leafe Christian offers essential resources for and catalogs the oh-so-many pitfalls as well as delights of visiting and joining a community. *Finding Community* is like having an explorer's compass and a roll of charts under your arm as you embark upon unknown waters. All the more important to learn these essentials before you're out at sea!

— Richard Register, author, *Ecocities: Rebuilding Cities in Balance with Nature*;
president, Ecocity Builders; founder, International Ecocity Conferences

Diana Leafe Christian has done it again! Her first book, *Creating a Life Together*, has become something of a bible for would-be community founders. *Finding Community* promises to be just as important. Thoughtful, thorough, and engaging, and enlivened by stories from the trenches of real community life, it's a must-read for anyone seriously seeking community.

— Liz Walker, author, *Eco Village at Ithaca: Pioneering a Sustainable Culture*;
cofounder and director, EcoVillage at Ithaca

This charming and commonsensical guide to approaching intentional group living should be read by every serious community-seeker. It offers an amazingly knowledgeable perspective, warmly sympathetic but sometimes wryly humorous toward both communities and those who visit and join them.

— ERNEST CALLENBACH, author, *Ecotopia*

An amazing, comprehensive, collaborative and kaleidoscopic achievement! By showing community seekers practical living examples of cohousing projects, ecovillages, and other intentional communities, *Finding Community* has the potential to change the suburban way of life and help North America reconcile its ecological footprint.

— PROFESSOR DECLAN KENNEDY, architect, and member of Lebensgarten Ecovillage, Germany

This stunning overview of ecovillages and intentional communities is not only a terrific read, but abounds with essential, profoundly important information for anyone seeking more community and a sense of belonging in their lives.

— JOAN MEDLICOTT, author, *The Ladies of Covington Send Their Love* series and *The Three Mrs. Parkers*

Finding Community is full of wisdom and "Convenient Truths" for anyone wanting to join an ecovillage or intentional community, and packed with advice for ecovillages and communities wanting new members, too.

— MAX LINDEGGER, cofounder, Crystal Waters Ecovillage, Queensland, Australia; director, Global Ecovillage Network Asia/Oceania

Heartwarming and fun, *Finding Community* will help readers make informed choices about joining a community. Diana Leafe Christian knows what people want!

— HILDUR JACKSON, cofounder, Global Ecovillage Network (GEN); co-editor, *Ecovillage Living: Restoring the Earth and Her People*

Finding Community

How to join an Ecovillage or Intentional Community

Diana Leafe Christian

NEW SOCIETY PUBLISHERS

Cataloging in Publication Data:
A catalog record for this publication is available from the National Library of Canada.

Cover design by Diane McIntosh. Cover image copyright (c) Sally A. Sellers.
From an original hand-made quilt entitled "Excess Pleasure".

Printed in Canada.
First printing March 2007.

Paperback ISBN: 978-0-86571-578-3

Inquiries regarding requests to reprint all or part of *Finding Community*
should be addressed to New Society Publishers at the address below.

To order directly from the publishers,
please call toll-free (North America) 1-800-567-6772,
or order online at: www.newsociety.com

Any other inquiries can be directed by mail to:

New Society Publishers
P.O. Box 189, Gabriola Island, BC   V0R 1X0   Canada
1-800-567-6772

New Society Publishers' mission is to publish books that contribute in fundamental ways to building an ecologically sustainable and just society, and to do so with the least possible impact on the environment, in a manner that models this vision. We are committed to doing this not just through education, but through action. We are acting on our commitment to the world's remaining ancient forests by phasing out our paper supply from ancient forests worldwide. This book is one step toward ending global deforestation and climate change. It is printed on acid-free paper that is 100% old growth forest-free (100% post-consumer recycled), processed chlorine free, and printed with vegetable-based, low-VOC inks. For further information, or to browse our full list of books and purchase securely, visit our website at: www.newsociety.com

NEW SOCIETY PUBLISHERS   www.newsociety.com

≈ Contents ≈

SECTION 1: COMMUNITIES: AN OVERVIEW

SECTION 2: RESEARCHING

SECTION 3: VISITING

SECTION 4: JOINING

Acknowledgments

I AM GRATEFUL TO THE Fellowship for Intentional Community (FIC) for kind permission to excerpt liberally from *Communities* magazine, and to FIC board member and *Communities Directory* editor Tony Sirna for exceptional, invaluable assistance in every chapter.

And grateful to ecovillage activists on three continents — Lois Arkin, Liz Walker, Albert Bates, Jonathan Dawson, Robert Gilman, Hildur Jackson, Max Lindegger, Ina Meyer-Stoll, and Achim Ecker — for making sure the information on ecovillages is accurate and up-to-date. And for the same kind of help with cohousing communities: Michael McIntyre, Elana Kann, Bill Fleming, Raines Cohen, Betsy Morris, Chris ScottHanson, Zev Paiss, and Neshama Abraham. And for housing co-ops: Lois Arkin, Deborah Altus, Tree Bressen, and Jim Co-op Jones; Camphill Communities: Claus Sproll; Christian communities: Joe Peterson; and income-sharing communes: Tony Sirna, Tree Bresson, and Parke Burgess. And to Martha Harris, Arthur Rashap, and Geoph Kozeny for the right advice at the right time.

Special thanks to Lee Warren and other Earthaven members who've enlarged and enhanced my understanding of community membership issues — Sue Stone, Ivy Lynn, Mihaly Bartalos, Peter Bane, Chris Farmer, Brian Love, Arjuna daSilva, Martha Harris, Lee Finks, and Patricia Allison. And to the people who shared stories about delightful, awful, or funny experiences with community visitors: Holly Baumgartner, Mary DeDanan, Darren Geffert, Elana Kann, Ivy Lynn, Bill Metcalf, Betsy Morris, Valerie Renwick-Porter, Warwick Rowell, and Phil Tymon.

Much appreciation to the communities in the Pacific Northwest that shared their joining costs, and those all over North America that shared their visitors policies or membership processes: Twin Oaks, Red Earth Farms, Mariposa Grove, Abundant Dawn, Walnut Street Co-op, The Farm, Whole Village, EcoVillage at Ithaca, Lost Valley Educational Center, and Dancing Rabbit.

I gratefully acknowledge the communities movement writers and contributors to *Communities* magazine whose works I've excerpted or quoted from briefly: Jan Martin Bang, Frank Beaty, Tree Bressen, Bevelyn Carpenter, Nina Cohen, Maril Crabtree, Keenan Dakota. David Franklin, Kristin Gardner, Emily Headley, Hilary Hug and Robin Bayer, Larry Kaplowitz, Kat Kinkade, Nancy Lanphear, Virginia Lore, Orenda Lyons, Chris McLellan, Bill Metcalf, Tim Miller, Zev Paiss, Julie Pennington, Valerie Renwick-Porter, Michael G. Smith, Ted Sterling, Scott Thomas, Blair Vovoydic, Liz Walker, Shimon Whiteson, Roberta Wilson, Anna Young, and Irwin Wolfe Zucker.

And especially Liz Walker, Jane Gyhra, Sue Stone, Patricia Greene, Larry Kaplowitz, and Jan Steinman, whose insights were compelling enough to warrant their own chapters in this book.

Much appreciation to the wonderful folks at New Society Publishers, including publishers Chris and Judith Plant and editors Ingrid Witvoet and Murray Reiss.

And last but not least, much gratitude to communitarians Lois Arkin, Scott Horton, Carol Wagner, and Jan Steinman, whose steadfast friendship, affection, and humor during the months I wrote this book kept my heart open and spirits high.

Foreword

by Richard Heinberg

LIVING IN COMMUNITY has a primal appeal. We humans evolved in small hunter-gatherer bands; thus roughly 99 percent of our history as a species has been spent in groups of 15 to 50 individuals where each knew all of the others, and where resources were shared in a "gift economy." Even in recent centuries, the vast majority of people lived in villages or small towns. Little in our evolutionary past has prepared us for anonymous life in mass urban centers, suburbs, and exurbs. Therefore the goal of living in an intentional community with friends of like mind carries a deep and perennial psychic resonance.

Intentional communities can be influential centers of social and artistic innovation, as was the case with the Shaker villages, Brook Farm, and Oneida in 19th century America. However, at their worst such communities can be as dysfunctional as any troubled family. The word "cult" has acquired severely negative connotations for good reasons. If a group has strong authority figures whose opinions must be accepted unquestioningly, abuses of power are inevitable. A strong sense of group identity is often accompanied by feelings of superiority to outsiders. And while members may share high ideals, sometimes they merely convince themselves that they are making a difference in the world while in fact they are fairly insulated from the rest of society and concerned mostly with the promotion and welfare of the group itself.

Of course, not all intentional communities are cults, and in fact many mainstream institutions (including some corporations, religions, and military organizations) are far more cultic than most communes. Indeed, some communities make it a point to develop the critical thinking capacities of their members. This book would not exist, and I wouldn't be writing the foreword to it, if the path of intentional community were inevitably a dead end.

Nevertheless, the statistics are clear: most communal experiments cease after only a few months or years, and most people who devote themselves to building community wind up moving back to the mainstream world as communitarian refugees.

I speak from experience. I was once one of those refugees.

I helped organize a commune in Toronto in 1973, motivated by the realization (already clear over thirty years ago) that our culture is in a state of emergency. My friends and I envisioned two alternative responses: either we could try to create a miniature alternative culture as a model with which to demonstrate solutions to society's problems; or, we could band together simply to survive as the world disintegrated in chaos around us.

In that youthful freewheeling effort we made most of our decisions through a combination of psychic channeling, psychedelic group-mind expansion, consensus, and, if all else failed, voting. Conflict often centered on whether those who were contributing more money should have more influence in the group's direction. In retrospect, it was a rowdy, unfocused, but good-natured exercise that fizzled as most of the people involved gradually lost interest and left.

Then, in the late 1970s, I joined a spiritual organization that ran several well-established communities scattered mostly around North America, with a few also in Europe, Africa, and Australia. These communities functioned in a relatively stable and predictable way largely because the people in them obeyed a hierarchical chain of command. It took me what seems in retrospect to have been an extraordinary length of time to realize that I wasn't cut out for life in a spiritual community (I've since become an atheist). However, I met my wife Janet in one of those communities, and together we moved out in the early 1990s, eventually buying a house in the suburbs and accustoming ourselves to "normal" modern existence.

At its best, I found the communal experience deeply nourishing. It provided a sense of context, meaning, and purpose; there were opportunities for shared celebration and experimentation, and a sense of security engendered by the knowledge that "we're all in this together."

Janet and I made many good and close friends during those years — the kind of friends who, even if you've been apart for a decade or more, you feel deeply at home with the moment you see them. Even though I rarely spend time reminiscing about those days, I still find that, of the nighttime dreams I can recall upon waking, the most vivid are of being in community. There's something about the feeling of being able to walk a few steps to a friend's house to chat, watch a movie, or share a snack that gets under one's skin.

Today many people associate the idea of intentional community only with the hippie communes of the 1970s, but that flurry of collectivism was just the most recent of a series of waves of interest in experimental common living arrangements that goes back many centuries. The history of the earlier waves is told in many books, among which one of the first and most charming was Lewis Mumford's 1922 classic *The Story of Utopias*, which affectionately cataloged utopias of both escape and reconstruction.

As Mumford and others have pointed out, these waves often coincide with periods in which society as a whole becomes uninspiring or unbearable. Economic depressions spawn utopian experiments, as do times of cultural decline. In retrospect, the 1970s fit that description well: a generation of young people, disillusioned and alienated by a pointless and costly war in Southeast Asia and surrounded by a culture of soulless consumerism, understandably struck out on their own for other destinations, founding thousands of communes and communities as they went — some of them still in existence, such as The Farm in Tennessee and Twin Oaks in Virginia.

Any competent analyst of social trends would have to conclude that we are today entering a period in which the potential for economic and cultural decline far outstrips that of the 1970s.

Then, the world staggered from the effects of temporary oil shocks; today we stand on the verge of the granddaddy of oil shocks — the all-time peak of global petroleum production.

Then, the economy suffered from stagflation; today, the bursting of the mortgage, derivatives, and debt bubbles threatens to unleash a tide of foreclosures, bankruptcies, and currency devaluations not seen since the 1930s.

Then, we were witnessing the end of America's oil supremacy and the sunset of its resource-extraction and manufacture-based economy, to be replaced by imports, globalization, and debt.

Today, the debt-import model is itself unraveling, and the threat is not just to America's economic leadership, but to the basis of the entire global industrial system.

Then, America was mired in an unwinnable and unnecessary imperialist war in Vietnam; so far, today's American military project in the Middle East has been less deadly for US soldiers, but the conflict is hardly winding down; instead, it threatens to expand to include more countries, and its ultimate consequences may be dramatically worse than those of the Vietnam war. Then, we had Nixon. Today, we have Bush.

Then, pollution of air and water was the focus of the emerging world environmental movement. A controversial book, *Limits to Growth*, foretold that, if society continued on its path, collapse would ensue by the mid-21st century. Today, we are well into the new century and collapse appears increasingly likely due to climate chaos, water scarcity, and a growing list of other environmental problems.

In order to establish a different path we will need not just a few new policies, but the invention of a whole new culture — a culture not of growth, but of material modesty; one not of militarism, but of cooperation and negotiation. How and where will the needed new attitudes and practices be pioneered, if not in small experimental communities?

Moreover, if hard times lie ahead, what would make more sense than to band together with people of like mind so as to ride out the storm together, sharing resources and companionship along the way?

In short, this may be the most propitious moment in history to join an intentional community.

I have already noted the fact that most communal experiments persist for only a relatively short time.

If longevity is a goal in community building, then most folks who aim for utopia are doing something wrong. The evidence suggests that founding or joining a community is hard work that requires preparation and skill. How to avoid the traps of personality conflicts and unrealistic expectations? How to arrange finances in a fair and practical way? How to select and purchase land and hold title to it collectively? How to select an existing community without being drawn into the wrong one, or without inadvertently making oneself unwelcome in the right one? On all of these points and more, potential communitarians need information and assistance.

Diana Leafe Christian answered many of those questions in her previous book, *Creating a Life Together* (2003). She has as much knowledge of the current communities scene as anyone, and she put that knowledge to work to produce what is clearly the indispensable, state-of-the-art, "how-to" book on starting a community from scratch.

Now she brings the same knowledge and skills to bear on questions surrounding the project of joining an existing community. Together, these two books form an indispensable compendium of information that should be the constant companion to everyone interested in the communitarian path.

Finding Community has the most helpful table of contents of any book I've seen in years. That may at first seem like faint praise, but actually it is the reader's first and best clue that the book is well organized, well thought-out, and easy to access. The information is not only clearly ordered; it is of high quality, being based on good research and long experience. The reader will learn from members of a wide range of ecovillages, communes, cohousing developments, and co-ops, discovering the range of options, and getting a sense of what it takes to successfully make the leap from "normal" urban life to intentional community living.

Having disclosed some biographical information about myself in this foreword, I should perhaps proactively answer a question that has likely crossed the minds of a few readers: If I see the need for intentional communities today, and have had the experience of living in them, why I am not pursuing that path currently?

My personal strategy, at this stage in life, is to try to maximize the survival prospects for communities by making the inevitable collapse of fossil fuel-based industrial society a manageable one. I do not expect that national or municipal governments will handle the coming crises of economy, energy, food, water, climate, geopolitics, and population successfully, but nevertheless there is a wide range of scenarios for how events could unfold. The worst case would be very bad indeed, and if it were to eventuate then even the best-planned ecovillage might fare no better than the rest of society.

That is not to say that other people should shift their focus away from community-building to do what I'm doing: we each have our role to play in the unfolding transition, and I have enormous respect for my colleagues in communities like Dancing Rabbit ecovillage in northeast Missouri, Occidental Arts and Ecology Center in northern California, The Farm in Tennessee, and Earthaven in North Carolina. Perhaps, one day in the not too distant future, I will come knocking on one of their doors.

Meanwhile, here is my advice to you, the reader: if you feel drawn toward community, then join the wave. Waste no time. But prepare yourself with the wise counsel of Diana Leafe Christian.

Richard Heinberg is a journalist, editor, lecturer and the author of The Party's Over: Oil, War and the Fate of Industrial Civilizations, Powerdown, *and* The Oil Depletion Protocol: A Plan to Avert Oil Wars, Terrorism and Economic Collapse. *His is widely acknowledged as one of the world's foremost Peak Oil educators.*

⁐Introduction⁐

Ecovillages and Other Intentional Communities

IF YOU'RE SEEKING to create more of a "sense of community" in your life, or to live a more sustainable lifestyle in the good company of friends — especially now with the emergence of Peak Oil issues — this book can offer valuable insights and how-to advice. While you may know little about ecovillages or other kinds of intentional communities, the men and women you'll meet in these pages will show you what these communities are about and why they're increasingly appealing. So, whether you're one of the "cultural creatives" who would like to know more about ecovillages and intentional communities, or if you're actively seeking a community to join, let the stories in these pages inspire you.

What this Book Can Do For You

You'll find an overview of ecovillages and other kinds of intentional communities and what they're doing; how to contact them; and how to visit them enjoyably and evaluate them intelligently. If you find a community you'd like to join, you'll learn how to make a good impression on the group and enter into your new community life with grace and confidence.

If you're interested in this topic generally, my hope is to pique your interest and inspire you to learn more. If you're already planning to join a community, my hope is to help you evaluate and compare communities wisely and discern what may lie under the surface. I'd like you to be able to consider each potential new home in terms of your own long-term social, spiritual, financial, and legal well-being, and to evaluate how you can best stay in harmony with your personal vision and closely held values. This book will show you what to look for and how to look for it.

Community seekers also need to know how to avoid the common blunders that well-meaning but inexperienced people can make when first visiting and joining communities. You'll learn what to expect, how to join a community with more assurance, and how to enjoy the experience. This book will caution you to avoid impossibly high expectations, for example that living in community will solve everything. It will offer a realistic perspective, based on years of experience — my own, and those of experienced colleagues living in ecovillages, cohousing neighborhoods, and other kinds of intentional communities.

I'd like to guide you on this journey because I've explored the subject from several perspectives — from those of community seekers, community founders, and communities seeking new members. As editor of *Communities* magazine since 1993, I've been privy to dozens of anecdotes and stories from communities across North America about what works and what doesn't work in terms of new people joining them — and dozens of similar stories from people who have visited communities and found those that impressed them and those that seemed troubled. I've helped friends visit and join communities, and sought and successfully joined a community myself, Earthaven Ecovillage, where I now focalize its Membership committee. I've also researched what it takes to start successful new communities, and written a book on the subject — *Creating a Life Together: Practical Tools to Grow Ecovillages and Intentional Communities* — published by New Society Publishers in 2003. I give workshops and speak at conferences about these topics all over North America, where I meet more community members and community seekers and have learned even more about this topic. This book is an opportunity to share what I've learned with you.

Who This Book is For

This book is first for "cultural creatives" — people who value environmentally sustainable living, cooperation, and a sense of community (and who perhaps have a spiritual practice) — but may not know much about ecovillages or intentional communities and would enjoy learning more. It's for people who want to know more about folks who live off the grid, grow their own food, or create their own biodiesel fuel, for example, or who share meals with friends and neighbors, raise their children cooperatively with others, work at jobs they find fulfilling, create their own home-grown entertainment — and thrive. People exactly like this visit ecovillages and intentional communities every week. "We didn't know a place like this existed!" they often say.

It's also for people who might consider joining an ecovillage or intentional community sometime in the future — and who'd like some guidance in the meantime about how to go about it.

Lastly, it's for active "community seekers" — people engaged in the process of seeking an ecovillage or another kind of sustainable intentional community — who would like some tips and pointers on how to make the journey far easier.

What is an Intentional Community?

My favorite definition of an intentional community is Bill Metcalf's in *The Findhorn Book of Community Living* (Findhorn Press, 2004): "Intentional communities are formed when people choose to live with or near enough to each other to carry out a shared lifestyle, within a shared culture and with a common purpose." Most intentional communities share land or housing or live in adjacent properties, though a few are non-residential. Most govern themselves with some form of participatory democracy, such as consensus decision-making, super-majority voting, or majority-rule voting. Relatively few (usually spiritual or religious communities) are governed by a spiritual or religious leader or a group of leaders.

The common purposes of communities vary widely. *Ecovillages*, for example, are intentional communities which model and demonstrate ecologically sustainable lifestyles. They can be urban or rural. My favorite definition of an ecovillage comes from Robert and Diane Gilman, in 1990: "A human-scale, full-featured settlement, in which human activities are harmlessly integrated into the natural world in a way that is supportive of healthy human development and can be successfully continued into the indefinite future." Ecovillage members tend to live as sustainably as they can, which often includes (depending on their setting) growing much of their own organic food, living in passive-solar homes made of natural materials such as strawbale or cob, generating their own renewable energy, car-pooling and/or using biodiesel fuels, and so on. We'll explore ecovillages much more thoroughly in Chapter 4.

The almost 100 *cohousing communities* in North America offer great family neighborhoods owned and managed by the residents themselves — ideal places in which to raise children or grow older. In fact, elder cohousing, a new but growing trend in the cohousing movement, offer seniors an appealing alternative to retirement communities. In cohousing communities people live in smaller-than-normal housing units, often in two-story townhouse-style dwellings, and share common ownership of a large "common house" with kitchen, dining room, meeting space, children's play area, laundry facilities, and other shared amenities, and in which they share optional meals several nights a week.

Urban group households of various kinds offer their residents lowered housing costs, shared expenses, and a lively social scene. Some urban communities are organized as housing co-ops, including student housing co-ops, elder housing co-ops, and limited equity housing co-ops. These allow students, elders, and people with limited funds, respectively, to share ownership of their housing, share resources, make decisions cooperatively, and enjoy a closer connection to their neighbors than they would simply living in apartment buildings or condos.

Rural back-to-the-land homesteads offer their members the opportunity to grow much of their own food and practice rural self-reliance skills. Communities organized as conference and retreat centers, holistic healing centers, and sustainability education centers are often rural, food-growing settlements as well, offering workshops and courses to the public.

Spiritual communities such as yoga ashrams and Buddhist meditation centers provide spiritual teaching and common spiritual practices, while spiritually eclectic communities welcome members with a variety of different spiritual paths, and often offer public workshops on a wide variety of spiritual and personal growth themes. Some spiritual communities, such as the over 100 Camphill Communities in Europe and North America, serve the needs of developmentally disabled adults or children in a community setting.

Christian communities offer Christian fellowship and shared worship. Some are income-sharing, some are not. Some Christian communities also provide needed services to others, for example, the Catholic Worker communities in many cities offer food and shelter for the urban homeless. By the way, most scholars of intentional communities include Catholic monasteries and convents, which they consider the most long-lived form of intentional community in the Western world.

In most income-sharing communes, members operate one or more community businesses. Each member receives room and board, and the community either pays them a small stipend or pays for their basic needs, such as clothes, toiletries, nutritional supplements, medical care, and so on. In some income-sharing communes members work outside the community, and pool their salaries or wages, with the same arrangement — receiving room, board, and a stipend, or the community pays for their basic needs. I use the term "commune" in this income-sharing sense, and not as a synonym for "intentional community," as many journalists mistakenly do.

We'll look at each of these kinds of communities more closely. But to start with, let's look at why anybody would want to live in an intentional community.

Communities: an Overview

Chapter 1

Why Community?

HERE ARE SEVEN reasons why you might enjoy living in an ecovillage or intentional community.

- It's **more environmentally sound.** You can live on the planet with a smaller ecological footprint.
- It's **safer.** You can raise a family or grow older in a wholesome, safe environment.
- It's **healthier.** Medical researchers find that people live healthier lives if they have many close social connections, particularly as they get older.
- It's **cheaper.** Shared resources and economies of scale reduce the cost of living.
- It's **more satisfying.** You can experience a sense of connection and support with like-minded friends and colleagues.
- **You'll grow as a person.** You will undoubtedly become more self-aware, and possibly more tolerant and compassionate. You'll learn better communication skills, and will become better at participating in meetings. You can learn new skills in other realms. And you'll probably develop more self-confidence.
- It's **more fun.** You can experience the child's delight of sharing life's pleasures with friends.

But first, what do we mean by "ecovillages and intentional communities?"

"Intentional communities are formed when people choose to live with or near enough to each other to carry out a shared lifestyle, within a shared culture and with a common purpose," writes Bill Metcalf in *The Findhorn Book of Community Living* (Findhorn Press, 2004). Ecovillages, cohousing neighborhoods, urban group households, housing co-ops, service-based communities, therapeutic communities, organized neighborhoods, Christian communities (including monasteries and convents), rural homesteading communities, conference and retreat center communities, income-sharing communes, spiritual communities, and yoga ashrams and Buddhist meditation centers are all intentional communities. They all share land or housing, share some resources, and have common agreements. Most govern themselves with some form of participatory democracy, such as consensus decision-making, majority-rule voting, or an agreement-seeking method (such as 90 percent voting), however a very small number (often spiritual or religious communities) are governed by a leader or a group of elders. What's different about each of these kinds of communities is their shared lifestyle and common purpose, which I call a community's "mission and purpose." We'll take a much closer look at ecovillages (Chapter 4), cohousing communities (Chapter 5), and other kinds of intentional communities (Chapters 6 through 10).

Now, back to the reasons you might enjoy living in such a place.

1. You'll live on the planet with a smaller ecological footprint.

Clearly sharing resources not only saves money but reduces environmental impact. If we cluster housing, we're using less land for buildings and have more land to grow food (or leave as wilderness). If we use common-wall housing units with shared foundations and roofs we're saving building materials such as wood and reducing the impacts on air, water, and soil of manufacturing concrete, sheetrock, plywood, paint, rebar, and metal lath and fasteners. If we share common utility systems, and, as many communities do, build passive solar buildings, and/or use gravity-fed spring water or roof-water catchment, we're saving on energy use and conserving water. If, as many communities do, we recycle graywater or compost or otherwise use our kitchen, human, or packaging waste, we're reducing the need for sewage services and reducing landfill space. If, as some communities do, we grow our own food, particularly with compost we make ourselves, we reduce the use of fossil fuel-created commercial fertilizer, petroleum-based plastic, and paper for packaging, and the impacts on air, water, and soil of transporting food long distances and storing and refrigerating it at distribution points and retail stores. And if, as some communities do, we organize a carpool or community vehicle co-op, and/or use biodiesel fuel, we are obviously benefiting the environment.

Most intentional communities and certainly ecovillages do many of these practices. Chances are that if you lived in community, you'd be impacting the Earth more beneficially, or at least less harmfully.

Several European ecovillages have found ways to measure their ecological impact. For example, Munkesoegaard, a 100-household ecovillage near Copenhagen in Denmark, learned that they used 38 percent less water than the average Danish household, and 25 percent less electricity. Carbon dioxide emissions from their wood-pellet heating system and from their electricity consumption are both 60 percent lower than the average Danish household, and Munkesoegaard residents who carpool drove only 5 percent of the Danish average.

Similarly, researchers at the University of Kassel in Germany compared carbon dioxide emissions from the daily lifestyles of the average German household, three local "ecological households," and two German ecovillages: Kommune Niederkaufungen and Ökodorf Sieben Linden. The researchers measured CO_2 emissions along the chain of events to create, use, and/or transport electricity, heating, water, and food (including the transport of food grown elsewhere to the local markets). They also measured the CO_2 emissions of each member's work and vacation travel. Given the current number of people on the planet, they determined a baseline for an acceptable level of CO_2 emissions. (Not surprisingly, they found that the average German household emitted six times the minimum acceptable level of CO_2 emissions.) The researchers found that the CO_2 emissions of the two ecovillages were still higher than the minimum acceptable baseline, although the CO_2 emissions of Ökodorf Sieben Linden, for example, were only around 28 percent of the average German household. When it came to heating their buildings, Sieben Linden's emissions were only ten percent of the national average, and they achieved a level of six percent of the national average in all the processes involved in constructing their buildings, the materials used, etc. They also found that the two ecovillages used far less water, electricity, heating fuel, and fossil-fuel for heating and food (including transporting food), than either the ecological households or the average German household. This was because the ecovillagers lived in shared, clustered, passive-solar housing with high insulation and efficient heating systems; ate mostly vegetarian diets; grew much of their own food; and earned a living on their homesites rather than traveling to other locations very much.

The 400 members of Findhorn Foundation in northern Scotland have a 40 percent smaller "ecological footprint" than the UK average, according to a 2005 study. An ecological footprint analysis measures a given population's impact on the environment by translating the impact of its activities — buildings, clothes, food, water, energy, and all products and services used — into the amount of biologically productive land needed to create and maintain these activities. By dividing the total number of biologically productive acres on the Earth by the global population (and allowing for other species' needs), environmentalists have determined that each person's "fair share" — how much land one would ideally use to support their activities — is about three acres per person. While many Third World countries use far less than their fair share, with people in Nepal, for example, using less than half an acre per person, typical North Americans use about 30 acres per person and Europeans use about 15 acres per person. Yet Findhorn found that the ecological footprint of the average community member was about 8 acres, or 60 percent of the UK national average.

Cohousing communities — small, close-knit urban and suburban neighborhoods owned and managed by the residents themselves — often use "green" building materials, recycle, and use super-energy-efficient heating, power, and water systems as well. In the late 1990s Australian architect Graham Meltzer surveyed 278 households in 12 cohousing communities in Canada, the US, Japan, New Zealand, and Australia. He found reduced car use, more efficient land use, and more sustainable energy use. Specifically:

+ Seventy-two percent of the cohousers surveyed reported reduced driving as well as increased biking and walking, most likely because they coordinated casual errands with neighbors, and they had more social and recreational opportunities at home — and many stayed home to work in home offices. On average, driving was reduced nine percent.

+ Cohousing communities use less land and building materials than mainstream housing developments, while they vary widely in population density. Because housing is often common-wall and clustered, cohousing communities are usually more compact in their use of land. Suburban cohousing communities in the US and Australia are more than twice as dense as conventional suburban developments, and the units themselves are about half the size of typical new-built houses in the US.

+ A consistent five-to-six percent improvement in energy conservation practices was found in all cohousing communities surveyed, with a nine percent average improvement in water conservation habits. While most cohousing founders have strong environmental practices to start with, the strongest ecological impact is from people who learn to modify their practices after living in cohousing for awhile. It seems that the longer residents live in cohousing, the more likely they'll improve their pro-environmental practices.

2. You'll feel safer.

People feel safer living in an intentional community, since they're usually surrounded by people they know and trust. Even in urban communities they often live on a larger parcel of land than if they lived in a single-family home. This property is not only familiar and welcoming to them, but also serves as a buffer zone between them and outside property, creating kind of a "safe inside the nest" effect. People in group households in a large house in a city also feel more secure. When you are home there are usually a few other people there too. This helps people feel a sense of familiarity, comfort, and ease.

According to gerontologist Deborah Altus, who conducted a study with 60 residents of 3 rural senior cooperative housing communities, 95 percent said that living in the co-op had a good effect on their personal safety. (Altus, D. E., and Mathews, R. M, *Cooperative Housing Journal*, 1977.)

At Earthaven Ecovillage in North Carolina, where I live, people walk freely along the roads from one neighborhood to another, even late at night, with a feeling of complete familiarity and comfort.

Compared to the increasingly violent mainstream culture, intentional communities are islands of safety for women, who are much less likely to encounter abusive or threatening strangers near their home. They're much less likely to fear getting beat up or raped.

"There are almost no reports of attacks or physical violence at all in any of the communities I have visited or have knowledge of," writes Keenan Dakota, who has lived at Twin Oaks community in Virginia since 1984 and visited many others. "Except for armed survivalist communities, the members of every community I'm familiar with appear to be open and trusting. Compare this to the often constant caution and awareness of potential danger present in mainstream culture."

In community, children feel safe — and their parents feel relieved. Concern for their children's safety and well-being is a major reason some families join communities, in fact. Since people drive cars more slowly on community roads, or, as in cohousing communities, cars are confined to the edge of the property, children are in much less danger of getting hit by cars. Not only that, children are surrounded by caring adults besides their parents who look out for them.

Even domestic violence appears to be less common in communities, although people certainly *do* bring their emotional problems with them when they join communities. However, consider the "fish bowl effect" of living in community. Not much goes on in a household in community that one's neighbors aren't aware of. If the community is small enough, and close enough, people won't let abuse within a family continue. The group will call a meeting with the family to try to work it out, or send people with good processing and communication skills over to talk with the family. Even if such interventions are seen as unwelcome meddling, it does put the family members on notice that the "community eye" is upon them, and even that slight amount of social pressure can induce people to behave better towards one another. It not only "takes a village to raise a child," it takes a village to raise all of us!

3. You'll most likely be healthier.

Medical research has found there is a direct link between good health and living with a sense of community. People with strong social ties tend to have lower healthcare costs, recover faster from illness, and live longer — one of the reasons the Danish government has supported the development of over 100 senior cohousing communities since the mid-1980s.

"There is strong scientific evidence of the connection between community and healing," writes Blair Vovoydic, M.D., in *Communities* magazine. "Of all the many influences on our health, interpersonal relationships are not only a factor, but increasingly are being recognized as the most crucial factor. One study showed that people who said they did not have anybody that could help them out if they were sick or broke had three times the risk or premature death from all causes than those who knew they could get help if they needed it...."

More studies:

- In the late 1990s *The Journal of Emergency Medicine* published two articles demonstrating that good social support is the most predictive indicator of someone's chances of avoiding a second heart attack, more so than a person's cholesterol level, measurable heart function, amount of exercise, or whether or not the person smokes or has diabetes.

- In studies beginning in 1966, researchers from Harvard and Yale found that while most American men 55–65 have increasing numbers of heart attacks, in the close-knit town of Roseto, Pennsylvania, whose Italian-American residents were regularly looking after one another and were active in local social and service organizations, men 55–64 had almost no heart attacks, and men over 65 had half the death rate from heart attacks as the national average.

- A research team from Harvard University School of Public Health, Yale University School of Medicine, and Rush Institute for Healthy Aging in Chicago, found that social and productive activities were equally as significant as physical exercise in promoting longer, healthier lives in Americans 65 and older. (*British Medical Journal*, August, 1991.)

- Research by Bernard A. Shaw at State University of New York, Albany, found that neighborliness, and the expectation of help from neighbors, tend to be highly correlated with elder adults remaining more physically functional into their later years. (*Research on Aging*, Vol. 27, 2005).

How does it work, Dr. Vovoydic asks? "It is likely that people manifest healthier behaviors, such as eating better, when they're with other people. They also tend to do more 'self-correcting' with a higher degree of social interactions. Living with other people usually results in getting feedback that can serve to steer us back on track if we're behaving in ways that we don't realize are unhealthy." (*Communities*, Spring, 1999.)

4. You'll save money.

After the initial expense of joining an ecovillage or another form of intentional community and the expense of building or buying a home there, the cost of living is often a lot less than in mainstream culture. Usually members share the expenses of property taxes, property insurance, and maintenance and repair costs of common physical infrastructure. The group can share many expenses and might only need one tractor, snow plow, laundry room, or crafts room, for example — each household doesn't need its own. If there's a community garden, many people can share the costs of garden fencing, sheds, carts, and soil amendments, seeds, plant starts, etc. Depending on the group's agreements and degree of trust, the expense for chainsaws, weed-eaters, large power tools, or a whole woodshop or sewing room can be shared, reducing the cost for everyone. According to Deborah Altus's study mentioned earlier, for example, 69 percent said living in a senior housing co-op had a positive impact on their financial situation.

And for every meal a community eats together, the cost of food is less from buying at a volume discount. "We're proud of how much money our food committee has saved members while providing delicious, nutritious food," observes Nancy Lanphear of Songaia Cohousing in Bothell, Washington. "We serve five common meals a week, and stock our community pantry, from which our members can take any food items they need for preparing meals at home, for $80 per month per adult member. The fee for children is $5 per year of the child's age; for example, a three-year-old is $15 per month. I believe it's possible for members to live well on our community-purchased food alone, without needing to purchase additional food, although of course they can and often do. Obviously it's a lot cheaper to live a community lifestyle when it has a well-organized food system like this." (*Communities*, Fall, 2002.)

Most communities are well aware of the money-saving factor. "Our mission," write the founders of St. Anthony Park Cohousing in St. Paul, Minnesota, "is to be a community for people who want to live simply among friends rather than extravagantly among strangers."

"We live simply and well," say members of Lost Valley Educational Center in Oregon.

Of course your cost-of-living expenses in community will vary widely with regional property values, the scale of your lifestyle and amenities of your dwelling or homesite, and the number of other community members among whom common expenses are shared.

SHARED HOUSING, REDUCED COSTS

At Magic, a residential service-learning community in Palo Alto, California, seven adults and two children live comfortably by North American standards, and luxuriously by global standards. We do this on less than half the average per capita income in our area, and with less than half the per capita pollution and resource depletion of an average US resident. We earn our livelihoods by studying and teaching how people can learn to apply ecological principles to further the common good, and enjoy round-the-clock access to each other's thoughtful counsel. We can afford all this by living in community.

Sharing housing can help improve personal well-being, reduce social inequality, and protect environmental quality. Renting or purchasing a four-bedroom home or apartment is less than four times as expensive as renting or purchasing four comparable one-bedroom dwellings. Providing a kitchen and bathroom for every bedroom increases environmental impacts and labor burdens as well.

The average US household contains between two and three occupants, and between one and two bathrooms. Because at Magic we lay claim to fewer than 'our share' of bathrooms — about one-tenth of a bathroom per person instead of one-half

— we've avoided $100,000 of capital expenditures. We also reap savings by cleaning one, rather than five bathrooms.

Seven adults in the US each living alone, typically pay for seven phone lines. They either answer their phones, let a machine do it, or miss their calls. At Magic we share two lines. We take calls for each other, serving callers and called, and becoming better acquainted with each other's family and friends in the process. For being each other's personal assistants, each enjoys the services of several personal assistants.

A high-speed Internet connection costs less and is faster and more reliable than seven dial-ups. Our single utility bill is a fraction of what we would pay if each of us lived alone. We've one washer and one dryer to purchase and maintain. We clean and repair less than two thousand square feet of floor space, including workspace, and we service one, rather than two or five or seven, of everything from an ax to a zoom lens. Our pooled tools, books, vehicles, musical instruments, recreational equipment, etc. are so extensive that friends and neighbors regularly borrow from us. The list goes on and on.

— Hilary Hug and Robin Bayer,
Communities magazine, Fall 2002.

5. You'll grow as a person.

"In my years at Twin Oaks I've been passionate about understanding what community is and how it affects people," writes Keenan Dakota, "so I've talked with hundreds of members (and particularly ex-members) of other communities who have come through here. I've also visited over 20 other communities and attended many communities conferences. So, based on this extensive, broad-based, and yet informal research, here are some tentative conclusions.

"People appear to experience personal growth and at times profound transformation from living in community, even in communities which are not focused on personal growth per se. Community members report common results, regardless of the size, focus, location, or governance structure of their communities. Here, in no particular order, are what current and ex-community members most often report as the changes they've experienced:

- *Increased self-confidence.*
- *Better communication skills.*
- *Broader perspective.*
- *Clearer thinking.*
- *Less idealism.*
- *Increased responsibility.*
- *Broader set of skills.*
- *Broader general (useful) knowledge.*
- *Increased awareness of personal limitations.*

"What makes communities tend to foster these similar patterns of personal change? First, communities are small social entities so the social relationships among members are intimate and intense. And because communities are self-selecting, inevitably more homogeneity is present than in the culture at large. And most communities are, to some degree, socially self-reliant.

"A byproduct of living in mainstream culture is the sense of being cut off from contact with other people — variously called alienation, isolation, or anomie. While members of communities may not always find the intimacy they desire, communitarians at least seem to accept each other and encourage personal challenge and exploration. In community, without fearing of harsh judgments or negative consequences, it's much easier to take personal risks. Many community members find this profoundly liberating.

"All of these factors taken together seem sufficient to explain why community members may become more confident, are better able to communicate, develop a broader perspective, and become more responsible. But why should living in community make them more aware of their personal limitations?

"I suspect it's this: community living provides a brutally accurate mirror. We see each other, and we see our selves in more detail than most people were accustomed to before coming to community. Some members can't handle this incidental and unavoidable openness, and leave, seeking more privacy. But for most of us, observing that even wonderful people around us also have glaring imperfections is a release from our own expectations of perfection, and from self-punishment for our failings.

"The community mirror reveals our capabilities and keeps us from effectively hiding our shortcomings. We tend to blossom with previously unknown strengths, and accept and shrug off the revelation of any shortcomings, rather than being devastated by them.

"It is true that not everyone is cut out for community, and I doubt that any one communitarian will experience growth and change in his or her life exactly as I have outlined, as I certainly didn't conduct a rigorous empirical study. Nevertheless, I have found these trends to be generally true. If you join a community, you will almost certainly find your life enriched as a person — often in ways you never could have imagined." (*Communities*, Spring, 1995.)

6. You'll experience connection and support with like-minded friends and colleagues.

In Deborah Altus's study of 60 members of rural senior housing co-ops, 92 percent reported that living in the co-op had a good effect on their life satisfaction. "An overwhelming majority of respondents also indicated that the co-op had a positive effect on the quality of their contact with friends (83 percent), the amount of contact with friends (82 percent), their happiness (81 percent)."

In the Spring, 1995, issue of *Communities* magazine, Orenda Lyons wrote:

I was raised in an alternative community where cooperation, acceptance, and support were the codes of life. The Miccosukee Land Co-op near Tallahassee, Florida, was started in the early '70s. My parents were among the first to buy land in the Co-op and I was born 11 days after they moved into a yet-to-be-completed house. Nestled deep in the pine and cypress wetlands, miles outside the city limits, the roads, property, community center and the entire Co-op was — and is — my playground.

Growing up, I had many families: my Co-op playmates were my siblings and their parents were also my parents. As children we had preschool in each other's homes and roamed the community freely. I remember once my best friend Kristin's yard flooded and about six of us carried a canoe a half mile to her house; we then canoed through her yard and up a path to another friend's house. We believed that the Co-op belonged to us, but as we grew we found that in actuality, it possessed us.

The memories of my childhood lie every-

where, from the creek beds we would tromp through to the room in our house where my sister was born. I have seen changes in the land and in the people. I've learned from disagreements among the children and among the adults of the community. I have found a home in the forests, swamps, and families, and hopefully, helped make a home here for others.

As people moved to the Co-op and new acres were developed, everyone helped with the building of the houses and the settling in of the new households. On the common land, the pool, community center, and boardwalks were all constructed by everyone giving up a weekend or two for the benefit of the neighborhood. We had a way of making something spring out of almost nothing.

As with any close group, the Co-op family has experienced tragedy. In 1988 a founding member of the community died of AIDS, and another, my uncle, died in 1989, just months after a teenage girl was killed in a car accident. Besides this, two houses have burned and two older men have passed on. Through all of it, everyone has always been there for each other. I remember going to see my friend and neighbor Gerry the day he died. We stopped by on the way home from school and arrived about 30 minutes after he passed away. He had been suffering from AIDS for quite a while and we (and many others) had prepared meals for him and helped him out for months. My mother was at his side when he died, and minutes later friends and relatives gathered to mourn his death, comfort each other, and celebrate his life. Such was also the case with Chip, who died on my 14th birthday. I went to see him, but walking out to his house I met up with my parents, who gave me the news. I still regret not being there at the end.

It is priceless what we can learn from disaster. But what is incredible, what really amazes me, is the way it brings people closer. People stick together so selflessly in times of need. One person's lack of strength is balanced out by ten strong hearts. One family's sorrow is felt by all. Fundraisers to help them, or friends to console them, are just the beginning.

There are other things which I have gained by living here. The vast diversity of the households encourages acceptance of every kind of living arrangement, culture, and belief. These are taught from parent to child, from child to child, and taken out into the world around us. Happiness abounds in our community through the birth of children, the marriages, the parties, and the celebrations of life and Earth — truly these are the heart of community. Looking back, I would never dream of changing one detail of growing up here. When I think of the ideal place to raise a family, I think of the Co-op. When I think of the most stable and largest family anywhere, I think of the Co-op. When I think of myself, I think of the Co-op. It has made me who I am.

7. You'll have more fun.

"I love the fact that sometimes someone will make a special treat for the whole house," writes David Franklin about living at Walnut Street Co-op in Eugene, Oregon. "I love when some of us will spontaneously decide to rent a movie, make popcorn, and pile onto someone's bed; or walk over to the neighborhood bar to shoot pool and sing *karaoke* together. I love being able to stop and talk with someone for a couple of minutes, to have people who can pick me up from the airport, and to laugh at meals with, or to know that if someone can't do something around the house that someone else will volunteer to cover for them. I love that

sometimes we can support each other around our struggles and difficulties, and help each other out." (*Communities*, Winter, 2004.)

In *EcoVillage at Ithaca: Pioneering Sustainable Community*, Liz Walker writes:

One of the most fulfilling aspects of our community life is celebrating together. And it doesn't take much to spark a party — just someone with inspiration and the energy to organize. Add some shared food or drink and a little music, dance, or ritual, and voila!

We celebrate Easter with an egg hunt and Chanukah with potato latkes (cooked by the dozen). Other Jewish holidays, Christmas tree decorating, a big Thanksgiving feast (complete with the option of vegan turkey), and occasionally a Buddhist-inspired ceremony or Earth-based spirituality ritual all take the spotlight during the year. We have corn roasts in the fall and a strawberry festival on the summer solstice. Birthday parties happen year-round. And we don't stop at ordinary parties. What makes our community extraordinary is that we often invent our own celebrations, drawing from many traditions — or creating a new one. We live for those times of creative and meaningful fun.

...At EcoVillage at Ithaca meaningful human contact is the norm and not the exception. I consider myself blessed to live here. I can maintain my privacy when I need to, but also have plenty of opportunity to form and develop my connections with my cohousing neighbors. Indeed, I think that living in community fills the deep longing for human love and connection that is shared by our whole species.

Excerpted with permission from EcoVillage at Ithaca: Pioneering Sustainable Community, *by Liz Walker (New Society Publishers, 2005).*

This all sounds fine, you may say, but what about the unpleasant or downright awful things that can happen to people who live in intentional communities? In the next chapter we'll closely examine some of the most common myths about life in community. Are the scary stories we sometimes hear about communities true?

Chapter 2

Ten Most Common Fears
about Joining a Community

THE FOLLOWING is adapted in part from the Fellowship for Intentional Community's "13 Myths About Intentional Community."

1. I don't want to live out in the boonies.
You don't have to. A total of 1,520 communities listed themselves in the Online Directory of the Fellowship for Intentional Community (FIC) in 2006. (*directory.ic.org*) Of the nearly 1,000 communities which noted whether they were urban or rural, four out of ten (412) said they were urban, suburban, or located in small towns. Six out of ten (592) said they were rural. In this sample, anyway, at least 40 percent of the communities listing themselves online were not located way out in the country.

2. I don't want to live with a bunch of hippies.
Few community members today consider themselves hippies. Some might identify themselves as non-mainstream or countercultural, others might identify themselves as relatively mainstream people who have an interest in community and sustainability. Many, such as members of cohousing communities, are essentially middle-class to upper-middle class people who live relatively normal lives — though more progressive, cooperative, and ecologically sustainable than most. Most communitarians are hard-working and responsible, not folks who fit the image of '60s-era hippie stereotypes. What do most communitarians have

in common? They tend to be health-conscious, environmentally aware, and politically and culturally progressive — the "cultural creatives" whom authors Paul Ray and Sherry Ruth Anderson describe in their book *Cultural Creatives: How 50 Million People Are Changing the World* (Three Rivers Press, 2001).

3. I don't want to live a "poverty consciousness" lifestyle with limited resources.
You'll find many different standards of living in ecovillages and intentional communities. Some embrace voluntary simplicity; others have full access to the comforts of contemporary life. Nearly all communities use the benefits of common ownership to allow people access to facilities and equipment they don't need to own privately — for example, hot tubs, saunas, pools, exercise rooms, yoga rooms, power tools, washers and dryers, pickup trucks, tractors, and so on.

Newly formed communities often start off with limited resources and thus their members tend to live simply. As the community gets more established over time, it tends to create a stable economic base and its members gradually enjoy a physically more comfortable life — according to their own standards.

4. I don't want to live with countercultural types who are trying to avoid responsibility.
Many people choose to live in community because

it offers an alternative way of life from that of the wider society, yet most community members still raise families, maintain and repair their land and buildings, work for a living, pay income and property taxes, etc.

At the same time, communitarians usually perceive their lifestyle as more caring and satisfying than that of mainstream culture, and because of this — and the increased free time which results from pooling resources and specialized skills — many community members feel they can engage *more* effectively with the wider society.

5. I don't want to have to join a religion or take up some spiritual practice I don't believe in.

You choose what kind of community you join, and you can choose from plenty of secular communities, or those which are spiritually eclectic and don't have a common spiritual practice. (See Chapter 8, "Spiritual Communities," and Chapter 9, "Christian Communities.") In the FIC's Online Directory listings (in 2006), of those which noted whether they had a shared spiritual path, 45 percent said they did, indicating that slightly more than half the intentional communities that listed themselves do not have a common spiritual practice.

6. I don't want to live in a hierarchical system or follow a charismatic leader.

Very few communities are hierarchical, and again, which one you join is your choice. The most common form of community governance is democratic, with decisions made by consensus or some form of voting. Of the 1,228 communities which checked the "governance" section of the FIC's Online Directory in 2006, nearly two-thirds (867) used a democratic form of governance, including consensus decision-making (747) or majority rule voting (120). About one-sixth (213) used a hierar-chical model, including a community leader (65) or group of elders (148), and about one-twelfth (148) used some other form of governance which they didn't specify.

7. I don't want to have to think like everyone else. What if it turns out to be a cult?

Is community living like living with the Borg on Star Trek? Do massive part-human, part machine cyborgs suddenly appear in front of you and announce in a monotone chorus of electronic voices: *"You will be assimilated. Resistance is futile."*? As every Trekkie knows, after the half-human/half-machine Borg suddenly materialize and deliver their chilling announcement, they beam you off to their starship where you are biomechanically morphed into a cyborg yourself — destined to an immortal, never-escape existence as one more cell in the Borg's "hive mind."

Fortunately, this won't happen. Unlike with the Borg on Star Trek, people who join communities don't get assimilated, and in most groups community members don't all think alike. Members of any given community do hold many more values and beliefs in common than a comparable group of typical neighbors, since the community is organized around a common vision or purpose. However, disagreements about what they want or how to spend their funds are a common occurrence in most communities, just as in the wider society. Community members certainly don't all live in a "hive mind," but can have widely diverging opinions. Just ask any process and communications consultants called in to help resolve disputes!

The concern about intentional communities being potentially dangerous "cults" is one of the most common and significant misconceptions held by people unfamiliar with the subject, so we'll examine it in more detail.

I agree with the view of the US-based Fellowship of Intentional Community (FIC), publishers of *Communities* magazine. In a Fall 1995 issue on "cults," guest editor Tim Miller, a professor of religion at the University of Kansas, noted that when people call a community a "cult," they're really saying that they don't like or understand the group's beliefs and practices. Tim Miller and the FIC encourage people not to call intentional communities "cults," which tends to slur all communities, but to just say "I don't like them," "I don't understand them," or "I strongly disagree with their methods," if that's the case. If you believe the group is lying, manipulative, and emotionally abusive, or that it is patriarchal and demeans women, the request is that you not refer to them as a "cult," but, rather, call them a "lying, manipulative, emotionally abusive group," or a "patriarchal group that demeans women." This is more straightforward, more truthful, and it doesn't slur the communities movement in general. And if you fear that a group is harming its members, please don't call them a "cult" — call the police.

The term "high-demand group" is sometimes used for communities with rigorous rules for conduct or highly structured schedules for one's time. Some Christian communities, Buddhist retreat centers, and yoga ashrams are high-demand groups, in that people are expected to follow the agreements about diet, the use of money, or relations between the sexes, and have set schedules for prayer, meditation, or other forms of spiritual practice. People join these communities *because* they offer a more rigorous way of life than one usually lives, one which supports the particular religious or spiritual path they seek, or because the group offers specialized spiritual or religious training. High-demand groups simply have a strong focus: consider, for example, the military, and Catholic or Buddhist monasteries and convents.

Only a small percentage of intentional communities could be described as high-demand.

Where does the concept of "brainwashing" come from? It's been shown that it literally takes captivity and physical abuse to effect brainwashing, as happened to prisoners of war in the Korean War. However, both the American Psychological Association and the Society for the Scientific Study of Religion have done research that refutes the idea that religious or other groups are systematically "brainwash" their members or interfere with their ability to think critically. In high-demand groups in which leaders are abusive or manipulative, the leaders mostly do this by psychological humiliation or peer pressure, not physical coercion. Most people who leave high-demand groups do so voluntarily: they get fed up by being treated this way and leave. However, it's easier to leave the group if the person is not economically dependent on the group, as in a high-demand group which is income-sharing or asset-sharing.

The mainstream culture's use of the word "cult" comes from essentially two sources. The first is the tiny percentage of high-demand groups whose members live together that physically abuse their members or who don't let them leave, and whose violence ends up in headlines worldwide. Then the term "intentional community" becomes tainted by these groups' harmful practices, much to the detriment of the real communities movement. It's the FIC's experience that the overwhelming majority of communities are considered good places to live by their members — and good neighbors by the people who live around them.

A second source of the common use of the word "cult" are the few high-demand groups with local reputations for, say, authoritarian leaders who punish community members who question their authority. Or groups which seem harsh, such as those with reputations for coercing their members to discipline their children through beatings. One or two high-demand organizations whose members live in community have reputations for characteristics like these, and these reputations follow the group around for years, never quite being substantiated, and never quite going away either. Perhaps it's because a state agency overstepped its bounds and violated the community's civil rights and the case is thrown out of court, so the accusations lose credibility. Or the community members who report abuse or beatings later withdraw their accusations before such cases ever get to court at all.

If the members of a group like this have independent finances (meaning that they retain their assets and use any money they earn as they wish), they can leave the group fairly easily. It may be psychologically difficult to leave, but physically, they can just drive on out of there. If, however, a high-demand group with a reputation for authoritarian leadership or harshness has asset-sharing (you donate all your assets to the group when you join), or income-sharing (your monthly income goes into the common pot and you either get a stipend or your expenses are paid by the group), or the group is both asset-sharing and income-sharing, it can be very difficult for someone to leave. This is not because they're being physically forced to stay against their will, but because they can't afford to move out. People in this situation can be trapped economically, since they may not own their own car anymore or have any savings with which to go someplace else, not to mention having enough cash for first and last month's rent on housing, or to tide them over while they look for a job. Please let me emphasize, the asset-sharing and income-sharing aspects of the community are not the problem — and if a community is asset-sharing or income-sharing it does *not* mean it has authoritarian or harsh leadership! On the contrary, secular

income-sharing communities have no single leader and they usually govern themselves by some kind of fair, participatory process of all the members, such as consensus or voting. The problem, is the combination of a high-demand group plus an authoritarian leadership, combined with the economic dependency of income-sharing and/or asset-sharing.

What if you're seeking to join a group with a shared spiritual practice or the shared worship and fellowship of a Christian community, or other religious community? How can you tell in advance if the communities you're considering might have practices like this? What if the group's website looks really good, and the community members you meet seem warm and welcoming, but the group has a lingering reputation for shady practices? My strong recommendation is that you Google the group for the websites of organizations that may study this group, or websites of its former members, and read what *they* say. I believe that where there's smoke, especially in repeated allegations of abuse that continue over decades — there's probably fire. In two such controversial high-demand communities with reputations like these, I found websites with accounts of former members, including children, who told stories that broke my heart. I would never join such groups, and I don't want you to either!

So, to summarize, unlike with the Borg, you don't get "assimilated" when you join a community. You have total control over which community you might join, and you can and should get abundant information about a community before you even consider joining it. In any case, if a community seems too high-demand or controlling for your taste when you read their literature or their website, you'll know not to visit them. And if a community seems kind of strange when you're already visiting, you don't have to stay.

8. I'm afraid I won't have enough privacy or autonomy.

In a well-planned community whose members value sustainability, people's needs for privacy are built into the site plan and building design. To do otherwise would likely drive many people to leave the community — which of course wouldn't make it sustainable! So most likely a community has planned, physically and socially, for its members' needs for privacy.

Once in Fort Collins, Colorado, I observed a meeting of the then-forming Grayrock Commons Cohousing community. Chuck Durrett and Katie McCamant, the architects who brought cohousing to North America, were leading a session on the community's overall site plan. Chuck was up at the front of the room with preliminary sketches of roads and clustered townhouse duplexes and triplexes. One couple had drawn their house across an internal road, at some distance from the other houses, because, the people said, they wanted to ensure their privacy.

Chuck was describing to the group how the physical design of a site totally affects the *social* aspects of community life — one of the original principles of cohousing design. "Please don't let the front porches of some housing units face into the backyards of other housing units because you're seeking privacy," he cautioned. "And please don't separate out some units from the others. It won't really create a sense of privacy but it will reduce the sense of community you'll feel with the rest of the group."

Katie, who was in the back of the room next to me, leaned over and said that in all the cohousing communities they knew, they'd never once heard a complaint about the lack of privacy. But they sure had heard plenty of concerns about the lack of community!

Cohousing architects build privacy into their site plans and densely clustered buildings in several ways: by facing the fronts of the houses towards a common green, with all backyards facing into fields or woods, often with backyard fences; by placing the more public rooms like the kitchen and entry hall on the front of the units, not far from the pedestrian pathway, and placing the "private" areas such as living rooms and bedrooms on the back side of the units, closer to the backyard; by staggering the placement of each unit in a duplex or triplex so people don't enter their homes all along the same flat plane; by putting plenty of sound-proofing between shared walls; and by arranging exterior windows so people can't see into the windows of adjacent buildings.

Non-cohousing communities, usually those founded in the 1990s or later, often utilize similar processes for preserving privacy.

However, this is not true at some alternative-culture communities founded in the 1960s through 1980s. For example, some rural income-sharing communities like Twin Oaks Community in Virginia and East Wind Community in Missouri don't value privacy much when it comes to uni-sex shower- or toilet-using, and you'll often find group shower facilities and two-seater outhouses. Communities built in those days didn't value sound privacy much either, or perhaps didn't know at the time how to build sound-deadening walls between living units. (However, more residences built in more recent years at Twin Oaks have taken significant care in sound-proofing between rooms.) And at Twin Oaks, most small-group residences have bathrooms with an open-door policy. "It's quite common for different members to be brushing their teeth, using the toilet, or bathing at the same time, and people will just walk into the bathroom regardless," says longtime resident Valerie Renwick-Porter. "Sometimes we joke about 'bathroom parties' or 'tooth-brushing parties' if there are four or five people in there at once."

But please realize that it's *you* who will choose those ecovillages and communities you might want to visit, and those you might consider joining. You can certainly assess them for their practices re privacy, and consider only those that match your values.

Of course there's also social privacy, and one has much less of this in community than in mainstream culture, since in communities everyone pretty much knows everyone else's business, very much like in a small town. But unlike a town, people have come together quite intentionally and with shared values and a common purpose. So, depending of course on the size of the community, the closeness or distance of the relationships, and the level of harmony, people's interest in one another tends to be based more in concern and compassion than in mere curiosity or as fodder for gossip.

9. I don't want to have to share incomes or give all my money to the community.
You don't have to! Approximately 90 percent of intentional communities' members have independent finances. As long as people pay what the community requires in annual dues and fees, they

LOVE RELATIONSHIPS IN COMMUNITY

"Could my marriage or love relationship be threatened when my partner comes into daily contact with all those other attractive community members?"

Don't laugh; lots of people have this concern. The answer is yes. And no.

It does happen that someone in a love relationship can become romantically attracted to someone else when they live in community, with all the attendant upset this can cause, but it's difficult to say whether this happens more frequently or less frequently in community than in mainstream culture, where, after all, many partners also find themselves drawn to others.

We can make two generalizations, though.

First, community, which serves as kind of "magnifying mirror" for one's personal issues, tends to make strong relationships stronger, and shaky ones shake apart faster. Strong relationships get stronger because each person in the partnership can meet many of their social and recreational needs (to hang out with friends who love touch football, to hang out with friends who love chamber music) with a wide variety of others. This takes pressure off the relationship: each partner isn't expected to meet all of their partner's social and recreational needs. Also, if the couple is having conflict, plenty of community-trained empathetic listeners and peer-counselors are nearby, not to mention the conflict resolution processes the community may offer members in need.

Conflicted relationships tend to become more stressed, however. This is because living in close, frequent contact with so many different personalities tends to bring one's unresolved emotional issues and projections up to the surface, and intensify them. More than one communitarian has referred to community as a "crucible" or a "boiling cauldron." This is not bad, just intense. Shaky relationships often can't take the heat and break up sooner than they would have had the couple not moved to community. Another factor is that since people in community are less dependant on their partners for their social needs, they might feel more confident breaking up. They're less afraid of being lonely if they do.

Second, if a couple breaks up, neither necessarily has to leave the community. Impartial, kindly community mates can often help both partners heal more quickly, and come to a place of acceptance.

are free to work at any job they choose and spend or invest their income any way they like. The pervasive idea that in all communities people work at a community business for a stipend or that one's outside salary goes into a common treasury with everyone else's comes from the '60s-era communes, fictional tales of community, and media accounts of some of the largest and most well-known income-sharing communities in North America such as Twin Oaks in Virginia, and (until they switched to independent incomes in 1984), The Farm in Tennessee. Roughly ten percent of the communities which listed themselves in the FIC's online communities directory (in 2006) noted they were income-sharing.

Many people also have the idea that you must donate all your assets to a community — and if you leave, you won't get any of it back! This is only the case in some Christian communities. But again, it's *you* who are in charge of which communities you'll visit and consider, and so if donating all your assets doesn't appeal to you, you have ample opportunity to avoid it.

10. What if we all can't get along? I don't want to live with a bunch of bad-tempered grumps.
There are many times when people in community don't get along. Conflicts can simmer, erupt, and ultimately get resolved to most people's satisfaction, leaving the whole group a bit wiser and more mature for having gone through it. Or conflicts can fester for years, spreading resentment or hostility between individuals or groups of individuals, leaving the community weakened and vulnerable to larger, more intense conflicts later on, just as a compromised immune system can result in having a lower-than-normal energy level and being vulnerable to opportunistic disease organisms. Or conflicts can explode and rip the whole community apart, with various members leaving, or even

the whole community disbanding, sometimes leaving broken hearts and crippling lawsuits in the wake.

This is where *your* discernment is needed as you visit communities. You'll want to assess communities for signs of health or imbalance, and get to know your top choices for a community home in a long, slow process of checking them out thoroughly, which I call "long engagements." (See Chapter 23, "The Membership Process.")

But let's say the community you join is relatively healthy, yet you keep running into conflicts and difficulties with other people — and they with you. Welcome to the club! This is also what community is like, at least at first. There's no place like community to meet yourself. That is, you'll learn what does and doesn't work well in terms of your own interpersonal communication skills. And you'll most likely get better at getting along with even the "difficult" people, and grow enormously as a person.

Other Common Questions About Community Living

Do I have to go nude?
No (unless you join a specifically clothing-optional community, in which case, after all, it's optional). The more counter-cultural or "alternative" the community, the more likely some people will be nude sometimes, particularly if they have a sauna, sweat lodge, hot tub, or swimming hole. But it's very unlikely that a group would *require* members to be nude. If you're wondering about this when you visit a community, ask them about their norms and expectations around nudity.

Do I have to go to a lot of meetings?
Probably, if it's a small community. And if it's small or large, you will want to attend meetings if you want to influence the decisions that will affect

your life there. In many communities you may have options to not attend meetings, with the understanding that you'll have to abide by the decisions the group makes in your absence. Many cohousing communities report that large numbers of their members don't attend meetings, or don't attend often. This can be looked at as "freedom" for individual cohousers, or a factor that can demoralize the group. Also, some rural communities in which each family or household owns their own property with a deed, and in which there's relatively little community life beyond shared road maintenance and maybe a shared community building, tend to have fewer meetings than in more closely knit communities. In any case, the work of community self-governance can be exhilarating, tedious, and/or rewarding — and it's usually time-consuming.

What if I yearn to live in community but my partner doesn't?

Then please don't join one! In my experience watching couples struggle through this, moving to community even though one partner doesn't really want to tends to make the unwilling person so miserable, and thus both people so miserable, that the couple leaves the community. Or they break up.

If you can hardly bear living in mainstream culture and yearn for a simpler, or more ecologically sustainable, or more socially connected life, and your partner likes things just as they are, or finds the idea of community vaguely distasteful or repellant — you've got a huge issue in your relationship *now*. Staying where you are and being miserable won't solve it. Moving to community won't solve it. I respectfully suggest deep, soul-searching communication between the two of you, and perhaps counseling, to resolve the issue. This may lead to your creating a mutually acceptable life in a way that will work for both of you — in com-

munity or not. Or it may lead to breaking up, so each of you can move on to the life path you most want. But please, don't think moving to community without doing this work will resolve anything. It won't!

Are intentional communities mostly middle-class white people? Are people of color welcome? Are there any communities comprised of people of color?

Most communities have a lot of white, middle-class, college-educated people. People from the owner class or working class are generally not found in community at the rates they exist in the wider culture, and one finds very few people of color from any socioeconomic background (though nearly all communities are open to people of color). Of course the demographic mix will vary from community to community depending on its structure, location, costs, and culture. Some cohousing communities, especially in college towns, tend to have some members of Asian descent, or members born in Asian or Middle Eastern countries. Communities in highly urban areas, or progressive Christian communities focusing on social-justice activism, tend to be multi-racial, including Koinonia in Georgia, Ganas in Staten Island, New York, Los Angeles Eco-Village, Jesus People USA and Sophia communities in Chicago, Enright Ridge Ecovillage in Cincinnati, and Order of Christian Workers in Tyler, Texas, to name a few examples.

One couple I know, the man African-American, the woman Hispanic, told me they wouldn't join a mostly white community, but want to start their own people-of-color community, which would include only those white people who had first seriously worked on transforming their own unconscious racism. I've also met people who are in the process of forming African-American intentional communities; however, I don't know of any African-American or Hispanic intentional communities which are up and running already.

Are gays and lesbians welcome in community?
On the FIC's Online Directory very few communities, mostly Christian, indicated that they were specifically not open to gays, lesbians, bisexuals and transgendered people as members. That said, gay, lesbian, bisexual, and transgendered individuals should expect as wide a range of tolerance, acceptance, and enthusiasm for their presence at communities as they do in the wider culture. A few communities are focused on gay, lesbian, bisexual, and transgendered culture for those specifically seeking such an environment.

Can "hermits" — people who need a lot of alone time — live in community?
Yes, depending on the community. In cohousing communities, and larger communities, there are usually so many different kinds of people that it's natural that some will be shyer, quieter, and/or participate less often than others. However, in most communities, everyone is expected to contribute to the ongoing work of community life, so shy or reclusive people will need to come out sometimes to participate in workdays and other projects. And although most cohousing communities prefer that everyone attends meetings and helps out in committees and work days, one does not literally have to as there are usually no enforceable consequences if one doesn't.

In smaller communities, though, it may not be acceptable to be reclusive, as everyone is expected to participate in meetings and work activities.

Now that we've laid to rest some common misconceptions, what is it like to actually *live* in one of these places? In the next chapter we'll take a look at a cohousing-style ecovillage on the outskirts of a progressive college town, as one example of community life.

≈ Chapter 3 ≈

Community Living Day-to-Day

Community living is different in many ways from what most of us are used to. When you read the following tale by Liz Walker about her life in community, please notice the sense of connection and "family feeling" among the members, which is typical in intentional communities.

EcoVillage at Ithaca, in upstate New York, first introduced in Chapter 1, is an experiment in sustainable living meant to appeal to mainstream folks. The community's 175-acre semi-rural site is located a mile and a half from downtown Ithaca and includes two adjacent cohousing neighborhoods, a 10-acre organic CSA farm, and a 55-acre permanent conservation easement.

I WAKE UP EARLY and stretch, looking out our bedroom window at the pink sunrise illuminating blue hills across the valley. From the second-story window of our passive solar home at EcoVillage at Ithaca I can see the buildings of Ithaca College campus four miles away, but in front of me there are acres of open fields bordered by tall pines. We're in a great location — just two miles from downtown Ithaca, New York, a bustling college town, yet enfolded in the quiet beauty of 175 acres of farmland, woods, and meadows.

My partner Jared is already up, doing yoga. My teenage son Daniel will sleep as late as he can before biking to his summer job downtown. Our French housemate Florian is not yet up. In a couple of hours he will take the bus to work at Ithaca College, where he does research on the environmental movement in France. When I come downstairs, Jared is already packing his panniers for his three-mile bike ride to work at the county health department. He is a nurse who works with special-needs children and he's starting a small computer ergonomics business on the side. With a big hug

and kiss, I send him on his way. I sip a cup of coffee (Fair Trade, of course) made from freshly ground beans from our local natural foods cooperative, and toast some delicious whole-grain bread from a local bakery. The jam I've made myself, from wild blackberries on our land.

My friend Rachael and I plan to meet at 7:30 for a short bike ride before our work days start. We live in adjacent cohousing communities. Rachael's is called "SONG," our nickname for the second neighborhood group. Mine is called "FROG," short for first resident's group. Although I was initially very sad when Rachael and her husband Elan moved from FROG to SONG, we've timed the walk between our houses, and it is a mere four minutes, door to door.

Rachael wheels her bike up the pedestrian path and I go out to greet her. We head out for a vigorous 35-minute ride. The main road is busy with cars and we are relieved to soon be on side roads — biking past horses, barns, open farm fields and white clapboard houses. It's hilly here, and we work up a sweat, while riding side by side, and catching up on our lives.

When I get home I hang my bike in the bike shed. It is filled with 15 bikes of all sorts: mountain bikes, road bikes, neon-colored kids' bikes, and a three-wheel stroller for running with a baby. There is also a community lawn mower, community garden tools, and a community chest freezer, filled with frozen berries and vegetables grown on the farm.

Grabbing my water bottle and a sunhat, I look at my watch — it's 8:15. I'll be a few minutes late for my shift at West Haven Farm, a community supported agriculture farm (CSA). I walk down a small dirt road, past the chicken coop, the four sheep, and the new, winterized greenhouse. The chickens run up, clucking eagerly for a handout. I cut across another field on a grassy, mown path. On one side are tall grasses, milkweed plants, and black raspberry bushes; on the other side is an acre of potatoes, the plants covered in purple-starred flowers. I walk along the hedgerow checking to see if the wild cherries are ripe. I eat one, but it is still tart. In another week, I'll go out with Daniel to pick enough cherries for a wild cherry pie.

Now, an eight-minute walk from home, I'm at West Haven Farm. This thriving 10-acre organic CSA farm feeds about 1,000 people a week during the growing season. It is a small business, run by my next-door neighbors, John and Jen Bokaer-Smith. In March each year Jen and John collect cash subscription "shares" from 170 participating families. From late May through early November shareholders get a generous portion of freshly picked organic veggies, herbs, and flowers. Jen and John have a guaranteed market for their veggies, and consumers enjoy delicious, highly nutritious produce, as well as feeling connected to the land. Jen and John also sell some of their produce to the public at the Ithaca Farmer's Market, and some to EcoVillage at Ithaca for our four meals a week in the Common House.

Every Tuesday morning I help harvest veggies in exchange for my family's CSA share. Although the exchange rate works out to be only about $6/hour, I love the work, as it's a wonderful, relaxing part of my week. I'm outside in the sun chatting with my fellow workers who are mostly Cornell graduate students, harvesting nature's abundance. In three hours we pick and wash two kinds of peas, green beans, long yellow wax beans, zucchini, crooked neck squash, romaine, basil, dill and the first cherry tomatoes. My hands smell of herbs the rest of the day. I walk home, dirty and happy.

I use three large woks to create a stir-fry for 80.

I decide to check on my emails before washing off with a dip in the pond. Once I sit down at my computer, though, it's hard to stop. Perhaps 5–10 of my 55 new emails since yesterday are informational requests from students or potential visitors outside EcoVillage at Ithaca. The rest are from community members. With about 100 adults and 60 kids, our community is wired together with Internet cable, and we have continuous, unlimited access to high-speed Internet connections for just $15/month. Even though we see each other in person frequently, we also use email constantly — almost, I think, like a group brain, muttering to itself.

The EcoVillage at Ithaca business in my inbox includes committee meeting minutes, requests from researchers, and nonprofit business items. There's an agenda for our twice-monthly FROG meeting this Sunday, from 2–5 pm. One issue involves accessibility. (We're currently embroiled in controversy about accessibility issues — are we ready to make a major community investment to spend $50,000 to pave our gently winding pedestrian paths? It's a lot of money, but as our Aging and Accessibility committee points out, our current gravel paths have very poor drainage and are icy and hazardous in the winter, and too often muddy in the spring and fall. Walking on gravel is hard for our elderly and disabled members, let alone pushing a wheelchair or walker.) I print out on recycled paper the 10 pages of material to read before the meeting: minutes, agenda, three proposals, and a mini-survey.

I scan the village-wide announcements and discussion. Another hot topic raging on email right now: SONG is busily designing its own Common House, but in the meantime is using FROG's. Do we really need two complete kitchens and dining areas — one in each Common House for two adjacent cohousing neighborhoods? If SONG continued to share FROG's space, would meals be too crowded? Or could we be more creative about using the existing space? What could the SONG Common House provide to FROG residents? Heated emails advocate each side of the issue, interspersed with thoughtful, creative ideas. This is a tough issue that won't go away soon.

I've had enough emails after an hour. I'm still sweaty so I change into a swimsuit and walk down to the pond, halfway down the neighborhood.

Our clustered housing in FROG takes up just three acres, with the Common House at one end and a one-acre pond on the south side. Now, at 12:30, it's about 85 degrees, with a slight breeze. The pond is cheerfully crowded with kids and adults — talking, playing, and swimming. The older kids are playing a lively game involving throwing each other off a rubber raft. Toddlers play in the shallows, catching minnows and creating little dams. I greet friends, then plunge into the

My hands smell of herbs the rest of the day.

cool water, swimming the length of the pond several times. It feels so refreshing. No need for air conditioning when your body tingles with cool water. I climb out dripping, wrap a towel around my middle and join five other people, including Rachael's husband Elan, at the awning-shaded picnic table. I eat the sandwich I've brought, and someone offers me chips and salsa. Someone else passes around a jug of cold lemonade. I get into a discussion with a visitor from Spain who is doing her graduate work on intentional communities.

At 1:00 it's time for Elan's and my meeting on EcoVillage at Ithaca education programs. We've had an educational mission from the beginning: to provide a model of a more sustainable way of living that would be easily accessible to students, visitors, and academics. Recently, in partnership with the Ithaca College Environmental Studies Program, we received a three-year, $149,000 National Science Foundation grant. Now, in addition to hosting regular visitors and tour groups, and working with interns, we are also teaching semester-long courses on "Sustainable Communities," "Energy Conservation and Renewable Energy," and others. Elan and I are paid a small amount to coordinate the EcoVillage at Ithaca portion of the grant — a never-ending stream of student projects, course evaluations, and mentoring a team of EcoVillage at Ithaca educators. It's exciting and sometimes overwhelming. Elan and I have just an hour to meet and talk about our new grant proposal with Ithaca College. After another quick dip in the pond, where we swim side by side and talk, we move our meeting to towels on the grass far enough away from the crowd at the pond that we won't get distracted. It feels great to work outside with a friend. This is not unusual here. Out of 100 adults, many are stay-at-home parents or retired.

About 80 percent of the remaining 66 wage-earners work at least part-time on site — as farmers, builders, therapists, software engineers, graphic artists, environmental writers, health professionals and more. It's satisfying to have work, play, food production, and nature in such close proximity.

I say goodbye to Elan and hurry home to change into a summer dress and sandals. At 2:30 I meet a group of architecture students at the Common House to give them a tour. Thirty students from Rhode Island have arrived in three vans, with the assignment to design a third neighborhood for EcoVillage at Ithaca. This is their first visit, and they have done extensive preparation by reading our website and a variety of articles. I spend a couple hours showing them around, touring the Common House and sample homes in FROG and SONG. They are full of questions. "What green building features do you use?" "How are the two neighborhoods different?" "What would you do differently if you designed them again?" I point out several environmental features that may not be so immediately obvious:

I tell them we chose land close to the city to cut commuting distance yet still have a farm. We're building on just 10 percent of our 175 acres, and preserving 90 percent of our land as open space for organic agriculture, meadows, woods and wetlands. We plan to eventually build a third neighborhood and an education center.

I tell them all homes are passive solar, super-insulated, densely clustered duplexes. Back-up space heating and hot water are provided by boilers for each two to eight homes. We use about 40 percent less natural gas and electricity than other homes in the northeast. About half of the homes in SONG generate their electricity from solar

I plunge into the cool water, swimming the length of the pond several times.

panels. Buildings use local lumber when possible, and environmentally friendly building materials.

As we tour the Common House, I show them our dining room, our sitting room (which functions as a comfortable meeting or hang-out space), the sound-proof toddler playroom, community laundry, eight private offices, guest room, and multi-purpose room.

After the tour it's time for me to help cook tonight's community meal. I meet my two main assistants from the cooking team in the Common House kitchen. Each adult in the community is expected to put in at least two hours a week on a work team. Several children, from four to ten years old, offer to help out. We spend the next two hours chopping veggies from the CSA farm, cooking rice, and cutting locally made tofu into bite-size pieces. I use three large woks to create a stir-fry of broccoli, red peppers, and yellow squash with a spicy Indonesian peanut sauce for 80. We prepare cheese and apple slices to add to the children's table. At 6 the dinner is ready, and one of the kids rings the gong outside the Common House. Soon people drift in, chatting with their friends and giving hugs. We hold hands in a large circle for a moment of silence, then several visitors are introduced, and we have quick announcements. Time to eat! Jared and Daniel arrive a little late, sweaty from their bike rides up the hill, and I save them a place at the table. Sometime during the meal there is a thunderous sound as people bang on the tables and shout out "Yay, cooks!" I grin, feeling very appreciated for my efforts, and introduce my fellow cooks. There is special applause for the three children who helped. As the dish team is cleaning up dinner, I buy a quart of leftovers for a dollar, for lunch tomorrow. After dinner we celebrate a member's 60th birthday with cake and ice cream. Later, a group of kids gather with two adults in the sitting room for story-telling. A parent's group meets downstairs to discuss some recent behavior issues among the pre-teens. A men's support group meets in the guest room. Jared holds a short meeting with the maintenance team committee.

I go home to spend the rest of the evening with my family. I check in with Jared and Daniel about their days, and we make plans for a family hike over the weekend. After such a social day it is nice to have some quiet time. Another two hours working on the grant proposal, and it's time for bed.

And I look forward to the next summer day.

Liz Walker is cofounder and director of EcoVillage at Ithaca and author of EcoVillage at Ithaca: Pioneering Sustainable Community *(New Society Publishing, 2005). The community's website is www.ithaca .ecovillage.ny.us. Excerpted with permission from* Communities *magazine, Summer, 2004.*

YOU KNOW YOU LIVE IN COMMUNITY WHEN...

By Virginia Lore and Maril Crabtree

- You don't have to go to a bookstore to find a good read.
- You can't remember the last time you took the trash out.
- You can always find someone to take you to the airport, watch your pets, water your plants, and eat your brownies.
- Someone's always up for a hike or a hot tub.
- You've talked about world peace, the global economy, and the Bush administration — all before breakfast.
- You know at least one person who has been arrested for demonstrating their beliefs.
- You know what "polyamory" means.
- You feel guilty about your TV viewing habits — if you have any.
- You have to try 14 keys to find the one you want.
- You know a dozen ways to cook tofu.
- Your parenting style regularly comes up for review.
- Your spending habits regularly come up for review.
- There's always something fattening in the kitchen.
- The leftovers are still there only because you hid them in a yogurt tub.
- Laundry day is any day the washer is free.
- You've had to sell your kayak because the community already has two.
- The question "but where will we put it?" plays a big role in your buying decisions.
- Honoring the process is more important than making the decision.
- Deciding when to start planting the community garden requires the negotiation skills of Bishop Tutu.
- You know someone who has carried a grudge since 1972 when the mailboxes were reorganized without consensus.
- You hate to admit it, but you're that person.
- You fantasize more about winning a weekend getaway than about winning the lottery.
- Other people's kids call you "Mommy."
- You know where to go for a hug.

Virginia Lore is a cofounder of Duwamish Cohousing, an urban cohousing neighborhood near downtown Seattle, Washington (www.duwamish.org).

Maril Crabtree, Virginia's mother, is a cofounder of Heart-haven, a six-member urban community sharing a large home in Kansas City, Missouri (rjm@shadowcliff.org).

Excerpted with permission from *Communities* magazine, Fall, 2004.

As you might already realize, there are many more kinds of communities than this combination eco-village and cohousing community. In the next chapter we'll begin considering the wide variety of communities you have to choose from, starting with ecovillages.

Chapter 4

Ecovillages: For Future Generations

Ecovillages are the newest and most potent kind of intentional community, and in the vanguard of the environmental movement that is sweeping the world. I believe they unite two profound truths: that human life is at its best in small, supportive, healthy communities, and that the only sustainable path for humanity is in the recovery and refinement of traditional community life.

— Robert J. Rosenthal,
Professor of Philosophy,
Hanover College, Indiana

ACCORDING TO the Global Ecovillage Network (GEN), ecovillages are urban, suburban, or rural communities where people value both a supportive social network and a low-impact, ecologically sustainable way of life. They can include intentional communities, as well as traditional indigenous villages whose members focus on ecological and social sustainability, such as the many villages in Sri Lanka's Sarvodaya movement. Jonathan Dawson, co-director of GEN-Europe and president of GEN, suggests there may be perhaps 1,500 ecovillage projects worldwide.

Depending on its location and circumstances, being a "low-impact, sustainable human settlement" might mean an ecovillage uses permaculture principles for its site design, grows and raises much of its own organic food, builds passive-solar natural-built homes, uses roof-water catchment and/or constructed wetlands, generates renewable energy, bicycles, car-pools, uses biofuels, uses consensus decision-making, and/or uses a local currency. Not all ecovillages do all these practices; however, these practices most likely are the goals of many ecovillages.

The organized ecovillage movement began with a seminal meeting of ecovillage thinkers in Denmark in 1991, and the Global Ecovillage Network officially launched an international ecovillage conference at the Findhorn Foundation in Scotland in 1995. GEN-Europe is a subsidiary organization, with 80 member ecovillages in 30 countries in western and eastern Europe, the Middle East, and Africa, including Turkey, Egypt, Ghana, Senegal, Nigeria, and Zimbabwe. Global Ecovillage Network-Asia/Oceania has member ecovillages in Australia, New Zealand, Sri Lanka, The Philippines, Thailand, and Bangladesh. Ecovillage Network of the Americas (ENA) has member communities in South, Central, and North America.

Ecovillages — Multiple and Various

The settings and circumstances of ecovillages vary widely and they can physically look quite different from one another. Consider these ecovillages, for example:

• *Yarrow Ecovillage, British Columbia:* Twenty ecovillage pioneers create community in white clapboard houses on a former dairy farm on the main street of a tiny town in the Fraser Valley, with spectacular views of the nearby mountains.

+ *EcoVillage at Ithaca:* At the edge of a progressive college town, 160 people live in passive-solar townhouse dwellings in two adjacent cohousing neighborhoods on 175 acres of rolling hills and meadows, with organic CSA farms onsite.
+ *Los Angeles Eco-Village:* Forty urban ecovillagers rent 48 units in 2 adjacent stucco apartment buildings in a working class Korean-Latino neighborhood near the heart of downtown LA.
+ *Huehuecoyotl, Tepotzlán, Mexico:* Eleven artists, artisans, and performers live in community in adobe brick homes with red tile roofs (with a dining room/theater colorfully decorated with murals and mosaics), on a tree-covered plain in the mountains of central Mexico.
+ *Torri Superiore, Ventimiglia, Italy:* Twenty ecovillagers are restoring a 14th-century stone village with 160 rooms linked by arches, narrow passages, and stairways on a steep hillside near the Italian Riviera.

As you can see, on the surface these ecovillage projects all seem fairly different. What they have in common is dedication to social and ecological sustainability, and to sharing what they learn with others. To get a better sense of this dedication to sustainability and helping others, consider the following ecovillage mission/vision statements:

"We are a group of families from a variety of backgrounds who…are creating an ecovillage in conjunction with a biodynamic farm…. We are concerned about loss of genuine community in our society, increasing urbanization of rural areas, and impoverishment of farmland. Our intent is to show, by example, that these trends are neither inevitable nor irreversible — that a community that preserves natural land can be sustainable."

— Whole Village, Ontario

"Dedicated to caring for people and the Earth, and recognizing the Oneness of all life, we come together to create and to sustain beyond our lifetimes a learning community village, by gaining the skills, cultivating the attitude, and sharing with the public the resources for a holistic, regenerative culture."

— Earthaven Ecovillage, North Carolina

"To create a society, the size of a small town or village, made up of individuals and communities of various sizes and social structures, which allows and encourages its members to live sustainably. To encourage this sustainable society to grow to have the size and recognition necessary to have an influence on the global community by example, education, and research."

— Dancing Rabbit Ecovillage, Missouri

"We demonstrate the processes for creating a healthy neighborhood ecologically, socially, and economically. We try to reduce our environmental impacts while raising the quality of neighborhood life. We share our processes, strategies and techniques with others through tours, talks, workshops, conferences, public advocacy, and the media."

— Los Angeles Eco-Village

Human-Scale, Full-Featured Settlements

As noted in the Introduction, the ecovillage definition I like best is Robert Gilman's: "A human-scale, full-featured settlement, in which human activities can be harmlessly integrated into the natural world in a way that is supportive of healthy human development, and can be successfully continued into the indefinite future." In recent years Gilman has added another phrase to this definition: "Multiple centers of initiative."

Human-scale means the settlement has a population which is large enough to function well, but small enough that everyone is able to know and be known by others in the community, and is able to influence the community's direction. How many people is this? The ecovillage projects I'm familiar with in North America have roughly 20 to 160 people. GEN-Europe wrestled with the "how small is too small" issue for several years, and finally concluded that an ecovillage project was not too small to be considered an aspiring ecovillage if at least eight people lived full time on land that they owned. Lois Arkin, founder of Los Angeles Eco-Village, notes that there is considerable practical evidence that in modern industrialized societies the upper limit for such a group may be roughly 500 people. (And some people believe you need at least 500 people for a settlement to be called a "village.") And Albert Bates, GEN activist and director of the Ecovillage Training Center at The Farm, notes that in settlements where the turnover is smaller, much larger populations of several thousand people can indeed know everyone, the names of their children and grandparents, and so on. In any case, Findhorn in Scotland has close to 500 people, Damanhur in Italy has 1200 people, and Auroville in India has around 2,000. There are no hard and fast rules about the population size of ecovillages and what is or isn't human scale. Rather, there's a growing grassroots interest in human settlements becoming more humane, people-friendly, and ecologically sustainable — and starting an ecovillage is one way many groups are moving towards this goal.

Full-featured settlement means that, ideally, ecovillage residents live and work onsite (or perhaps within a short bike ride), and grow much of their own food, buy many goods and services, and enjoy their social and spiritual lives there. While people could certainly leave the property anytime, they could also choose to do many of their daily life activities onsite. Another, slightly different way to understand "full-featured," suggested by GEN's Jonathan Dawson, is that the settlement is active on all the key sustainability-related fronts: governance, human relations, Earth restoration, energy, food, village-scale economy, and so on. Most ecovillages are not full-featured settlements yet. While some indigenous, sustainably oriented villages are full-featured, most that are also intentional communities are "aspiring" or "in process" ecovillages, whose members don't yet all work onsite, or who don't yet grow most of their food onsite, or who can't yet purchase most needed goods and services onsite, and so on. (One exception may be the Findhorn Foundation, an educational center and community in northern Scotland, where many residents live and work, and are able to buy or trade for needed goods and services, and food that is grown or raised onsite.)

Human activities harmlessly integrated into the natural world means that ecovillagers live, work, grow food, generate power, and basically try to carry on their daily lives in ways that do not harm the air, water, soil, or the creatures they share the land with. They try to build homes with building materials which are the least polluting, most local, and/or have the most recycled content, given economies of scale and the need to use building materials that aren't prohibitively expensive. Food is grown organically. Waste is recycled. If they can afford it, they're wholly or partially off the grid. If they drive vehicles, ideally they car pool, have a car co-op, and/or use biofuels.

So are most aspiring ecovillages "harmlessly integrated into the natural world?" No — most are still aiming for it. Given the economic necessity to travel to and from jobs, and given the need to use materials from PVC pipe to concrete, from photovoltaic panels to soil amendments (which may be manufactured elsewhere and shipped far distances), most aspiring ecovillages are still a long way from "harmless."

In a way that's supportive of healthy human development means the people living in ecovillages are enjoying their sustainable lifestyle and have time to relax. They're not burnt out. They're living lives that balance their physical, emotional, mental, and spiritual needs in a healthy way. Of course this is an ideal, and not always achieved. For instance, in the earlier, start-up years, many ecovillage founders work long, hard hours building their community, and don't spend as much time relaxing and playing until they've achieved a certain basic level of physical and organizational infrastructure.

Multiple centers of initiative means that while the ecovillage as a whole funds and manage certain projects, individual ecovillage members, or groups of members, can also initiate, fund, and manage projects themselves, such as onsite businesses, organizations, or amenities. The individuals do the work; the whole community reaps the benefit and the credit for having these projects. At EcoVillage at Ithaca, for example, two members own and operate a ten-acre organic CSA farm onsite, offering produce to community members and neighbors six months of the year. Another member owns and operates a CSA berry farm onsite. These individual community members did all the work, yet EcoVillage at Ithaca itself can claim: "We have two CSA farms in our ecovillage."

Successfully continued into the indefinite future means that in terms of using resources wisely and preserving the quality of the air, water, soil, beneficial microorganisms and so on, we aren't borrowing from future generations. Our descendents and future residents will still be able to live sustainably on the property (and on the Earth!). Of course we won't know for many generations whether this part of the definition applies to many current aspiring ecovillages.

Max Lindegger, director of GEN-Asia/Oceania, adds that ecovillages also need to include good design for ecological and social sustainability right from the beginning.

In any case, the Gilmans and Max Lindegger's ideals are more principles to aspire to than descriptions of most ecovillages that exist now. "There may be…no single example of an 'ecovillage' in the sense of a full-featured human community untainted by earlier technologies, or polluting material flows, or which hasn't engaged in theft of our future natural heritage to some extent," writes Albert Bates. (*Communities* , Spring 2003.)

As you might expect, ecovillages are uneven in their manifestation of ecological sustainability, and may be strong in one aspect of sustainability while being undeveloped in another. For example, O.U.R. Ecovillage in Shawnigan Lake, British Columbia, innovated a precedent-setting change of local zoning to include a new "sustainability" zoning category, which they now operate under, and have built several outstanding natural buildings with the blessing of the local building department. This means they can be a model demonstration project for their way of life and host visitors and produce workshops and other educational programs without fear of being fined or forced to change their structure. Other ecovillage projects in North America, however, operate "under the radar" because they violate local zoning regulations by having more residents than permitted, or they use natural-building methods not covered by the local code, or build smaller and more simple dwellings than the code allows. While the under-the-radar ecovillages are doing the best they can to live out their sustainability values (perhaps waiting for zoning regulations and building codes to become more progressive), they're not able to serve as model demonstration sites and share what they're learning with the public, for fear of exposure.

In other examples, both Dancing Rabbit and Earthaven have off-grid power, natural buildings, and homemade composting toilets, the last of which is fine with their local counties where most rural folk have outhouses (or at least remember them). Dancing Rabbit also encourages bicycling, operates a car-pooling car co-op which runs on biofuels, and doesn't allow privately owned cars. However, as of 2006, Earthaven members still drive to town in individual vehicles, although there are plans afoot to change this. Earthaven doesn't grow much of its own food yet, but Ecovillage at Ithaca (which also encourages bicycling, carpooling, and public transportation), has two CSA farms onsite. Yet so far only a few homes at Eco-Village at Ithaca have composting toilets or are off the grid. And while residents of Los Angeles Eco-Village recycle their trash, compost their kitchen scraps, and grow some fruits and vegetables in their apartment courtyard, they're almost entirely dependent on grid electricity (so far only three apartments are off the grid), and they buy most of their food at local stores. But Los Angeles Eco-Villagers are enthusiastic bicycle and public transportation activists — and get twenty dollars off on their rent if they don't own a car!

Some ecovillages, such as the 80-member ZEGG Eco-Village in Germany, while creating passive solar buildings, organic gardens, and constructed wetlands, put considerable attention on creating a socially as well as ecologically sustainable culture. "We question what seems to be normal," reads ZEGG's mission and purpose statement. "We follow the vision that we can choose cooperation instead of competition and place human contact and trust in the centre of attention. What kind of life supports the development of our human beauty, compassion, and ability to love and to live nonviolently with each other and with the Earth?"

Besides ecological and social sustainability, ecovillages also seek economic sustainability. In larger communities this can include developing a village-scale economy by its members earning, spending, saving, and investing onsite whenever possible. At Findhorn Foundation in Scotland, for example, people earn a living in trades such as construction, maintenance, agriculture, various healing modalities, administrative work, and the arts. The educational center buys goods and hires services from community members, and members buy goods and hire services from each other whenever possible. Community members also invest in Findhorn's projects and one another's onsite businesses, including the wind generator co-op, woodlot co-op, CSA farm, and the Phoenix community store. They save in Findhorn's community-owned bank, and use its local currency, the Eko.

Global Ecovillage Network also emphasizes spiritual sustainability. To me, this means community members being open to and supporting one another's various spiritual beliefs and practices, and being willing to be open, honest, and transparent in their dealings with each other — and doing this with a sense that they and the plants and animals they share the land with are part of something larger than themselves, something sacred.

Five Characteristics of Ecovillages

Jonathan Dawson of GEN is particularly versed in European and African ecovillages. He points out that ecovillages in the North — in Europe and North America (as well as Australia and New

Zealand) — are often characterized by a desire to repudiate the alienation and materialism of industrialized society in favor of a more humane, heart-centered, and connected feeling of community with others. Ecovillages in the South — in Africa and Latin America — are often also characterized by the desire to throw off the influence of industrialized nations and return to the values and practices of their traditional cultures.

But South or North, he observes that ecovillages can be identified by five essential characteristics. I've paraphrased from his book *Ecovillages: New Frontiers for Sustainability*, (Green Books, 2006):

1. Ecovillages are not projects started by governments or corporations, but private citizens' initiatives. They're grassroots.
2. Ecovillage residents value community living.
3. Ecovillage residents are seeking to regain a measure of control over their own community resources: they're not being overly dependent on government, corporate, or other centralized sources of water, food, shelter, power, and other basic necessities.
4. Ecovillage residents have a strong sense of shared values, which they often characterize in spiritual terms.
5. Ecovillages serve as research and demonstration sites, and many offer educational experiences to others.

But Is it Really an Ecovillage?

"Ecovillage" has recently become kind of a buzzword. As more than one long-standing intentional community has grown more ecologically conscious over the years it has added the term "ecovillage" to its community name. Does installing solar panels and building a greenhouse make an intentional community an ecovillage? Sometimes housing developers call their new subdivision projects "ecovillages." Recently at a conference where I was

ECOVILLAGE OVERVIEW ONLINE

For a quick online overview of various ecovillage projects, including those mentioned in this chapter, see:

- O.U.R. Ecovillage, British Columbia: *ourecovillage.org*
- Yarrow Ecovillage, British Columbia: *yarrowecovillage.ca*
- Whole Village, Ontario: *wholevillage.org*
- Dancing Rabbit Ecovillage, Missouri: *dancingrabbit.org*
- Earthaven Ecovillage, North Carolina: *earthaven.org*
- EcoVillage at Ithaca, New York: *ecovillage.ithaca.ny.us*
- Emerald Earth Sanctuary, California: *emeraldearth.org*
- Los Angeles Eco-Village: *laecovillage.org*

- Lost Valley Educational Center, Oregon: *lostvalley.org*
- Huehuecoyotl Ecovillage, Tepotzlán, Mexico: *huehuecoyotl.net* (English)
- Quilla Tunari Ecovillage, Marquina, Bolivia: *communities.msn.com/pictures* (English)
- Findhorn Ecovillage, northern Scotland: *findhorn.org/ecovillage*
- The Village, Tipperary, Ireland: *thevillage.ie*
- ZEGG, Belzig, Germany: *zegg.de* (English)
- Tamera, Portugal: *tamera.org* (English)
- Torri Superiore Ecovillage, Ventimiglia, Italy: *torri-superiore.org* (English)
- Crystal Waters, Queensland, Australia: *ecologicalsolutions.com.au/crystalwaters*
- Kookaburra Ecovillage, Queensland, Australia: *kookaburra.eco-village.com.au*
- Somerville Ecovillage, Perth, Australia: *sev.net.au*

speaking a member of the audience said, "Ecovillages aren't 'sustainable' at all; they're exorbitantly expensive to join!" Turns out he was referring to an upscale rural-gentry cohousing project which had stuck the marketable term "ecovillage" in its name.

In 1998, attendees of a sustainability and education conference in Denmark affirmed that a community is an ecovillage if it specifies an ecovillage mission in its organizational documents, community agreements, or membership guidelines — and then makes progress toward that goal. The Global Ecovillage Network, however, doesn't even try to establish criteria or regulate which projects can and cannot call themselves an ecovillage, but rather encourages ecological and social sustainability in communities wherever possible. If you're wondering whether a place calling itself an ecovillage really is one, I advise you to explore their website, e-mail them, visit, and see what you think. If you like the place and would like to live there, that's what really counts.

"Lifeboat Communities," Future Generations

I'm especially enthusiastic about ecovillages because the people who live in them aren't just doing all this hard work for themselves; many are also creating model demonstration sites — sharing what they're learning with others through tours, workshops, and internships. Their focus is on

ECOVILLAGE RESOURCES

Websites:
- Global Ecovillage Network (GEN): *gen.ecovillage.org*
- Ecovillage Network of the Americas (ENA): *ena.ecovillage.org*
- Canadian Ecovillage Network: *enc.ecovillage.org*
- FIC's Online Directory: *directory.ic.org*
- Urban Ecovillage Network: *urban.ecovillage.org*
- Global Ecovillage Network-Europe: *gen-europe.org*
- Eco-Village Network UK: *evnuk.org.uk*
- Global Ecovillage Network-Oceania/Asia: *genoa.ecovillage.org/genoceania*
- Ecovillages and Cohousing Association-New Zealand: *converge.org.nz/evcnz*

Reference Directories and Books:
- *Communities Directory, Fellowship for Intentional Community* (new editions every 18 months) *store.ic.org*
- *Eurotopia: Directory of Intentional Communities and Ecovillages in Europe,* Volker Peters, Martin Stengel, editors. Volker Peters Verlag (2005). *eurotopia.de/englindex*

- *Directory of Ecovillages in Europe,* Barbro Grindheim and Declan Kennedy. *gen-europe.org*
- *Ecovillages and Communities Directory: Australia and New Zealand,* Global Ecovillage Network Oceania/Asia, Inc. (GENOA). *genoa.ecovillage.org*
- *EcoVillage at Ithaca: Pioneering Sustainable Community,* Liz Walker, New Society Publishers, 2005.
- *Ecovillages: New Frontiers for Sustainability,* Jonathan Dawson, Green Books, London, 2006.
- *Ecovillage Living: Restoring the Earth and Her People,* Hildur Jackson and Karen Svensson, Editors, Gaia Trust, 2003. *ecovillage.org*
- *Ecovillages: A Practical Guide to Sustainable Communities,* Jan Martin Bang, New Society Publishers, 2005.
- *The Post-Petroleum Survival Guide and Cookbook: Recipes for Changing Times,* Albert Bates, New Society Publishers, 2006. *thegreatchange.com*

changing our culture, and not just for us, but for generations to come. At O.U.R. Ecovillage in British Columbia, you can learn permaculture and natural building. At The Farm's Ecovillage Training Center in Tennessee, you can learn permaculture, ecovillage design, and setting up off-grid power systems. At Earthaven you can take workshops ranging from natural building to natural birth control. At Los Angeles Eco-Village you can learn how to build a bicycle from recycled parts, or set up an urban community land trust. At Lost Valley Educational Center in Oregon you can take the "Ecovillage and Permaculture Certificate Program." Ecovillages are essentially charged to be fruitful and multiply. "They can be likened to yogurt culture," says Jonathan Dawson, as they are "small, dense, and rich concentrations of activity whose aim is to transform the nature of that which surrounds them."

Ecovillages are also increasingly being seen as potential "lifeboat communities" during the widely predicted hard times ahead. In *Powerdown* (New

LEARNING IN AN ECOVILLAGE SETTING

Each of these organizations or individual ecovillages offers workshops and courses on subjects ranging from permaculture design to natural building, organic gardening, off-grid power, and starting your own ecovillage.

- **Living Routes Study Abroad in Ecovillages**, Amherst, Massachusetts. Interdisciplinary academic and internship programs in Scotland, France, Senegal, India, Mexico, Brazil, Peru, and the US. *livingroutes.org*
- **Gaia Education**. Global Ecovillage Network-sponsored and United Nations-affiliated hands-on courses and workshops held onsite in "living and learning centers" in ecovillages worldwide, according to a curriculum worked out by a consortium of 12 leading ecovillage founders and educators from ecovillages in Europe, Australia, and South and North America. *gaiaeducation.org*
- **Gaia University**. Courses and workshops in ecological sustainability and other topics, held in ecovillages in North America and Europe. *gaiauniversity.org*
- **O.U.R. Ecovillage**, British Columbia. Permaculture and natural building. *ourecovillage.net*
- **Ecovillage Training Center**, The Farm Community, Tennessee. Permaculture, ecovillage design, natural building, off-grid power. *thefarm.org*

- **Ecovillage at Ithaca**, New York. Courses in "Creating Sustainable Communities: The Ecological Dimension." *ecovillage.ithaca.ny.us*
- **Earthaven Ecovillage**, North Carolina. Permaculture design, natural building, starting a successful ecovillage, herbal medicine, fertility and natural birth control, fermented foods. *www.earthaven.org*
- **Lost Valley Educational Center**, Oregon. Ecovillage and Permaculture Certificate Program, Heart of Now. *lostvalley.org*
- **Occidental Arts & Ecology Center**, northern California. Permaculture design, natural building, organic gardening and seed saving, watershed organizing, starting your own intentional community. *www.oaec.org*
- **Center for Appropriate Technology (CAT)**, Powys, Wales. *cat.org.uk*
- **Findhorn: Ecovillage Training**. *findhorn.org/ecovillage*
- **EcoLogical Solutions, Crystal Waters Ecovillage**, Queensland, Australia. *ecologicalsolutions.com.au*
- **Ökodorf Sieben Linden**, Germany. *oekodorf7linden.de*
- **Z.E.G.G.**, Germany: *zegg.de*
- **Torii Superiore**, Italy: *www.torii-superiore.org*

Society Publishers, 2005) an exploration of various possible responses to the challenges of Peak Oil, author Richard Heinberg describes friends of his in various intentional communities and ecovillages worldwide. "While they engage in activism on many fronts," he writes, "participating vigorously in the anti-globalization, peace, and environmental movements — they also have established rural bases where they save heirloom seeds, build their own homes from natural and locally available materials, and hone other life-support skills that they and future generations will need. I admire those people unreservedly: if there is a sane path from where we are to a truly sustainable future, these folks have surely found it."

"Our ecovillage movement is blessed with diversity," writes Albert Bates (*Communities*, 2003). "From rural to urban, neighborhood experiments to large districts in transition, in many cultures and geopolitical climates, people are reading the handwriting on the wall and getting on with the work that must be done. They are not waiting for government or foundation grants. They are picking up shovels and hoes and building the future, often without a blueprint or even the ability to read and write. It is on the shoulders of these pioneers that the dreams we all have now rest — for peace, security, prosperity, family, and happiness into the coming generations of our children — whether they, or we, recognize it yet."

≈ Chapter 5 ≈

Cohousing Communities

The common denominator of the thousands of people I know who live in cohousing…is that these folks believe that it's more readily possible to live lighter on the planet if they cooperate with their neighbors, and their lives are easier, more economical, more interesting, and more fun.

— Chuck Durrett,
Communities magazine, 1999

We are creating a community where lives are simplified, the Earth is respected, diversity is welcomed, children play together in safety, and living in community with neighbors comes naturally.

— Mission and Purpose statement,
Sunward Cohousing, Ann Arbor Michigan

COHOUSING COMMUNITIES are small, close-knit urban, suburban, and sometimes rural neighborhoods owned and managed by the residents themselves, and ideal places in which to raise families or grow older. This is perhaps the fastest growing kind of intentional community in North America, with (in 2006) approximately 94 completed cohousing neighborhoods and 110 cohousing projects in the forming stages in Canada and the US. The first cohousing community in the US began in Davis, California, in 1989. The average cohousing community has about 26 to 30 homes and perhaps 50 to 60 members.

Like the ecovillage movement, cohousing is an international phenomenon with hundreds of cohousing communities worldwide — especially in Denmark, Sweden, the Netherlands, Canada, and the US, but also with cohousing communities in Germany, France, Belgium, Austria, Australia, New Zealand, and Japan.

Cohousing was first designed by Danish architects in the late 1960s to address the alienation of modern suburbia, where there's little sense of community and few people know their neighbors. The Danish architects consciously designed site and buildings to encourage and facilitate social contact. Typically, smaller-than-normal housing units face each other across a common green or courtyard with pedestrian pathways, leaving lots of open space on the site, and lots of opportunity to meet neighbors on a daily basis. Generally, cars are parked on the edge of the property or clustered in a single parking lot near the common house.

The housing units — often two-story townhouse-style duplexes and triplexes, but sometimes free-standing houses or stacked flats — contain all the features of conventional homes: kitchen, living/dining room, bedrooms, and bathrooms, although not usually laundry rooms or guest rooms. The housing units are often designed so the most active part of the home, usually the kitchen, faces into the common green or courtyard, which allows more sense of ownership of the common space, more of a sense of security, and the ability to keep an eye on children playing. Usually the more private areas of a home, the living room and bedrooms, are placed to the back of the housing unit, where there is more visual and sound privacy. Residents also have access to one or more common greens or courtyards, children's play areas, a community garden, parking, and a large, centrally located community building called the common house. The common house, which is often visible from the front door of every dwelling, typically includes a kitchen, large dining room, sitting area, children's playroom, laundry facilities, one or two guest rooms, and sometimes a workshop, library, exercise room, and/or crafts room. The common house is essentially an extension of everyone's private home and cohousers use it continually.

Cohousers share cooking and clean-up duties for optional group meals in the common house, generally at least three evenings a week. The common house is also the site of community meetings, where residents make decisions, usually by consensus. Making decisions together and taking care of their shared property together tends to create a sense of connection, trust, and mutual support among cohousers.

For a quick overview of cohousing, please see:
- Canadian Cohousing Network: *cohousing.ca*
- Cohousing Association of the United States: *cohousing.org*

As noted earlier, most cohousing communities are urban or suburban. Some are right downtown such as Swan's Market Cohousing, a 20-unit project on 3 floors of one side of a restored 1920s art deco-style market building in the heart of Oakland, California. The market building, which covers a whole city block, includes a café, shops, art galleries, a children's art museum, office space, affordable rental homes (which aren't part of Swan's Market Cohousing), and a courtyard in the center.

THE SIX PRINCIPLES OF COHOUSING

Kathryn McCamant and Chuck Durrett, the architects who brought cohousing to North America in the early 1980s with their book *Cohousing*, identify six primary characteristics of cohousing.

1. **Participatory Process.** Future residents participate in the design of the community.
2. **Neighborhood Design.** The physical layout and orientation of the buildings encourage a sense of community.
3. **Common Facilities.** The common house and other shared facilities are designed for daily use and are an integral part of the community. Except on very small urban sites, cohousing communities often have playground equipment, lawns, and gardens as well. Since the buildings are clustered, larger sites may retain several or many acres of undeveloped shared open space.
4. **Resident Management.** Cohousing communities are managed by their residents, who participate in committees, help maintain the property, rotate preparing common meals, and meet regularly to make community decisions.
5. **Non-hierarchical structure and decision-making.** Cohousing residents share power; most cohousing communities use consensus decision-making.
6. **No shared community economy.** Everyone has independent incomes. There are no community-owned businesses; people work at their regular jobs.

The "common green" of Swan's Market Cohousing is a second-floor outdoor promenade overlooking the courtyard below. A few cohousing communities are relatively close to towns but look and feel rural, such as Blueberry Hill near Vienna, Virginia; Island Cohousing on Martha's Vineyard in Massachusetts; and Heartwood in Bayfield, Colorado.

Is cohousing sustainable and "green"? Many cohousing communities built in North America in the '90s tended to seek green and sustainable building practices, and put into effect those they could afford. For example, Winslow Cohousing on Bainbridge Island, Washington, completed in 1992, used compact florescent lighting fixtures throughout the project, airtight buildings with thickly insulated walls and ceilings, and air-to-water heat exchangers heating all the domestic hot water with the exhaust air from the ventilation system. Some cohousing projects use passive solar design, shared heating systems, and other green features such as thermally efficient buildings and central heating plants for radiant floor heating and hot water. At Heartwood Cohousing in Bayfield, Colorado, with detached single-family homes on adjacent lots, many residents built their homes with natural building methods such as strawbale and cob. And EcoVillage at Ithaca in upstate New York, which is comprised of two adjacent cohousing neighborhoods, uses passive solar design; in the second neighborhood several houses are built of strawbale, and have rooftop solar hot water systems and/or off-grid power. Cohousing developer Chris ScottHanson points out that just having clustered common-wall housing units in a town is more green and sustainable than the alternative. "A single-family home off the grid five miles from town," he notes, "uses significantly more energy than a cohousing unit of comparable size in a small town, within walking distance of services."

The Costs of Cohousing

Members of cohousing communities own their own homes. The have a deed to their housing unit and the property directly beneath it, or they have a mortgage, using traditional institutional lending to make the purchase. They also share ownership of the land, common house, and other common facilities along with other community members, through membership in a homeowners' association or condominium association (and in a few cases, a housing cooperative), depending on their preferences and the legal entities and financing available in their state or province. A small number of cohousers rent or home-share.

The cost of buying a home in cohousing can seem slightly higher than comparable market-rate housing for similar-sized housing units in the area, but it's really not, since each homeowner's cost of the common house and other shared facilities are part of the asking price. Some cohousing units can cost less than local market-rate housing, though. For example, Berkeley Cohousing, which has a 100 percent limited equity agreement, keeps housing unit prices down to around half the price of similar housing in the same neighborhood. At Jamaica Plain Cohousing in Boston over half the members qualified for affordable housing. The group managed to keep costs under control through their five-year development process, and moved in with the value of the homes estimated to be about 85 percent of the market rate in their neighborhood. At Fordyce Place Cohousing in Ashland, Oregon, the property was purchased at below-market rates, a savings passed onto buyers — but with limitations on how much units could later be sold for, so no one would buy low and sell high. In Boulder, Colorado, Nomad Cohousing and Wild Sage Cohousing were both built with government subsidies (and for some units, sweat equity help from Habitat for Humanity) so 60 and 40 percent respectively of the units sold at below-market rates to qualifying households. (Cohousing communities rarely offer the opportunity to use sweat equity to partially offset the cost of buying in, unless an organization like Habitat for Humanity helps them create an option for affordable housing, as it did, for example, with Nomad Cohousing and Wild Sage.)

Even though cohousing units are not more expensive than market-rate housing, cohousing communities nevertheless cost considerably more to join than most other kinds of intentional communities. Joining a cohousing community essentially means buying a house — which means qualifying for a mortgage, having enough cash to make the down payment, and paying monthly mortgage payments as well as community fees and dues.

Joining a Cohousing Community

The original way to create cohousing involved a group of people who planned, financed, purchased, and developed their property themselves, while hiring and managing architects and contractors to design and build it. This usually resulted in taking three to six years or more to finish their project, and often being tens of thousands to hundreds of thousands of dollars over budget, with the price of even the smallest units rising beyond the means of one or more of its founders, who, sadly, could no longer afford to buy in. Next came the developer-driven model — a housing developer builds the project from scratch — which was more likely to get built more cost-effectively and on a shorter timeline. If you're interested in cohousing, you should know that experienced cohousers see a trade-off between efficiency and having a sense of community when they finally begin living together. In cohousing circles it is generally believed that the more people in a start-up group are involved in decisions about their intended neighborhood throughout the development process, the more closely they will have bonded as a group by the time they move in. The less they're involved at the outset, the less connected they will feel when they move in.

However, Elana Kann, developer-resident of Westwood Cohousing in Asheville, North Carolina, points out that groups can always bond *after* they move in, and do. "What creates bonding among cohousers," she says, "is doing things together that specifically create bonding." She also points out that many cohousers are now saying that the process and communication skills learned during the fast-paced, get-it-done development phase don't really apply as much after people move in to their new community. They must learn a whole new set of interpersonal skills for the slower-paced living-in-community mode. "It's like starting over again," some of them say.

In any case, the "streamlined" development model — in which an experienced housing developer partners with a forming cohousing group, offering expertise, development cash, good credit, and credibility with local officials and lending institutions — tends to create more on-time, on-budget cohousing communities with a good sense of community connection at move-in time as well. Another model is for the group to serve as the developer and remain in charge of everything, but use the development management services of an experienced developer to build their project in a more efficient and cost-effective manner. These are the development methods most cohousing activists recommend today.

To live in cohousing, you can join a cohousing core group that is in the process of forming and developing cohousing, and attend weekly or biweekly meetings for the number of months or years it will take before the community is built. Or you can buy or rent into an already established cohousing neighborhood when a housing unit becomes available for sale. Most cohousing communities have a waiting list for buyers, and you might have to wait awhile. Some cohousers suggest that you get to know various cohousing communities before you consider buying into one, by visiting several, staying in their guest rooms, and getting to know folks there before asking to be placed on their waiting list.

Cohousing has had a hugely beneficial influence on the wider communities movement, and on green building in North America, with positive articles in *The New York Times, Wall Street Journal, Washington Post, Boston Globe* and many other major newspapers across North America. "Commune Living Goes Upscale" reads a typical (if somewhat misleading) newspaper headline, with a glowing account of how these neighbors live cooperatively

COHOUSING RESOURCES

Networks
- Canadian Cohousing Network, *cohousing.ca*
- Cohousing Association of the United States (Coho/US), *cohousing.org*
- UK Cohousing Network, *cohousing.org.uk*
- Ecovillages and Cohousing Association — New Zealand, *converge.org.nz/evcnz*

Tours
- Coho/US and regional groups organize regularly scheduled bus tours of cohousing communities in the Denver-Boulder, Washington, D.C., Massachusetts, and San Francisco Bay Area/Sacramento/North Bay regions. *cohousing.org/news/tours*

Books
- *Cohousing: A Contemporary Approach to Housing Ourselves,* Second edition, Kathryn McCamant and Charles Durrett with Ellen Hertzman, Ten Speed Press, 1994.
- *Reinventing Community: Stories from the Walkways of Cohousing,* Dave Wann, Editor, Fulcrum, 2005. *reinventingcommunity.com*
- *Senior Cohousing: A Community Approach to Independent Living,* Chuck Durrett, Ten Speed Press, 2005. *seniorcohousing.net*
- *Sustainable Community: Learning from the Cohousing Model,* Graham Meltzer, PhD., Trafford Publishing, 2005.

- *The Cohousing Handbook: Building a Place for Community,* Revised Edition, Chris ScottHanson and Kelly ScottHanson, New Society Publishers, 2005.

Regional Alliances in the US
- Regional networks support each other, cross-train, cross-facilitate, co-educate, co-market, do common-meal exchanges, hold conferences, and more. Some groups, like NICA, serve the full spectrum of local intentional communities, not just cohousing.
- Mid-Atlantic Cohousing, Washington, D.C. area, *cohousing.org/regions/midatlantic*
- East Bay Cohousing, Oakland-Berkeley, California, *ebcoho.org*
- Northern California, *norcalcoho.org*
- Southern California, Greater Los Angeles, *socalcoho.org*
- Cohousing for San Diego, San Diego, California, *cohousingforsandiego.org*
- Chicago Cohousing Network, *chicagocohousing.net*
- Northwest Intentional Communities Association, Washington and Oregon: *ic.org/nica*
- Colorado Cohousing Council, Denver-Boulder area, *cohousing.org/regions/colorado*
- Twin Cities Cohousing Network, Minneapolis-St. Paul, *mn.cohousing.org/tccntop.htm*

and have fun in the process. For the communities movement as a whole, this recent media affection for cohousing is a long-needed shot in the arm.

Like most people drawn to community living, many cohousers are visionaries, and many, as the widely-quoted cohousing phrase says, are "building a sustainable society one neighborhood at a time." They often fall in love with the heart-opening moments of community living, from the congenial shared meals and lively conversations to the solid support of neighbors who are there for you just when you need them. "Only in cohousing," you sometimes hear, "do you find people who_____" — and then they fill in the blank with the warm fuzzy moment of the day. This is usually from people new to cohousing and not much aware of the wider communities movement. While I applaud cohousers and the movement they are creating, some of us in the wider communities movement would like the cohousers new to community to know that it's not only in cohousing that these wonderful things happen.

Cohousing Communities and Non-Cohousing Communities

As a new housing phenomenon in North America, cohousing is radical. Imagine, from a mainstream culture's perspective, suburban neighbors who actually know each other, make decisions together, share resources, and eat together several times a week — and not only that, why, they even recycle and make compost! Cohousers tend to be mainstream-but-progressive retirees with savings or two-income or single professionals with substantial borrowing power, as well as many single women. (Chris ScottHanson points out that two-thirds of those living in cohousing are women, and half of those are single, with children or post-children.) While non-cohousing communitarians are often adept at good group process — sharing

circles, the talking stick process, check-ins, and heartshares — many cohousers tend not to be drawn to such processes, and some seem to have an aversion to "that damned touchy feely stuff." But unlike many non-cohousing communitarians (some of whom wouldn't know a business contract, promissory note, or strategic plan from a hole in the wall), the founders of successful cohousing projects tend to know very well how to work the system — they're adept at creating budgets and cash-flow projections, evaluating properties, and securing loans.

In the first decade or so of cohousing in North America, from the mid-1980s through the 1990s, there was a certain amount of distance between cohousing activists and the wider intentional communities movement. Early cohousers feared being associated with "hippie communes" in the minds of local zoning and lending officials, whom they had to convince to grant zoning variances and loans for housing projects that seemed, well, unorthodox to say the least. In spite of the fact that the communities movement is broad and varied, and nowadays contains relatively few hippies or communes, many cohousing leaders and activists formerly tended to look down their noses at other kinds of communities. This prejudice worked both ways, too. Longtime communitarians tended to look askance at cohousers as well, for being too middle-class. "They're not building community," sniffed a long-time community veteran. "They're building *buildings*."

The mutual suspicion has mellowed quite a bit in recent years. Now the Cohousing Association of the US (Coho/US) regularly invites activists from the Fellowship for Intentional Community (FIC) to present workshops at their biennial national conferences. *Communities* magazine, which is published by the FIC, features cohousing in every issue, and developing cohousing communities support the magazine with their advertising dollars. The webmasters of the FIC and Coho/US regularly collaborate and share data for their communities directories. And two cohousing activists are board members of both organizations.

This is good, because in my opinion, cohousers and non-cohousers have much to learn from one another. When I began researching communities in the 1990s, I saw that roughly only ten percent of newly forming communities ever got built. The other 90 percent disbanded before they ever got off the ground. (See *Creating a Life Together: Practical Tools to Grow Ecovillages and Intentional Communities*.) But Chuck Durrett believes one cohousing start-up in three gets built, which suggests that cohousing community founders are considerably more successful than non-cohousing founders. It's obvious why. People attracted to cohousing, and who can afford it, tend to be proficient in the real-world skills needed to locate, finance, and develop property. Non-cohousing community founders can learn a lot from the practical, step-by-step methods used by the cohousing groups who get their projects completed. At the same time, cohousers often have more conflict and need more outside help from community process consultants than most non-cohousing communities — which I assume results from their relative inexperience with (and perhaps impatience with) that "touchy feely stuff." So cohousers can learn a lot from veteran communitarians as well — and they do. Three experienced communitarian friends of mine travel around the US regularly to teach consensus, consensus facilitation, and conflict resolution to forming and already-existing cohousing communities.

How do cohousing communities and ecovillages compare? Let me tell you a story. I love to visit Westwood Cohousing when I'm in Asheville, just 50 minutes from Earthaven. Two dear friends live

there, and many people I'm friendly with. Sometimes I do workshops, consultations, or my ecovillage slide show for Westwood residents. And they, bless their hearts, put me up in their common house guest room when I need to stay overnight in town. Once when I had a *Communities* magazine deadline the solar system on my homesite at Earthaven broke down, rendering my laptop, printer, and water pump useless. I drove to Asheville to stay in Westwood's Common House for a few days, where I had — lo and behold! — grid electricity and hot running water. (In fact, the hot water was from their rooftop solar hot water system.) I got the magazine issue out on time, and enjoyed long, wonderful showers, thanks to friends in cohousing. A few months later I stopped by and met several Westwood folks on their pedestrian path. "We visited Earthaven last Saturday and took the tour," they said, giving me a knowing eye and giggling. I knew why they found this funny. *They* live in a beautiful, finished community with attractive landscaping and nicely painted, normal-looking housing units with ever-ready electricity and hot water (solar heated), a centralized zoned radiant floor heating system, and a paved parking lot full of clean cars. Their community was privately financed before building, designed by an architect and mechanical engineer, built by a contractor, and — bang! — finished in 16 months. What they'd seen the previous Saturday, however, where *I* live, was tiny earth-plastered huts heated with woodstoves, projects under construction, roof-water catchment and cisterns, tiny wooden outhouses, mud-splashed trucks parked along gravel roads and multiple stacks of useful salvaged items — also known as unsightly piles of junk. Our community was financed by what our founders had in the bank at the time or could borrow from friends, designed by enthusiastic visionary amateurs, built on-and-off, homemade-style, by first-time owner-builders and self-taught carpenters, and it isn't finished yet and won't be for decades. *They* walk on paved paths, turn on faucets, and flip switches in a clean environment; *we* live amid earth and mud, limit our use of water, electricity, and propane, and daily "chop wood, carry water."

"What's the difference between a Westwood person and an Earthaven person?" I asked, suddenly seized by amusement. "What's the difference? Huh? Do you give up?" I held out my outstretched hands, palms down. "Show me your hands," I said. "See? Westwood people have clean fingernails; Earthaven people don't." We all cracked up. I thought the metaphor was hilarious — and apt. I still do.

"In our view," write Raines Cohen and Betsy Morris in the Summer, 2005 issue of *Communities* magazine, "cohousing expands the intentional communities movement by teaching people the basics of dealing with the realities of real estate and housing markets — essentially offering a strong set of lessons on the get-it-built aspects of creating community. The cohousing movement builds on widespread social practices, such as private financing of homes, and offers a process for others to follow within that system. It also offers a context where people feel they can become more of who they'd like to be, environmentally and socially."

If you feel drawn to cohousing, you're in luck. The phenomenon is growing so fast that if you live anywhere near a mid-sized city, there is probably a cohousing community near you, or soon will be.

Elder Cohousing

"Senior cohousing" or "elder cohousing" is a new and growing subset of the cohousing movement, designed for older people who seek an alternative to retirement communities and retirement homes, people who want "age in community" within a close-knit group of neighbors. These cohousing communities have ground-floor apartments with extra-wide doors for accessibility, and sometimes common houses with studio apartments as living quarters for home health aides whose services may be shared by several residents. For example, here's the mission and purpose statement of Glacier

COHOUSING COMMUNITIES CITED IN THIS CHAPTER

- Sunward Cohousing, Ann Arbor, Michigan, *sunward.org*
- Swan's Market Cohousing, Oakland, California, *swansway.com*
- Blueberry Hill, Vienna, Virginia, *blueberryhill.org*
- Island Cohousing, Martha's Vineyard, Massachusetts, *icoho.org*
- Heartwood Cohousing, Bayfield, Colorado: *heartwoodcohousing.com*
- Winslow Cohousing, Bainbridge Island, Washington, *winslowcohousing.org*
- EcoVillage at Ithaca, New York, *ecovillage.ithaca.ny.us*

- Berkeley Cohousing, California, *berkcoho-info@coho.org*
- Jamaica Plain Cohousing, Boston, Massachusetts, *jpcohousing.org*
- Fordyce Place Cohousing, Ashland, Oregon, *ashlandcoho.com*
- Nomad Cohousing, Boulder, Colorado, *nomadcohousing.org*
- Wild Sage Cohousing, Boulder, Colorado, *wildsagecohousing.org*
- Westwood Cohousing, Asheville, North Carolina, *westwoodcohousing.com*

Circle Senior Community in Davis, California: "To create and maintain a small cooperative-style housing community of seniors who share some expenses, skills and visions in mutual support and friendship. We are committed to being a welcoming community of independent outlooks and shared values."

Senior cohousing began in Denmark in the 1980s, and in the early 2000s became a growing phenomenon in North America as well. For a quick online overview, see ElderSpirit Community in Abingdon, Virginia (*elderspirit.net*), and Silver Sage Village in Boulder, Colorado (*silversagevillage.com*).

According to the US Census Bureau, one American turns 50 every 7 seconds and 10,000 turn 59 every day. The baby boomers are going gray. But unlike indigenous cultures, or southern Europe and most of Latin America, where people live out their elder years with their extended families, in North America, northern European cultures, and industrialized Asian nations, most elders live on their own, in assisted living centers, retirement homes, or nursing homes. People in the global South house, feed, and nurse their elders. In the North, we isolate them.

But increasing numbers of North Americans don't want this at all. According to an *AARP Bulletin* article, "Communes for Grownups" (November, 2004), "22 percent of 500 respondents aged 50 to 65 said they'd be interested in building a new home to share with friends that included private space and communal living areas." Long-time elder care administrator Emily Headley interviewed residents in an assisted living center, asking the question: "What brings you fulfillment at this time in your life?" The overwhelming response of each person she interviewed centered on one theme: *human connection*. And author Joan Medlicott has written a series of best-selling "Covington Ladies" novels, about three friends over 60 who live together happily in shared housing. Joan is continually being asked by her older women readers how they, too, can live with other women this way.

"Elders are looking for ways to enjoy the company of friends in a supportive setting providing independent housing and the benefits of community," write elder cohousing activists Zev Paiss and Neshama Abraham of the Elder Cohousing Network (*eldercohousing.org*). "In elder cohousing residents can grow older meaningfully, consciously and independently in a self-managed, close-knit community."

It's not just cohousers who are getting involved in communities for elders. The well-known geriatrician Dr. Bill Thomas, author of *What Are Old People For?* (VanderWyk and Burnham, 2004), chose the cohousing model for his planned Elder-Shire communities — multi-generational yet "elder-rich" communities with special physical and social features to benefit seniors (*eldershire.net*).

Yet, some older people attracted to elder cohousing become even more interested in multi-generational cohousing once they learn about it, since multi-generational cohousing resembles an old-fashioned village, where younger friends and neighbors might help elders in various ways as they get older. Multi-generational cohousing, however, is not set up to provide the nursing and hospice care that elder cohousing activists envision.

The communities movement isn't all ecovillages and cohousing, though. In Chapters 6 through 10 we'll consider the many other kinds of intentional communities you can choose from.

≈ Chapter 6 ≈

Urban Communities:
Group Households and Housing Co-ops

"URBAN COMMUNITIES" refers to a location rather than a particular kind of community, since urban communities are as diverse in structure and purpose as the communities movement as a whole. Some ecovillages, for example, are urban, and most cohousing communities are urban or suburban. Many of the communities we'll look at in upcoming chapters are sometimes located in a city, including spiritual communities, Christian communities, and income-sharing communes. What many urban communities have in common is that most community members have local jobs outside the community, and sometimes members pay rent rather than co-owning a shared property. Also, many urban communities are organized as housing co-ops, as we'll see below.

Urban Group Households

The reasons people live in urban communities can include sharing expenses and saving money, reducing one's environmental impact, and enjoying the company of friends and fellow community members. Sometimes this means buying a large house together and living together as co-owners (perhaps renting out some bedrooms to tenant-members) as in Ganas Community in Staten Island, New York. In other urban communities everyone rents, like at Bob, the House, in Seattle.

"We are an urban community of six members who seek to model a way of living from the heart that involves living responsibly, nonviolently, and

ecologically," says Hearthaven, in Kansas City, Missouri. "Most of us think of ourselves as a bonded, caring, hard working, fun-loving, extended family," says Ganas.

It's not uncommon for an urban community to have a specific purpose to assist others. Magic in Palo Alto, California, for example, serves as a home base for a small group of environmental activists.

Some urban communities offer food, hospitality, and other assistance to the urban poor, such as Jesus People USA, whose members live in a renovated office building in inner city Chicago, the many Catholic Worker communities with a similar mission, or the many L'Arche communities which offer a nurturing environment for developmentally disabled people. You can read more about these communities in Chapters 8 and 9.

We already know most cohousing communities are urban or suburban, and some ecovillages are urban too, such as Los Angeles Eco-Village, and Ecovillage Detroit. And urban ecovillagers sometimes rent rather than own property. As we've seen, LA Eco-Villagers rent housing units in two adjacent apartment buildings. Residents of Maitreya Ecovillage rent 25 shared houses and apartments on five adjacent lots near downtown Eugene, Oregon.

Sometimes a community can have two locations: one urban and one rural. Members of Community Alternatives Society in British Columbia, for example, can choose between Community Alternatives Co-op in the False Creek area of downtown Vancouver, with all the stimulation of big city life, or Fraser Common Farm an hour away near Langley, where they can relax in the fresh air and quiet atmosphere of the country — and residents of either location can visit the other any time. And an urban community can also look and feel as if it were rural. Members of Tryon Life Community Farm, for example, a community-based sustainability education center, live in two large farmhouses among meadows and woods, where they raise goats and tend large organic gardens, surrounded by the native forest of the 650-acre Tryon Creek State Park. However, they're located inside the city limits of Portland, Oregon, just a half-hour bike ride from downtown.

Organized Neighborhoods

Sometimes when people want more community in their lives, they organize their neighborhoods to make a kind of intentional-community-right-where-we-live. The founders of Los Angeles Eco-Village organized a small part of their downtown neighborhood, and a supportive nonprofit bought two adjacent apartment buildings for them and other people to renovate and move in to as tenants. In Davis, California, over a period of several years a group of friends bought up houses around a city block on N Street, tore down the backyard fences to create a large common area with gardens and children's play areas, and, turning one of the houses into their common house, called it N Street Cohousing. Ganas Community in Staten Island is similar, with most of its houses on one block, with fences removed and large common gardens between them (with single houses on adjacent blocks). Cincinnati neighbors living on both sides of Enright Avenue, a half-mile dead end street surrounded by woods, are creating Enright Ridge Ecovillage as an organized neighborhood. Two brothers, Brad and Rod Lancaster, are creating an ecologically oriented virtual community in a working class neighborhood in Tucson, Arizona. Permaculture teacher Andrew Millison is helping create an organized "Eco-Hood" in a working class neighborhood in Prescott, Arizona.

Housing Co-ops

Many urban communities are organized as housing cooperatives, or "housing co-ops." This is a legal term for one way people can share property ownership together. (Sometimes people also use the term "co-op household" in a non-legal, more colloquial sense, meaning any kind of urban group household where people live together in one or more houses.) In true housing cooperatives in the legal sense, in most cases people buy shares in the co-op and become co-owners of the property, and each co-op member leases a particular unit from

ORGANIZED NEIGHBORHOOD RESOURCES

- *Superbia! 31 Ways to Create Sustainable Neighborhoods,* Dan Chiras and Dave Wann, New Society Publishers, 2003.
- Los Angeles Eco-Village, *ic.org/laev*
- N Street Cohousing, *nstreetcohousing.org*

- Enright Ridge Ecovillage, Cincinatti, Ohio, "A Home-Grown Ecovillage on Our Street," *Communities* magazine, Winter 2005.
- Eco-Hood, Prescott, Arizona. "Prescott's Sustainable 'EcoHood'," *Communities* magazine, Summer, 2006.

the co-op. However, in many student co-op houses students just pay rent.

Here we're talking about limited equity housing co-ops, sometimes called affordable housing co-ops, and not market-rate housing, such as certain high-rise co-ops in Manhattan. In limited equity co-ops, members who leave can't sell their shares at a rate that earns them a profit; however, their shares can be sold at a higher price according to a formula set by the co-op's board of directors, but at a rate the board feels is low enough to keep the housing affordable. People who buy in take over the lease to a particular housing unit and the monthly payments of the departing member. This keeps the buy-in price affordable. (Sometimes, however, a co-op house is organized differently. At the ten-bedroom Walnut Street Co-op in Eugene, Oregon, people don't buy shares, and they don't take over the lease to a particular unit.)

Sometimes housing co-ops are small, family-like homes, like Walnut Street Co-op, or a group of such homes in a given city, such as the 11 houses of Madison Community Co-ops in Wisconsin. Sometimes they are high-rise apartment buildings, such as the senior housing co-ops managed by Co-op Services, Inc. in Michigan. Not all housing co-ops are urban; some are rural, such as Miccosukkee Land Co-op near Tallahassee, Florida, in which co-op members hold leases on different plots of ground, with the whole property owned by the whole group.

The overall co-op movement, which includes consumer co-ops, such as local food co-ops, and worker-owned co-ops, as well as housing co-ops, shares certain values in common. "Cooperatives are based on the values of self-help, self-responsibility, democracy, equality, equity, and solidarity," according to the values stated by the North American Students of Cooperation (NASCO). "In the tradition of their founders, cooperative members believe in the ethical values of honesty, openness, social responsibility, and caring for others."

The co-op movement didn't originate in the intentional communities movement, but in the labor movement. In 1844 a group of weavers in Rochdale, England, created an alliance within the weaving trade, the Rochdale Society of Equitable Pioneers, to protect their rights and to cooperatively own and manage a store to sell goods to their members at reasonable rates. Their organizing principles were amazingly progressive for the times, and for more than a century and a half they have guided co-ops worldwide.

People who join limited equity housing co-ops are generally politically progressive, and often are social justice and environmental activists (though not always: sometimes people join low-income housing co-ops and high-rise urban senior co-ops, which cost less than similar local housing, out of economic necessity). "Stone Soup is an urban intentional community of three co-op houses dedicated to joy and justice," says Stone Soup Co-operative in Chicago. "Our members are organizers, teachers, social workers, students, artists, and others doing creative work for social change. We support each other's commitment to social justice with a caring, creative, and fun living environment."

"Our mission is to provide affordable cooperative housing for a diverse membership through cooperatively owned property, communal living, and resource sharing, while upholding principles of sustainability, peace, racial and economic justice, lifelong cooperative living, and involvement in local community," says Hei Wa House in Ann Arbor, Michigan.

Most urban communities and housing co-ops value ecological sustainability. The "greenest" are urban ecovillages and many urban group households and affordable or student housing co-ops. Most of these buy or grow organic food, compost and recycle their waste, bicycle or use public transportation when possible, and when they renovate their houses, retrofit them in more energy-efficient ways. Senior housing co-ops and urban Christian service-oriented communities don't seem to value these practices as much.

Senior Housing Co-ops

Senior housing co-ops were created in order to offer seniors affordable housing and an opportunity to own and manage their own housing themselves. Approximately 100 senior housing co-ops are operating in the United States, administered primarily by the Senior Cooperative Network in St. Paul, Minnesota, and Co-op Services, Inc. in Warren, Michigan. Most senior housing co-ops in North America are located in Minnesota and Michigan, with several in Massachusetts, Maryland, and California, and in Eastern Ontario in Canada. Some senior co-ops are market-rate co-ops and some are limited equity co-ops.

The media is catching onto the appeal of sen-

ior housing co-ops too: "Co-ops Could be Housing Answer for Aging Baby Boomers, Elderly," was a headline in the September 10, 2005 issue of the *Washington Post*, for example.

"The opportunities for growth and well-being in our senior co-op are endless," writes South Bay Co-op member Bevelyn Carpenter in the Winter, 1995 issue of *Communities* magazine. "Living here has helped me to realize how much more I can do, how much more I have to offer, and how much more wisdom or knowledge I have than I ever thought. The elderly living out lonely years alone in a big house is no longer necessary. The belonging, working, sharing, and personal growth in the years of retirement, or any age, can be much richer in community."

Some senior housing co-ops can certainly be identified as intentional communities; their residents have a common purpose (to live healthier, safer lives in a setting where they co-own their shared housing and make cooperative decisions about it) and a high degree of cooperation and

---

URBAN COMMUNITIES CITED IN THIS CHAPTER

- Bob, the House, Seattle, Washington, *bobthehouse@lists.riseup.net*
- Hearthaven, Kansas City, Missouri, *rjm@shadowcliff.org*
- Ganas, Staten Island, New York, *ganas.org*
- Magic, Palo Alto, California, *ecomagic.org*
- Jesus People, USA, Chicago, Illinois, *jpusa.org*
- Catholic Worker Communities, North America, *catholicworker.org/communities*
- L'Arche Communities, Canada, *larchecanada.org*
- L'Arche Communities, USA, *larcheusa.org*
- Los Angeles Eco-Village, Los Angeles, California, *ic.org/laev*
- EcoVillage Detroit, Michigan, *ecovillagedetroit.org*

- Maitreya Ecovillage, Eugene, Oregon, *melanie@rios.org*
- Community Alternatives Co-op, Vancouver, B.C.
- Fraser Common Farm, Langley, B.C.
- Tryon Life Community Farm, Portland, Oregon, *tryonfarm.org*
- N Street Cohousing, Davis, California, *nstreetcohousing.org*
- Walnut Street Co-op, Eugene, Oregon, *icetree.com/walnut*
- Stone Soup Co-op, Chicago, Illinois, *stonesoupcoop.org*
- Hei Wa House, Ann Arbor, Michigan, *ic.org/heiwa*

social interaction. Others seem more like normal apartment buildings, with a less significant level of connection between the residents.

Student Housing Co-ops

Like senior housing co-ops, student co-op houses offer students relatively low-cost urban housing (and in the Midwest, sometimes, semi-rural housing) and the opportunity to manage the assets and earnings of their houses themselves, and to make

decisions cooperatively. The students are expected to work an average of five hours per week for the co-op, for example, cleaning, cooking, and participating in house meetings.

More than 100 student co-op houses have been organized in North America. They are owned and administered either by a university, or by a nonprofit organization which purchases and helps develop multiple co-op houses in their university towns. North American Students of

HOUSING CO-OP ASSOCIATIONS

Affordable Housing Co-ops
- National Association of Housing Co-ops (NAHC), Washington D.C., *coophousing.org*
- Seaway Valley Co-ops, Kingston, Ontario, *tmoz.com/svco*
- The Co-operative Housing Federation of British Columbia, *chf.bc.ca*
- Boston Community Cooperatives, Massachusetts, *bostoncoop.net/bcc*
- Madison Community Cooperative, Wisconsin, *madisoncommunity.coop*

Senior Housing
- Senior Cooperative Foundation, St. Paul, Minnesota, *seniorcoops.org*
- Cooperative Services, Inc., Warren, Michigan, *csi.coop*

Student Housing
- North American Students of Cooperation (NASCO), Ann Arbor, Michigan, *nasco.coop* NASCO's website lists all the associations of multiple student co-op houses as well as individual student co-ops, in Canada and the US. If you don't see your city listed here, check the co-op directory part of the NASCO website; there very well may be a smaller association or individual student co-op house near your college or university. Some of the largest student co-op associations include:

Canada
- Waterloo Co-operative Residence, Inc., Montreal, *wcri.org*

US
- Chateau Student Housing Cooperative, Minneapolis, *chateau.coop*
- College Houses, Austin, Texas, *collegehouses.coop*
- Davis Campus Cooperatives, California, *daviscampusco-ops.net*
- Franklin Student Housing Cooperative, Minneapolis, *franklin.coop*
- Inter-Cooperative Council at the University of Texas, Austin, *icaustin.coop*
- Inter-Cooperative Council, Ann Arbor, Michigan, *icc.coop*
- Madison Community Cooperatives, Madison, Wisconsin, *madisoncommunity.coop*
- MSU Student Housing Cooperative, East Lansing, Michigan: *www.msu.edu/user/coop*
- Oberlin Student Cooperative Association, Oberlin, Ohio, *osca.wilder.oberlin.edu*
- Oregon State Cooperative Housing, Corvalis, Oregon, *uhds.oregonstate.edu/halls/coops*
- University Cooperative Housing Association, Los Angeles, *uchaonline.com*
- University Students' Cooperative Associatio, Berkeley Student Co-op Housing, *usca.org*

Cooperation (NASCO) advocates for, helps develop, and offers operational assistance to student co-op houses, and networks of student co-op housing, in the United States and Canada.

Students who live in student housing co-ops are sometimes profoundly affected by the experience. In "Ruined for American Culture" (*Communities* magazine, Winter, 2004), Shimon Whiteson, who lived at a student co-op in Austin, writes, "What a great resume-builder! When prospective employers ask me what experience I have with financial responsibility, I can say I served as treasurer for a student-run co-op, managing the food budget of 20 people. When they ask me what leadership experience I have, I can say I served on the board of directors of a nonprofit organization with an annual budget of a million dollars. When they ask me what experience I have mediating personal conflicts, there will be too many examples to count."

Living in a student co-op can also inspire its members to join an intentional community, or start their own, after they graduate. Two members of Sunflower House co-op in Lawrence, Kansas, for example, moved to Twin Oaks community after graduating, and still lived there 15 years later. Three members of Synergy student co-op in Stanford, along with non-co-op friends, later founded Dancing Rabbit Ecovillage in Missouri. And residents of N Street Co-op in Davis, California, enjoyed the experience so much they didn't want to leave after they graduated. They saved up their money and bought the house, and they and other friends later bought other houses on the same block — creating N Street Cohousing.

"I firmly believe I learned as much about life living at Lothlorien as I did in the classrooms of Berkeley," writes Ted Sterling , who now lives at Dancing Rabbit Ecovillage. "It is impossible to convey the immense joy of life there, of living as a family of 55, any of whom you would support to the ends of the Earth." (*Communities*, Spring, 2001.)

If you're about to head off for college and want to live in community, ask NASCO for the names and contact information for student housing networks or individual student co-ops for the areas of the schools you're applying for. Living in a student co-op could be one the best things you ever learned in college.

Chapter 7

Rural Homesteading Communities, Conference and Retreat Centers

L IKE "URBAN COMMUNITIES," the term "rural communities" refers to a location rather than a specific kind of community. In this chapter we look at three kinds of rural communities: homesteading communities, conference and retreat centers, and gay and lesbian communities.

Homesteading Communities

Classic back-to-the-land rural homesteading communities focus on growing food and/or raising livestock, and practicing the necessary homesteading skills for living a self-reliant country life. In some homesteading communities everyone works on the land, for example, when the community has a farming or food-producing operation. In others, while people grow much of their own food onsite, they also earn income through their own small onsite businesses or by working in nearby towns.

The 11 members of Birdsfoot Farm live on a 73-acre agricultural property in upstate New York with woods, a stream, and community buildings. In their two-acre vegetable garden they grow certified organic produce for their CSA farm, local retail outlets, the local farmer's market, and their own use. They also operate Little River School, employing three teachers and serving local students from kindergarten to 12th grade. Their vegetable business and Little River School provide income to some of their members, while others work in jobs off the property. As in many rural commu-

nities, Birdsfoot Farm members are active on social justice and environmental issues.

Sandhill Farm, in rural northeast Missouri, has 135 acres and 5 year-round members, assisted by many interns who live onsite during the growing and harvesting seasons. Sandhill Farm's land includes gardens, orchards, woods, hayfields, cropland, bee yards, and pastures. An income-sharing commune, Sandhill members earn money by growing organic sorghum, soybeans, and herbs, and processing and selling sorghum syrup, tempeh, garlic, mustard, horseradish, and honey. They also generate an income by doing administrative work for the Fellowship for Intentional Community (FIC), whose office is on their property. One Sandhill member offers group process consulting nationwide; another is an organic farm inspector. "We like to keep our lifestyle simple and healthy," they note on their website. "We tend to work hard, especially during the growing season, and get satisfaction from providing for ourselves as much as we can while maintaining close ties with neighbors, friends, and other communities. Core values include cooperation, nonviolence, honesty, and working through conflict."

The 7 members of Edges community, who live on 94 acres of wooded and cleared hills near Athens, Ohio, also grow and put up much of their own food from their organic gardens. And while community members do many homesteading tasks, including gardening, ordering community food, maintenance, construction, land restoration, and permaculture projects, many also have full-time work on the property or offsite. One Edges member operates a successful renewable energy design and installation business; two others operate an onsite bed and breakfast and Wellness Center; and one is a psychologist at Ohio University. Other members work at a cooperative bakery in Athens, do book editing at home, or market eco-friendly air filters.

The dozen members of Windward Community, on 111 acres near Klickitat, Washington, raise fiber sheep and dairy goats. Part of their mission and purpose, notes their website, is to "interweave the skills of the past with appropriate technology to create a hands-on, back-to-basics way to practice right livelihood."

Sometimes a rural community has a village-like setting, such as Morninglory Community near Killaloe, Ontario, with 14 members in 9 separate households scattered over 100 hilly acres. "We homestead in varying degrees, use only solar electricity and wood heat, and grow organically most of our fruits and veggies. We've spent 30 years learning how to be good neighbors, which has been a worthwhile process." One community family runs a home-based, ecologically friendly business, Cool Hemp, providing an organic hempseed frozen dessert.

While many rural communities like these value ecological sustainability, and many grow much of their own food, they aren't ecovillages. Many were founded in the '60s and '70s, before the concept of ecovillages existed, and most are not attempting to be model demonstration sites or to influence the wider culture, per se. Some, in fact, are fairly insular, seeking to just live a simple life in the country with family and friends. Yet Sandhill Farm grows perhaps 80 percent of its own food, an amount far higher than most aspiring ecovillage

projects, and all of Morninglory's households are off the grid, which is not true yet of most ecovillages.

Some of the benefits of living in rural communities are obvious: for example, the opportunity to live where it's peaceful, quiet, and often beautiful, and to experience a pitch-black sky dotted with brilliant stars at night — to actually see the Milky Way. If you're interested in food self-reliance, living in a rural homesteading community offers an opportunity to grow much more of your own food than you could in an urban or suburban setting. In rural counties, unlike urban and suburban areas, you would be free to have chickens, ducks, goats, sheep, and larger livestock animals. Building codes are often less enforced in rural counties, and there are often few to no zoning regulations. This means that a rural community has more freedom to have many members live there, to build smaller-than-normal dwellings, and to build with strawbale, cob, or adobe bricks, or to use compost toilets, constructed wetlands, roof-water catchment, and so on. Another advantage for people moving from urban areas is that people tend to need less money for housing and monthly expenses living in rural communities that they would in urban areas.

The primary disadvantage, however, is the relative lack of job opportunities in rural areas. As you can see in the above examples, either everyone works on the farm or in the garden (as at Birdsfoot Farm and Sandhill Farm), or works partly at the homesite and earns money from home-based businesses, or works in town. In must rural towns there are few job opportunities, and usually those that exist are of the most rudimentary, minimum-wage kind. Local employers tend to prefer hiring people they've known all their lives, not necessarily newcomer city slickers from the local intentional community. Rural communities tend to work well for telecommuters, people with home-based businesses, people who can easily plug into community-based farm work, people who already have a source of income, or people willing to travel offsite frequently to earn money, such as consultants. Other disadvantages include the need to travel long distances to get most places, which can use up a lot of gas, and the sense of isolation that can occur in a rural community, particularly if the community has relatively few members and is culturally different from, or not much connected with, its rural neighbors.

Conference and Retreat Centers

Conference and retreat center communities, located in rural or semi-rural locations, offer their own workshops — on ecological sustainability, environmental activism, personal growth topics, and/or spiritual subjects — and often provide a venue for the courses and workshops of other groups as well. Sometimes these centers also operate schools or summer camps. Usually a small number of members live there year-round, assisted by a large number of interns or work exchangers who live in the community only during the guest season.

Lost Valley Educational Center, for example, is an 87-acre property of meadows, forest, and a creek, not far from Eugene, Oregon. Lost Valley members grow much of their own food in their large gardens and greenhouses, and operate a 150-bed conference and retreat center. Besides renting these facilities to outside groups who host workshops and courses, Lost Valley offers its own programs, including a two-month residential Ecovillage and Permaculture Certificate Program and the Heart of Now personal growth workshops. About 18 people live in the community year-round, some of whom work in the conference center quarter-time to full-time, and others who work at other home-based businesses or commute to Eugene.

Another example is Sowing Circle Community in Occidental, California, which leases most of its 80-acre property and its two locally famous heirloom organic gardens to its affiliated nonprofit, Occidental Arts and Ecology Center

THE MANY FACES OF COMMUNITY

As you can see, many urban and rural intentional communities don't fit in any single "kind of community" category, but in several all at once. In fact, the idea of "kinds of communities" and "categories" is an oversimplification, used just to give a quick overview of what's out there.

For example, EcoVillage at Ithaca is both an ecovillage and cohousing. Temescal Commons in Oakland is a Christian community and a cohousing community. Jesus People USA in downtown Chicago is a Christian community and a large urban group household. Miccosukee Land Co-op in Florida is a rural community and a co-op.

Some homesteading communities with a spiritual focus, such as The Farm in Tennessee are also spiritual communities. Some gay men's communities, such as Ida and Short Mountain, are also homesteading communities. Some retreat and conference centers, like Rowe Camp and Conference Center, are also Christian communities; others, like Breitenbush Hot Springs and Mount Madonna Center, are also spiritual communities. Lama Foundation, Ananda Village, and Abode of the Message (see Chapter 8) are spiritual communities as well as retreat and conference centers. Camphill communities are simultaneously spiritual communities, rural homesteading communities, service communities — and some believe they're also ecovillages.

(OAEC). The Center offers public courses in permaculture design, bio-intensive organic gardening, heirloom seed saving, and even how to start new intentional communities. Like many communitarians, Sowing Circle members are dedicated environmental activists, so OAEC also runs environmental ethics and activist programs, for example, to train environmental activists, stop local pesticide spraying, outlaw genetically modified foods in their county, add water-resource management to the county's General Plan, and establish organic gardens and organic gardening education in northern California schools. About half the 11 community members work for OAEC; the rest have teaching or activist jobs in Sonoma County or nearby Santa Rosa.

Rowe Camp and Conference Center is a 45-acre Christian community (Unitarian Universalist) in the Berkshire Mountains of Western Massachusetts. Some of the community's 15 year-round members serve as resident staff for the conference center and their annual children's summer camp, assisted by temporary work-study members who live there from 6 weeks to a year. Other community members work at jobs offsite.

Breitenbush Hot Springs Retreat and Conference Center, an off-grid spiritual community on 155-acres with a hot springs by a river in Oregon's

GAY AND LESBIAN COMMUNITIES

Most gay and lesbian communities are also rural. The Susan B. Anthony Land Trust is a 150-acre women's outdoor education center and land trust in the foothills of the Appalachians near Athens, Ohio. The community's purpose is to offer safe, congenial, inexpensive living space for women. They have a campground and offer workshops on topics such as racism, nature and the arts, and practical skills for women. Six resident members live on the property, and friends in the wider community support the group's vision and contribute financially.

Easton Mountain Center, in upstate New York, is a conference and retreat center for spiritually oriented gay men, hosting workshops on spirituality and other topics. Like the Susan B. Anthony Land Trust, they also have a wider community of friends who support their vision and help financially.

The members of We'Moon Land, a 52-acre women's community near Portland, Oregon, publish the well-known annual datebook, the We'Moon Calendar, featuring women's art and poetry.

Zuni Mountain Sanctuary, in the Zuni Mountains of western New Mexico, is a community for gay men. Six resident land stewards live on a 320-acre land trust and host many visitors, with a purpose to provide an environment for spiritual growth and renewal. Zuni residents use the principles of permaculture design and holistic land management, conserving land and water resources, gardening organically, recycling, building passive solar buildings, and using solar power for electricity.

The 200-acre Short Mountain Sanctuary near Liberty, Tennessee, is also a community for gay men, with 18 members and many guests. "We strive to live lightly on the land and to maintain an environment that is open, free, and stimulating to each person's growth and creativity. Life here is simple and rustic. We drink spring water, use an outhouse, and heat with wood. What electricity we have we collect from the sun. We grow much of our food, herbs, and dazzling flowers. Goats supply us with milk and chickens with eggs. We publish RFD: A Country Journal for Queer Folk Everywhere, and host two faerie gatherings a year."

Queer in Community is a networking organization for members and supporters of gay, lesbian, bisexual, and transgendered people in community.

Cascade Mountains, uses geothermal and micro-hydro to generate power. The community's guests, up to 25,000 annually, soak in the hot springs and take courses on holistic healing, spirituality, and other topics. "Our primary service is to provide a healing retreat and conference center that promotes holistic health and spiritual growth," reads their website. "We mutually support and respect each person's dignity, and awaken to the Spirit within each of us that acknowledges we are all One." Long-term community members and many shorter-term members, ranging from 50 to 90 people total, run the retreat and conference center as a worker-owned co-op, and live their more private community lives in small dwellings across the river from the guest facilities.

Mount Madonna Center, also a spiritual community, is located on 355 acres in the Santa Cruz mountains of California. Led by the Indian teacher Baba Hari Das, Mount Madonna runs a conference center which hosts up to 14,000 work-shop participants each year. The community also operates a children's school, serving students from preschool through high school. Mount Madonna's 100 members focus on yoga and service, and many serve as volunteers for the conference center and school. "We share in work, vegetarian meals, spiritual practices, rituals, and play, and strive to live by positive values," notes their website.

Centers like these, like rural homesteading communities, offer the benefits of peaceful, quiet, beautiful settings, as well as the opportunity to serve others, and to take many courses and workshops onsite. Another benefit is that they provide jobs in the community-owned conference center business. The downside is that these jobs usually pay minimum wage, or just room and board in the community and perhaps a small stipend for workers, and there often aren't enough jobs for all community members, so some must work outside the community. A common dynamic in conference center communities is the tension between the

RURAL COMMUNITIES CITED IN THIS CHAPTER

- Birdsfoot Farm, Canton, New York, *steve@littleriverschool.org*
- Sandhill Farm, Rutledge, Missouri, *sandhillfarm.org*
- Edges Community, Glouster, Ohio: *edgesfarm@aol.com*
- Windward Community, Klickitat, Washington, *windward.org*
- Morninglory Community, Killaloe, Ontario: RR 4, Killaloe, Ontario, K0J 2A0 Canada
- Lost Valley Educational Center, Dexter, Oregon, *lostvalley.org*
- Sowing Circle Community/OAEC, Occidental, California, *oaec.org*
- Rowe Camp and Conference Center, Rowe, Massachusetts, *rowecenter.org*
- Breitenbush Hot Springs, Detroit, Oregon, *breitenbush.com*
- Mount Madonna, Watsonville, California, *mountmadonna.org*
- Susan B. Anthony Land Trust, Athens, Ohio, *frognet.net/~sbamuh*
- Easton Mountain Center, Easton, New York, *eastonmountain.com*
- We'Moon Land, Estacada, Oregon, *wemoon.ws/land*
- Zuni Mountain Sanctuary, Ramah, New Mexico, *zms.org*
- Short Mountain Sanctuary, Liberty, Tennessee, *radfae.org/sms*
- Queer in Community, *queerincommunity.org*

purpose of the business, which is usually to serve guests well and stay financially solvent, and the purpose of the community itself, which is usually to share resources, cooperate in decision-making and work tasks, and enjoy a sense of connection with one another.

Chapter 8

Spiritual Communities

By "SPIRITUAL COMMUNITIES" I mean both spiritually eclectic communities, such as Breitenbush Hot Springs, mentioned in the last chapter, the Lama Foundation, The Farm, and others described below, as well as communities whose members practice a specific spiritual path or religious tradition. The latter can include yoga and meditation centers and yoga ashrams, communities that draw on Native American traditions, Sufi centers, residential Buddhist meditation centers (Zen, Tibetan, and Vipassana) and so on.

Many people may think "guru" or "one leader" when they think of intentional communities. As you know, this is not true of the communities we've considered so far, or of most communities you'll read about in this chapter, which have no single leader and govern themselves with some form of participatory democracy. However, most spiritual communities which have a common spiritual practice do have a single spiritual leader or group of elders, such as the yoga and Sufi communities you'll read about in this chapter, Mount Madonna Center, mentioned in the last chapter, and most Christian communities.

To give you a sense of life in a spiritual community, here's a description of Lama Foundation in New Mexico:

Just after the break of dawn I hear them. The bells. Their sound has been present every single day since Lama Foundation was begun in 1968 here in Taos, New Mexico. To me, the bells define the reason we are here — to remember. They say it is now morning meditation time, or breakfast time, or practice time, or meeting time. They are always a gentle reminder of where the group mind is focusing right now.

We call Lama Foundation a spiritual community because of our practice of religious traditions and commitment to personal growth. The founders had a vision to create a family-oriented monastery for the investigation of "inner space." Since then, many of the practices taught and practiced here have included Sufi *zhikr*, Hindu chanting, Native American sweat lodge, Insight Meditation, yoga, Japanese tea ceremony, and other creative practices.

People come from all over the world to share teachings, many of which seep into our curriculum. Many Lama residents believe that personal growth comes from our connection to Spirit, however we perceive it to be, and this sometimes includes suffering. Like a bean in a stewpot, one must simmer until done, thoroughly. Among the '60s-era communes in the Taos Valley, Lama is the only one to have survived — even through a devastating forest fire — mainly because it wasn't committed to sex, drugs, and rock and roll, but to spiritual practice, karma yoga, and conflict resolution.

However, we're actually high all the time, literally. The 110-acre community is nestled in a mountain forest near the base of Lama Mountain at 8600 ft. in the southern Rockies. When looking out to the west, with a vast sea of land and sky equally sharing the landscape, one gets the feeling of being in the Heaven realms, with no other people on Earth.

Lama is unusual among spiritual communities in that no one teacher resides here permanently. The practice of living in community is the real teaching. The resident circle becomes the teacher. Few secrets survive here for long. Our commitment to community process is present in the way we cook, dance, do business, have fun, make decisions, and work. We make all our decisions in business meetings by consensus, and roles in these meetings include a facilitator, heart guardian, and keeper of the hearth. The facilitator sticks to the agenda, calls on people, and serves as a servant to the circle. The heart guardian, known to other groups as a "vibes watcher," will ring a bell (there it is again) if the discussion gets too unfocused. The keeper of the heart sits in full meditation for 20 minutes, as disengaged from the discussion as possible, in order to maintain a space of respect and acknowledgment that the "spirit of guidance" is moving the process, not any one individual. We circle for a brief prayer before a group activity like cooking, eating, building, or meetings, acknowledging again our inherent oneness.

An abiding principle of Lama is that all traditions, no matter how old, have a kernel of the truth hidden within the outer forms, and that it is possible for people from different backgrounds and faiths (or no faith) to come together to share the light. Practitioners of faiths usually at odds in the geopolitical realms are inspired to share the space and let go of attachments to "being correct" or "defending the faith" and simply be friendly. Many of us hope that this

is a way of inspiring others to do the same, to respect each other and not have to prove that theirs is the "true religion".

The experience can be truly transformational. Like the tiny bean in the stewpot, many of us depart softer and tastier than when we arrived. Hard edges are smoothed. Inner triggers are loosened. Inner light shines just a little brighter. We go into the world with more gladness, detachment, and optimism, knowing that the mountain will likely be there for us should world-weariness create the need to drink from the well once again. Enduring, life-long friendships are made. The web of connection is expanded. Light is increased in a world obscured by darkness. The candle in the prayer room continues to burn. And the bells continue to ring.

(Excerpted from "Rocky Mountain High," by Scott Thomas, in Communities *magazine, Fall, 2004.)*

Spiritually Eclectic Communities

Here are a few examples of spiritually eclectic communities, starting with the Lama Foundation.

Lama Foundation was founded in 1968 near Taos, New Mexico, with the mission: "To be a sustainable spiritual community and educational center dedicated to the awakening of consciousness, spiritual practice with respect for all traditions, service, and stewardship of the land." In May through late September, with 50 or more residents and summer interns, Lama hosts visitors in a program of workshops, retreats, and hermitages. In winters, with the community covered in deep snow for five months, a core group of about 10–15 year-round residents take more intensive personal time for contemplation, spiritual practice, and study. Lama Foundation is not a Tibetan Buddhist community ("Lama" refers to the mountain on which the community sits), and, as noted above, has no one spiritual practice. The community invites teachers and attracts residents with a wide variety of spiritual practices. It's the place where in 1970 Ram Dass wrote his modern-day spiritual classic, *Be Here Now*. Lama members grow organic produce; compost and recycle; use roof water catchment, graywater recycling, and photovoltaic power; and build Earth-friendly passive solar buildings. Every year the community hosts a well-known natural building gathering, "Build Here Now." Housing and facilities are rustic, and life at Lama can be strenuous, year-round. Nevertheless, visitors and community members are drawn to the community, some to live in a supportive environment for daily practice and remembrance, others to relax in the deep stillness and peace of the high-altitude setting.

The Farm, near Summertown, Tennessee, was founded in 1971 when young people from the San Francisco Bay area and their spiritual teacher, Stephen Gaskin, traveled across the country in a bus caravan looking for land for a community based on the principles of nonviolence and a respect for the Earth. They landed in central Tennessee, and built homes, raised children, taught themselves to farm, and for many years raised most of their own grains, soybeans, and vegetables. Today, with 1,750 acres and 175 members, The Farm is like a rural village where many community members work onsite in individually owned businesses, including Farm Soy, the Farm Store, Village Media, and the Book Publishing Company. The Farm Education/Conference Center hosts retreats and conferences for outside groups. The Farm School offers alternative education to members' and neighbors' children.

"We started The Farm with the goal of establishing a strongly cohesive, outwardly-directed community," reads their website. "We wanted, by action and example, to have a positive effect on the world." I'm personally a big fan of The Farm because they really *do* have a positive effect on the world, inspired by their spiritual beliefs. For example, they started Plenty International, a non-governmental aid and development organization that works with indigenous and impoverished people in the US and internationally. Co-founder Ina May Gaskin and other Farm midwives are largely responsible for reviving midwifery in the West, through their onsite education and training programs for midwifery students, offering Farm-based home births for thousands of women over the years. The Farm's Kids To the Country project brings at-risk children to the community to enjoy nature and study peace education. Their Swan Conservation Trust protects fragile ecosystems in Tennessee's Western Highland Rim. Their Peace-Roots Alliance represents the community in the global peace movement. Farm members work in public schools to counter military recruitment, and their More Than Warmth project helps public and private school students create peace quilts which are sent to Africa, Afghanistan, and Iraq. Their Ecovillage Training Center offers workshops on permaculture design, installing off-grid power systems, ecovillage design, and other sustainability topics.

Sirius Community was founded in 1978 on 90 acres of woods near Amherst, Massachusetts, by people who had lived at the spiritual community the Findhorn Foundation in Scotland. Today Sirius has 36 members. The community's mission and purpose is to be a demonstration center of spiritual principles based on respect for the individual and cooperation with nature. "We are committed to living our lives with spiritual integrity, recognizing that we are all in a process of growth with every experience in our life offering valuable lessons," notes their website. "Our individual paths vary, but they all lead to a place of personal reflection, a study of Self on a deeper level leading to greater awareness and more conscious living." Sirius members garden organically, and use composting toilets and biodiesel fuel. They have built several passive-solar natural buildings and are partially off the grid with photovoltaics and a wind generator.

Communities with a Common Spiritual Practice

Ananda Village was founded in 1968 in the foothills of the Sierra Nevada Mountains near Nevada City, California. It is one of the largest spiritual communities in North America, and today owns 840 acres with 190 adults and 70 children. Ananda members are disciples of Paramhansa Yogananda, the Indian spiritual teacher who wrote *Autobiography of a Yogi*, and they practice the Kriya Yoga techniques he introduced to the West. The community is part of a larger worldwide movement based on Yogananda's teachings. Ananda Village operates various community-owned businesses and nonprofits. The Expanding Light, for example, is a guest retreat facility offering yoga and meditation instruction. Living Wisdom Schools provide normal schooling as well as yoga and meditation, and Living Wisdom Performing Arts Camp is an arts-based boarding and day camp for children and youth. Crystal Clarity Publishers produces books, video tapes, and CDs on yoga and meditation. Individual community members also own and operate various onsite businesses, including a natural foods market with a deli and bakery, a construction company, a nature education foundation, a flower essence company, and — in Nevada City — the county's largest natural-foods market and vegetarian restaurant. Some single and married couple members take vows in the Ananda Monastic Order.

Abode of the Message is a Sufi community in the Berkshires of upstate New York. Founded in 1975 by Pir Vilayat Inayat Khan, the leader of the Sufi Order International, the Abode is owned and operated by Sufi Order International and serves as its headquarters. Some of the Order's spiritual goals include: "To realize and spread the knowledge of unity, the religion of love and wisdom...to help to bring the East and West closer together by the interchange of thought and ideals." The 425-acre property is the site of a historic Shaker community built in the 1850s, and Abode members use a common kitchen and dining room and live in rooms in the 150-year-old buildings. Some residents have built homes on the property. People begin each day with morning prayer and meditation, and are called to prayer three times a day. Many take classes in healing and esoteric studies, and each Sunday attend a Universal Worship Service. Individually owned and community-owned business and nonprofit organizations include a Sufi Retreat Center, a Bed and Breakfast, a retail store and mail order source of books on Sufism, a four-year spiritual training program, a private preschool and elementary school, and an organic CSA farm.

Many more eclectic spiritual communities, as well as yoga ashrams and meditation centers, and Zen, Tibetan, and Vipassana Buddhist retreat and meditation centers exist than these few examples. When I searched for Jewish communities in North America I found only one, and its website said it had stopped operation.

Camphill Communities

The Camphill Communities in Europe and North America (also called Camphill Villages) are spiritual communities based on the teachings of Austrian mystic Rudolf Steiner, and designed to serve people with developmental disabilities, with a strong emphasis on arts and crafts, music, celebration, ritual, and theater. "At Camphill," reads the website of Camphill UK, "we build intentional communities with people of all ages who live with disabilities, recognizing the potential, dignity, spiritual integrity, and contribution of each and every individual." Camphill members live together in family-like residences, usually in rural settings, with large Biodynamic organic gardens and specialty studios, such as woodworking shops, bakeries, weaveries, and pottery studios. Community members include people with developmental disabilities, sometimes called "villagers," and "co-workers," the residents who offer long-term service, as well as shorter-term volunteers. Co-workers serve as house parents in the group houses, as managers in the kitchens, gardens, fields, chicken and/or dairy operations, or by training students in vocational skills in the shops or schools. Volunteers assist the disabled residents in various ways, as well as help with gardening, maintenance, housekeeping and other tasks.

At Camphill communities, disabled people are included as important contributors to the well-being of the whole community. "Our household eats together as an extended family three times a day, and the bounty on our table reminds us daily how we all contribute," writes Jan Martin Bang, who lives at Solborg Camphill Village in Norway.

"Our tablecloth was woven by villagers at the weaving shop, and our candlesticks were made by villagers in our carpentry workshop from scrap wood. Our bread and pastries are baked by our baker and three villagers. The vegetables that appear on our table every day are lovingly tended by villagers in our gardens and greenhouses. In the 100 Camphill Villages worldwide we try to find a suitable job for each person according to his or her abilities, a job which contributes to the well-being of others. We try to create communities where we all look out after each other. And the way to do that is for everyone to work for the good of the community." (*Communities*, Fall, 2003).

Co-workers and volunteers join Camphill Communities for several reasons, including the opportunity to serve others, the personal growth opportunities of living in community, and the spiritual growth opportunities of learning to see developmentally disabled people as perfectly whole and not disabled in their souls, which is the basic premise of the 60-year-old Camphill movement.

Camphill Communities may be the most ecologically sustainable of all spiritual communities. In fact, Jan Martin Bang, who is a permaculture teacher, co-founder of the Green Kibbutz Movement in Israel, and the author of *Ecovillages:*

SPIRITUAL COMMUNITIES CITED IN THIS CHAPTER

- Lama Foundation, Taos, New Mexico, *lamafoundation.org*
- The Farm, Summertown, Tennessee *thefarmcommunity.com*
- Sirius Community, Shutesbury, Massachusetts *siriuscommunity.org*
- Ananda Village, Nevada City, California, *ananda.org*

- Abode of the Message, Mt. Lebanon, New York, *theabode.net*
- Providence Zen Center, Cumberland, Rhode Island, *providencezen.org*
- Camphill Communities in North America, *camphill.org* (All Camphill communities in Canada, the US, and Great Britain can be accessed from this site.)

A Practical Guide to Sustainable Communities (New Society Publishers, 2005), considers Camphill Communities "true ecovillages." Besides growing Biodynamic food in their farms and gardens, many Camphill communities build their buildings with natural materials and treat wastewater with ponds, reed beds, and "Flow Form" water cascades. "We are largely self-sufficient — we eat home grown, organic food; often recycle, compost, and treat our own waste; and attempt to integrate a spiritual world view into our everyday lives. We strive to create fellowship in our economic life, and a flexible equality into our social sphere. In short, Camphill ecovillages offer a self-reliant, deeply satisfying, sustainable way of life." (*Communities*, Spring, 2003.)

Spiritual communities appeal to people who want to live in a setting that encourages and supports their spiritual beliefs and spiritual practices, or, in the case of communities with a common spiritual practice, that helps strengthen their practice and usually offers an onsite teacher and ongoing instruction. If you have a meditation practice or other spiritual practice that you'd like to encourage and fortify, a spiritual community may be ideal. At the same time, one needs to follow the rules, and in some communities, the rules can be rigorous. Spiritual communities which require rather specific rules about paying attention, or about one's conduct, can be difficult for people who like to do pretty much what they want when they want. If the community requires residents to arise at dawn to meditate, for example, it can be challenging for folks used to sleeping in!

☞ Chapter 9 ☜

Christian Communities

PEOPLE JOIN CHRISTIAN communities as a way to experience shared worship, fellowship, and mutual support. While the Catholic monasteries and convents have their origins in the early desert hermits and their followers, most Christian communities are founded as a result of the biblical verses in the New Testament which describe the all-things-in-common lifestyle of Christian groups in the second-century Greco-Roman world. Many Christian communities do pool their incomes and share all goods in common.

Longtime Christian communitarian and Christian community scholar Joe Peterson writes:

> When visiting a Christian community, it is not uncommon to be examined about your beliefs, so its members can determine if you are a Christian, or even, the "right kind of Christian." For these community members, matters of truth and faith are at stake, and are taken quite seriously, usually more seriously than they may take the idea of community.
>
> This focus on "right belief" and doctrine especially affects the contact between non-Christian and Christian communities. Some Christian communities are so uninterested in or distrustful of other intentional communities that they decline being listed in the *Communities Directory*. While these folks certainly live a community lifestyle, they identify far more strongly with the rightness of their beliefs and mission than with being an intentional community as such.
>
> (*Communities*, Fall, 1996.)

"We have no interest in community for the sake of communal living," notes the website of the San Francisco-based Church of the Sojourners community, "but we believe that at the center of the Gospel is an invitation for people to share life in Christ together."

Joe Peterson also notes that many Christian communities are mission-oriented — converting non-Christians, making disciples, being closer to Jesus, waiting for the Second Coming, and learning to live truly well in community fellowship. Many are also service-oriented — inspired and illuminated by serving God through their works — with ministries which can include healing the sick, fighting oppression, helping the poor, helping immigrants, and so on.

Christian intentional communities seem to fall into four general categories:

1. *Places of fellowship where co-religionists can feel at home with and share fellowship with each other.* Beacon Hill Friends House, a Quaker housing co-op in Boston, provides a center where Friends and others can meet, worship and study. "We foster the principles of the Religious Society of Friends, offer opportunities for the development of leadership, and main-

tain a diverse, ecumenical, residential community guided by Friends' principles," their website reads. At Agape Lay Apostolate Community near Deming, New Mexico, community members share housing and manage a St. Vincent de Paul Thrift Store, a soup kitchen, and a homeless shelter. Agape members also work at regular jobs. On Saturday evenings they hold an in-house service with Communion, and once a month attend Mass in a local Catholic church.

2. *Contemplative Catholic orders and communities for lay monastics.* These communities focus on prayer, contemplation, worship, study, and service to the order, which might include offering spiritual retreat facilities. Nada Hermitage, a Carmelite-affiliated monastic order with both men and women, is one example. For an account of visiting several Catholic religious communities, see Chapter 15, "My Marathon Tour of Communities."

3. *Salvation-based Protestant communities which focus on prayer, worship, fellowship, and living an inspired, righteous life.* Members of these communities usually have the goal of being forgiven and saved, and seek this for others through evangelical outreach projects. They tend to withdraw from the world to some degree, which usually means sharing housing, working in community-owned businesses, and home-schooling their children or having their own community-based schools. These communities also tend to be conservative — politically, in terms of gender roles, in relationships between men and women, and in child-rearing practices.

4. *Service-based Protestant and Catholic communities.* While also focusing on prayer, worship, and fellowship, these communities also interact with the world at large, sharing their time, expertise, and resources with people in need. Jesus People USA in Chicago, for example, writes "We have always been a place of refuge for young, wounded individuals in search of a living, healing relationship with Christ and other Christians; believers looking for a fuller expression of discipleship; drug users and alcoholics trying to break away from old habits and haunts; men and women who met Christ in jail, have been released, and need a place to help them stay right with God; the unwed mother who needs friends and role models; those struggling with homosexuality who need fellow believers' support; and young teens whose parents need assistance in providing a nurturing yet structured home atmosphere."

Unlike most other intentional communities, which usually have some form of participatory decision-making among members, Christian intentional communities are often led by a spiritual leader or group of elders. In some communities governed this way the leader shares power and decisions are made through some form of participatory democracy. In others, the leader has absolute authority, meaning that community members are expected to comply with the leader's direction. Such communities often have no system of accountability or checks and balances for the leader's decision-making power. When scholars of new religious groups speak of "high-demand" groups, they're usually referring to those with one leader and a fairly rigorous set of agreements about belief and conduct. This includes many Christian communities, as well as various ashrams, meditation centers, and so on.

Also, unlike most intentional communities, which welcome gay, lesbian, and bisexual members, most Christian communities do not.

Some Christian communities, including many

Catholic Worker communities, value ecological sustainability, as do the more progressive Catholic communities lead by priests or nuns who focus on the ecospiritual work of theologian Thomas Berry. Others, however, don't mention environmental values in their literature or on their websites. Joe Peterson observes that some Christian intentional communities are in fact opposed to ecological sustainability, interpreting the Genesis 1:28 verse, "Be fruitful, multiply, and have dominion..." as a kind of biblical mandate that we might as well disregard Nature and use up all natural resources — there's no need to preserve anything since it was put here for humans to consume. This is similar to the view that, when Christ returns, the Earth and all its resources will burn up anyway, so why think about it now? However, Peterson notes that increasing numbers of Christians are taking a more proactive stance about "Stewardship of the Earth," while still maintaining their conservative views towards other contemporary issues.

I personally feel uneasy about organizations with a sole authority figure and no community-wide accountability, and sadness and distaste toward those that repudiate gay people or disregard the environment. And I'm inspired and moved by Christian communities which focus on seeking a deeper relationship with the Divine, and which focus on practicing kindness and generous, open-hearted service to others. So it's examples of these that I want to share in this chapter.

Service-Oriented Christian Communities

Koinonia Partners in rural Georgia is an interracial service community welcoming people of all faiths. It was founded in 1942 by Baptist theologian and social justice activist Clarence Jordan, who advocated for the rights of local African-American farmers, interracial harmony, and pacifism. Today Koinonia's service projects include programs for youth and elders through a community outreach center, the Heart-to-Heart home repair ministry (birthplace of the national Habitat for Humanity organization), and an educational program on peace and justice, religious faith, and other topics. "To us, following the teachings of Jesus means treating neighbors equally, loving our enemies as well as our friends, and living a simple, shared life," notes their website. Koinonia has 20 long-term members, 12 shorter-term residents, and, at any given time, up to 40 guests, students, and visiting groups living on their 573 acres. Their community activities include many neighbors. To earn income the community sells books, community-made arts and crafts, treats made from their pecan orchards, and baked goods through its on-site store and mail-order catalog, as well as receiving donations. "Our shared life together revolves around four elements: work, study, prayer, and service. We gather for morning and afternoon chapel each weekday, and work and serve together in the mornings and afternoons. Many of us serve privately and quietly through community service, visiting shut-in neighbors, church and civic group membership, peace and justice work, and more," their website continues.

A sister community is Jubilee Partners, also in rural Georgia, whose Christian service projects include resettling refugees from various countries, working to abolish the death penalty, visiting prisoners, peacemaking projects, and raising money to promote peace and justice in Nicaragua. Twenty-five people live on the 258-acre property; half are ongoing community members and half are short-term volunteers. Their website reads: "We seek to understand and live by the radical implications of following Jesus Christ and the biblical vision of 'Jubilee'.... We try to live a compassionate lifestyle. We want our life together to reflect biblical values rather than cultural values of materialism, consumerism, and individualism."

Lamborn Valley Community is a Christian intentional community in a fruit-growing area on a river near the town of Paonia, Colorado. Many of its 25 members are part of the four-generation family that started the community in 1987. Half the community members are young adults or children (and in fact a Lamborn Valley member founded *Mothering* magazine, which for many years was edited and published onsite). The community grows crops and produce and raises livestock on its 136-acre organic farm and orchard, and operates several businesses, including a health food store and restaurant specializing in locally grown organic foods, a solar construction company, Old River Road Trading Post, a wilderness camp for children, and Lamborn Valley School, an alternative school for about 35 students.

Jesus People USA (JPUSA), as noted earlier,

HUTTERITE AND BRUDERHOF COMMUNITIES

Hutterite and Bruderhof communities are Anabaptist (adult baptism), pacifist, income-sharing fundamentalist sects, founded in German-speaking Europe, similar to Amish and Mennonite sects. Both Hutterite and Bruderhof communities interpret Scripture literally and hold strict rules about their members' church attendance and conduct. They are considered high-demand groups by scholars who study them.

The Hutterites began in Austria in 1527. They moved many times, fleeing persecution, and lived in various eastern European countries until the 1860s and 1870s when they emigrated to South Dakota. Today an estimated 40,000 members live in 458 different farming colonies in the Canada and the US, mostly in the Midwest.

Hutterite colonies, which each have about 90 to about 120 people, are noted for being orderly and efficient. Hutterites own everything in common and raise crops and livestock with the latest agricultural technology. Men work with machinery; women cook, sew, and raise children. Most children stop school around age 16 to begin adult work full time. Everyone attends church daily. Each Hutterite colony is governed by an elder and deacons, who are elected to this role by the adult men. Gender roles and relationships between the sexes are strongly regulated, and celibacy before marriage and fidelity afterwards is expected. Other forms of romantic or sexual expression are considered "impurity," and, as the Hutterite website says, "Impurity is dealt with severely."

The Bruderhof communities began in Germany in the 1920s. The group soon emigrated to England, and as World War II broke out moved to Paraguay, and finally to the US in the 1960s. Today around 2,500 Bruderhof members live in 8 communities in the US as well as in England, Germany, and Australia. Although Bruderhof communities do farm and grow much of their own food, their primary occupation is not farming but two community-owned businesses: making safe and durable wooden play structures and toys for children, and making equipment for people with disabilities. In values, beliefs, lifestyle, gender roles, relationships between the sexes and childrearing practices, Bruderhof communities are similar to the Hutterites, however the Bruderhof have much more contact with the outside world. Bruderhof youth, for example, finish high school and often go to college. Bruderhof members interact with others in their immediate areas, and Bruderhof communities do outreach and cultural exchange with various communities in Europe and kibbutzim in Israel.

Both Hutterite and Bruderhof communities are asset-sharing as well as income-sharing, which means incoming members donate their savings and other assets to the group. If these members later leave, their assets are not returned.

was founded in 1972 by young people in the Jesus movement in the uptown neighborhood of Chicago's North Side, and later affiliated with the larger Chicago-area Evangelical Covenant Church. JPUSA (pronounced "Ja-*pu*-sah") is an interracial community of 500 people (350 adults and 150 children) who share a converted office building. JPUSA is also a church, with many members of the congregation living in their own homes in the neighborhood. Social service ministries include Cornerstone Community Outreach, a transitional shelter for homeless families; a soup kitchen; Friendly Towers, a senior citizens' residence; and Brothas and Sistas United, a neighborhood outreach to school kids. JPUSA also publishes *Cornerstone* magazine, a quarterly journal of culture, politics, and faith. Music ministries include hosting the annual Cornerstone Music and Arts Festival and their own record label. JPUSA is mostly self-supporting financially, generating about 90 percent of its income from a variety of community-owned and operated businesses, including a roofing supply house, T-shirt printers, and a sheet metal shop. Incomes are pooled and all goods and property are held in common. "We never started out to be a Christian community; our roots were in the early Jesus movement of the late sixties and the early seventies, notes their website. "When Jesus called, many of us were social rejects in search of something worth living for. You might say community living simply evolved as the practical expression of Christianity in our everyday lives, the working out of agape love."

Nada Hermitage in the 8,000-foot high desert near Crestone, Colorado, is a group of monastic, celibate men and women dedicated to contemplative life and affiliated with the Catholic Carmelite Order. Both genders are called "monks"; they live in individual small dwellings, called hermitages, and offer retreat space for the public. "We aspire to create a vital environment characterized by solitude, simplicity and beauty, where community thrives, love is nurtured, prayer flourishes, and the whole person can be transformed," their website reads. They spend half their time in silence and solitude and the other half in work, which they jokingly call "occupational prayer." Work at Nada Hermitage includes running the retreat center, publishing books and a quarterly magazine, and selling these and videotaped conferences, handmade pottery, and collections of their own folk music, as well as working in the garden and other physical labor. "Our life demands good physical and psychological health," continues their website. "We value our vows of poverty, chastity, and obedience, and enjoy a healthy man/woman celibate dynamic. Both genders have equal access to leadership positions."

Catholic Worker Communities

The Catholic Worker Movement, founded by Dorothy Day and Peter Maurin in 1933, is committed to "nonviolence, voluntary poverty, prayer, and hospitality." Over many decades, Catholic Worker houses of hospitality were established to serve the poor and disenfranchised, and members of Catholic Worker communities have taken part in nonviolent actions to protest injustice, war, and violence. Today there are over 185 Catholic Worker Communities worldwide, with 168 in the US, 6 in Canada, and 15 in other countries. Catholic Worker communities are independent of each other, and vary in their activities, in their relationship to the Catholic Church, and in how they incorporate Catholic Worker philosophy and tradition. "We are 20 people in seven adjoining households (some houses, some apartments)," notes the Toronto Catholic Worker, for example. The Catholic Worker tradition in which we try to live is one of prayer, hospitality, simplicity, non-violent resistance to oppression, and clarification of thought. In several of our houses we offer hospitality to people who need a supportive home, often temporarily. Our collective activities include weekly worship, gardening, publication of a paper, protest, lots of formal and informal discussions, coffeehouses, and retreats, and supporting each other in our individual pursuits and struggles."

L'Arche Communities

The ecumenical Christian L'Arche Communities (pronounced "larsh") provide an emotionally and spiritually nurturing community life for people who have developmental disabilities, offering "a vision of care-giving and community-building that fosters inclusion, understanding, and belonging." L'Arche means "the Ark" in French. Some developmentally disabled people live with caregivers in small private homes; others visit day centers with a family-like setting, but don't live there. The caregivers and volunteers have deeply committed to relationships with people with developmental disabilities, who participate in housekeeping tasks and crafts projects, contributing as they are able. The homes and centers are grouped into what L'Arche calls "communities." These are similar to Camphill communities, although L'Arche is not affiliated with the Camphill Movement. L'Arche arises from the work of the Canadian-born humanitarian and social visionary Jean Vanier, who founded L'Arche in 1964. Vanier saw disabled people as having special gifts to offer society, and believed that the wider society benefits when it realizes this. The mission of L'Arche communities is: "To create home where faithful relationships based on forgiveness and celebration are nurtured; to reveal the unique value and vocation of each person; to change society, by choosing to live relationships in community as a sign of hope and love." The L'Arche movement is worldwide, with 130 communities in 30 different countries, with 30 in Canada and 16 in the US. (They are not affiliated with the "Arche" communities in France, which focus on a shared spiritual life of work and prayer.)

Christian communities are ideal for people who seek a community setting that supports and strengthens their faith. Service-oriented Christian communities also offer the deep satisfaction of calling on reserves of kindness and generosity to help others.

As noted earlier, many Christian communities pool their incomes and share all goods in common. So we'll next look at income-sharing communities, both Christian and secular.

CHRISTIAN COMMUNITIES CITED IN THIS CHAPTER

- Koinonia, Americus, Georgia, *koinoniapartners.org*
- Jubilee Partners, Comer, Georgia, *jubileepartners.org*
- Lamborn Valley Community, Paonia, Colorado, *guques@hotmail.com*
- Jesus People USA, Chicago, Illinois, *jpusa.org*
- Nada Hermitage, Crestone, Colorado, *spirituallifeinstitute.org*
- Catholic Worker Communities, *catholicworkers.org/communities*
- L'Arche Communities, Canada, *larchecanada.org*
- Hutterites, *hutterites.org*
- Bruderhof Communities, *bruderhof.org*

Chapter 10

Income-Sharing Communes

As NOTED EARLIER, "commune" is an economic term, meaning an intentional community in which people pool their incomes and share a common treasury. About ten percent of intentional communities in North America which listed themselves in the FIC's online communities directory (in 2006) are income-sharing communes.

Radical Cooperation

In some income-sharing communes, often those in rural areas, people work in one or more community-owned businesses, as well as doing cooking, cleaning, maintenance, gardening, laundry, and/or childcare, and so on. The community members get room and board and the community either pays them a stipend or pays for their basic needs. Other income-sharing communes, often in urban areas, have no community businesses and members work at outside jobs and pool their incomes. Everyone's salaries and wages go into the common pot. Regardless of their differing salary contributions, everyone receives room, board, and a monthly stipend or else the community pays for each person's basic needs.

Income-sharing communes can be small, such as Skyhouse, a sub-community of Dancing Rabbit Ecovillage in Missouri, with 4 members, or Acorn in Virginia with 15 members. Or communes can be large, such as Twin Oaks in Virginia, with 90 members, or East Wind in Missouri, with 85 members. Income-sharing communes can be sec-

ular, like all of these just mentioned, or Christian, based on the "all things in common" lifestyle of early Christian believers. These include some of the communities mentioned in Chapter 9: Jesus People USA, Nada Hermitage, and the Hutterite and Bruderhof communities.

In an income-sharing community children's needs are taken care of, as the community pays for their food, clothes, school expenses, and so on. Elder community members may work fewer hours for community businesses, or no longer work at all, but they still receive room, board and a small stipend or else get their basic needs met. The community usually pays for elder members' medical insurance and any other medical costs unless they are covered by Medicare or other programs.

Income-earning activities in communes vary widely. East Wind in Missouri processes and distributes organic nut butters to health food stores and makes rope sandals to sell at craft fairs. Twin Oaks operates hammock-making, tofu-making, and book-indexing businesses. Acorn, also in Virginia, runs Southern Exposure Seed Exchange, an open-pollinated heirloom seed business, and a tinnery crafts business. Dandelion Co-op, in Enterprise, Ontario, makes hammocks, and through its gardens and livestock raises much of its own food onsite. Skyhouse offers computer programming, website design and hosting, and graphic design services to clients nationwide. Meadowdance, in Vermont, runs a typing and editing business for local and national clients. Ganas, in Staten Island, New York, operates "Everything Goes," neighborhood retail stores selling recycled clothing, furniture, and other items, and a bookstore and café. Alpha Farm, in Oregon, operates a café and gift store in the nearby town and has a rural mail-delivering contract with the local US Post Office.

Twin Oaks, East Wind, Sandhill Farm, and other communes are prosperous, even though the amount of money or the value-equivalent that individual commune members receive puts them below the poverty line. These communities have community buildings, kitchen and laundry facilities, group residences, outbuildings, cars, trucks, tractors, backhoes, other tools and equipment, farm animals, gardens, fences, feed, seeds, soil amendments — and money in the bank. "Communal" certainly does not mean "poor."

Some of the secular income-sharing communes cooperate with each other for mutual support in outreach, labor exchange, healthcare coverage and other programs, through the Federation of Egalitarian Communities (FEC) (not to be confused with the Fellowship for Intentional Community, or FIC).

What's It Like Financially?

Kat Kinkade, cofounder of Twin Oaks, where members receive a stipend, writes in *Is It Utopia Yet?* (Twin Oaks, 1994):

> We generate income almost entirely from onsite activities, and all of that money goes into a communal bank account, We are not employees, and we get no wages. Instead, the community takes care of all our needs.
>
> By "all our needs" I mean food, clothing, housing, medical and dental care, toiletries, furniture, automobiles and trucks and their maintenance, recreation, and a dozen other things. I do

THE FEDERATION OF EGALITARIAN COMMUNITIES

The Federation of Egalitarian Communities (FEC), a network of income-sharing communities in North America, includes six communities, three "communities in dialogue," and two allied communities. FEC communities cooperate and share labor and expenses on publications, conferences, recruitment efforts, community support systems including health care, and other mutually supportive activities. Their goal is not only to help each other, but also "to help more people discover the advantages of a communal alternative, and to promote the evolution of a more egalitarian world." Each FEC community:

- Holds its land, labor, income, and other resources in common.
- Practices nonviolence.
- Assumes responsibility for the needs of its members, receiving the products of their labor and

distributing these and all other goods equally, or according to need.

- Uses a form of decision making in which members have an equal opportunity to participate, either through consensus, direct vote, or right of appeal or overrule.
- Works to address and dismantle oppression of all kinds, including oppression based on race, class, creed, ethnic origin, age, sex, sexual orientation, or gender identity.
- Acts to conserve natural resources for present and future generations while striving to continually improve ecological awareness and practice.
- Creates processes for group communication and participation and provides an environment which supports people's development.

not mean "all our wants," which is different. The community buys food, but not candy. It keeps vehicles on the road, but not luxury cars and especially not new. It subsidizes parties, but within a modest budget. It does not buy cigarettes or private booze. It does not pay for much vacation travel.

The community reserves the right to determine what is and is not a "need," and this will vary according to our income. In spite of these exceptions, I consider that we have complete social security within the community.

Sick leave is unrestricted. If you get sick, you don't have to work. If a doctor sends you to the hospital, you don't worry about the bill.

Members don't have personal checking accounts, electric bills, or installment payments.... The pocket-money allowance this year is $50 per person per month, kept in the community's bank account until called for, and spent entirely at the member's discretion. (*Note: the stipend was $60 in 2006.*) This is where the gifts, cigarettes, phone calls, candy bar, etc. will come from. The allowance has no connection whatever with productivity. The person who was sick all month gets the same allowance as the people who managed a business. Children get an allowance too, about half the amount given adults.

Here's an example from Emerald Earth Sanctuary, a rural ecovillage in northern California, which until 2004 was income-sharing. It did not provide a stipend, but rather paid for most of its members' needs.

Currently we have eight adult members and two children. Six of the adults and both children are part of the income-sharing group; the two others contribute a fixed amount each month, based on an estimate of their share of food, phone bills, and other community expenses. Short-term residents and trial members don't participate in income-sharing.

Sharing incomes reflects the core of our community philosophy. We believe each person is best able to determine how much money and time he or she can contribute to the group and still balance personal and family needs. Unlike most intentional communities, we have no required number of hours that we must contribute to community projects, nor do we require members to spend a certain amount of their time earning income. We believe that sometimes the most valuable contribution someone can make to the health of the community may be reading to a child, meditating, getting a needed chiropractic adjustment, or taking a vacation.

Our ability to share money this informally is probably due to three circumstances. First, we're a small group and we're very compatible in values and needs. We trust each other's decisions about how we each allocate our time and money, so we don't have to work everything out in advance. Also, for the most part we are all physically able and enjoy contributing time and energy toward group needs, such as building, gardening, and earning outside income. And having no mortgage keeps our community expenses low.

At this point our income-sharing account covers food, rent, fuel, phone bills, automobile insurance, car repair and gas, entertainment, catastrophic health insurance, limited health care, and small personal items such as books and clothing. Overall, we are fairly successful at keeping our expenses low; our budget for eight people runs around $5,000 a month, roughly $625 per person. Certain choices based on our values, such as buying only organic food and running some of our vehicles on bio-diesel fuel, increase our expenses somewhat.

Our income-sharing account does not cover the cost of travel, expensive personal items (e.g. cars), prior debt, or gifts for friends and family. Although some of us see this as a compromise to our economic ideals, we haven't come up with a practical way to reliably cover these expenses while allowing individuals the freedom to make personal choices. We're in similar circumstances to those of a family with limited resources: if unforeseen expenses arise, such as major medical expenses, we work together to figure out how to support the person in need. We are aware that we also have a wider community of friends and family who can and do help us during difficult times.

The six income-sharing members contribute most, but not necessarily all, of their current income. They may retain a portion in order to build up some personal savings and to pay for items not covered by the income-sharing account. One family has no savings and needs to replace their car, for example, so they set aside part of their income each month. Another family already has adequate savings, so puts in 100 percent of their income.

Kristen Gardner and Michael G. Smith, *Communities* magazine, Fall/Winter 2002.

Why Are Income-Sharing Communities so Well Known?

Income-sharing communities are far more prominent in the communities movement than their actual numbers would suggest. When you first heard of "intentional communities" didn't you either think of a place where everyone pooled their money — or else had a guru? The sixth principle of cohousing, in fact, is "No shared community economy" — meaning, I think, "Unlike all those other intentional communities out there, we cohousers don't share incomes."

The first reason for this prominence, I think, is because income-sharing communitarians tend to be activists, if not enthusiastic proselytizers, for their radically non-competitive way of life. For them, having a close-knit and intimate group (in the smaller communes), pooling incomes, taking care of each other financially, and being on a level playing field with fellow members financially is a form of political activism, and they're proud of it. They invite the media to their communities to tell them about their way of life, write articles for *Communities* magazine, and lead workshops at the FIC's regional Art of Community conferences. The income-sharing Twin Oaks Community hosts an annual Communities Conference every August, drawing participants from all parts of North America.

The second reason for their prominence in the public eye, I think, is because during the '60s and '70s when there was so much media attention on the counterculture, most intentional communities *were* communes, literally. Popular magazines like *Life* and *Look*, and even *Time* and *Newsweek*, couldn't get enough of them. Movies too: everyone who saw *Easy Rider* knows what a commune is — or rather, was. Communes themselves generated their own media; for example, in its hippie heyday The Farm in Tennessee published several books by Stephen Gaskin about their colorful life on the commune. And, like baby ducklings who waddle after a moving lawnmower, thinking it's their mother because it was the first thing they imprinted on after hatching, many North Americans got media-imprinted in the '60s and '70s that intentional communities *are* communes. It's hard for many of us to stop following that lawnmower around.

Benefits of Income-Sharing

1. *Right Livelihood.* Income-sharing communities directly counter the widespread belief that people

should be compensated financially only to the degree to which they're skilled and productive, and that some work is more valuable, and should be more highly paid, than other work. In most income-sharing communities, people get stipends or the community pays their basic needs, whether or not they've worked a pre-arranged number of hours. Also, cooking, cleaning, childcare, and teaching children are valued as highly as construction, repair and maintenance, or legal or medical skills.

Also, in an income-sharing community you have freedom *not* to work at a job that closes your heart or deadens your soul. Tree Bressen is a long-time community activist who has lived at Acorn community and served as Executive Secretary of the Federation of Egalitarian Communities. She writes:

> My favorite thing about income-sharing is that it directly undermines capitalism. The exploitation and hierarchy that are part of the foundation of capitalism rely on pervasive fear and scarcity in order to operate. When we share with each other, we create abundance and security instead.
>
> In mainstream settings, people stay in jobs that they hate and that are immoral because they are afraid that if they don't, they won't be able to fulfill basic needs such as food, housing, and healthcare. If the other 9 or 90 people in my community all have income to contribute to the common pot, then we are not going to stay in crappy jobs where we are treated badly or forced to do things that destroy the planet, because we know that we can quit to find something better without becoming homeless or going hungry.

(Members of independent-income communities don't necessarily work at meaningless or demeaning jobs, however.)

2. *Deep and satisfying interpersonal connections, particularly in smaller communes.* Because people are more economically interdependent in income-sharing communities, a more skilled level of communication skill and trust-building is required, which can result in a deeper level of intimacy than in independent-income communities. Many small income-sharing groups are characterized by a close-knit family-like atmosphere with strong connections and strong feelings of caring, trust, and mutual support. Some people join income-sharing communities for this reason alone — because it feels good interpersonally — not just for political or economic reasons.

3. *Autonomy and sovereignty.* In this kind of community you would most likely self-manage your work hours, and be on relatively equal terms with everyone else in the community in terms of assets, spending power, material possessions and shared leadership. "Recently I hung up on an obnoxious phone solicitor who promptly called back to berate me for my rudeness and to demand to speak to my boss," writes Anna Young of East Wind Community in Missouri. "Imagine his surprise when I replied, 'I don't *have* a boss.' Sixty boss-less women and men own and operate three community businesses that gross more than $2 million a year. We mostly choose and schedule our own work; we're not required to follow the orders of any one person who can retain or dismiss us from our membership; we simply laugh at the idea of time clocks or dress codes." (*Communities*, Spring, 1997.)

4. *Learning new skills.* People tend to learn new skills living in community, regardless of its economic model, but this is considerably more true in larger income-sharing communities with one or more community businesses. Nina Barbara Cohen writes about her time at Twin Oaks:

I first trained at the community's sawmill, where the manager allowed me to drive the forklift. I discovered a hitherto untapped fascination with *big* things: logs, machines, towering stacks of lumber; they were like Tonka toys on steroids! I stuck with the sawmill, working shifts throughout my years there.

My newfound love of things large led me to the barn and its dairy cows. There I took on the most significant job of my life to date: managing the dairy program. I found myself with more responsibilities than I'd ever had before, and began cramming my head with facts about farming practices, bovine health, milking equipment maintenance, sanitation, record-keeping, and more.

Several years later, in 1994, when I left Twin Oaks to help start the new community of Abundant Dawn, I realized I had acquired an extraordinary education. As I decided how to make a living, created a business plan, and bought the portable sawmill for my new business, I found myself using the new skills and new attitudes that I'd picked up at Twin Oaks.

(*Communities*, Spring 1997.)

5. *Economic benefits.* Members of income-sharing communities that are financially successful tend to experience a high level of financial security. They don't have to worry about any money issues — how they'll meet their needs, pay their bills, or refinance their loans. They don't have to worry about whether they're using up sick time, whether their company will merge with a larger company and they'll lose their job, or whether their boss might fire them.

6. *More material benefits relative to the number of hours worked.* "The extensive resource-sharing that goes with income-sharing means we all have access to more material benefits, yet with a lower per-capita consumption rate," notes Tree Bressen. "A community might have a swimming pond, a recording studio, and various other facilities that we as individuals would not be able to afford. Quality of life goes up; personal time into earning money goes down. The income-sharing communities in the FEC typically put about 20 hours per person per week into income-earning activities, as compared with 40–50 hours on the outside."

7. *Usually no cost to join.* In communities with independent finances — whether ecovillages, cohousing neighborhoods, or housing co-ops — when you join you pay for the privilege: either through a joining fee, membership fee, and/or site lease fee, or in cohousing, the cost of buying your housing unit and a share of the commons. Once in the community, you'll pay annual (or quarterly) community dues and fees. Your monthly income is your own; you keep your salary, wages, or income from investments. Your assets, sources of income, and how much you earn a year or take home a month are your business and not the community's. This is probably similar to the way you're living now — paying rent or monthly mortgage fees and monthly expenses.

When joining an income-sharing community, however, in most cases you pay no joining fee, site lease fee, or property purchase fee. (I do know of one former commune, though, in which incoming members paid a one-time non-refundable joining fee of $7,500.) You pay no rent. You pay no annual dues and fees. If the commune has been around a long time, like Twin Oaks, which was founded in 1967, it most likely owns its property free and clear, and any annual expenses and monthly supplies are paid by the common treasury. If the community is still paying off its property purchase, through mortgage payments or private loan repayments, the common treasury pays this too.

Depending on the legal entity through which the community owns its property, there may be one financial idiosyncrasy, though. Some income-sharing communes that own their property through a nonprofit 501(d) legal entity interpret the tax requirements in a way that requires new members to place their assets out of reach before they join. In such communities members must live only on the community stipend and have no access to any of their individually owned assets, interest payments, stock dividends, or rental income. Members of these communities must place any savings accounts, IRAs, real estate properties, or stock market investments in trust for the duration of their membership. In contrast, some income-sharing communes, usually Christian ones, don't want you to place your assets out of reach, but rather to donate them to the community.

Challenges of Income-Sharing

1. *Too intimate.* The close-knit family-like atmosphere in smaller communes can be too intimate for some. It can be too time-consuming to process feelings about each others' spending habits and other issues of interdependence, both financial and personal. For some, it can feel overwhelming to be so much into each other's business.

2. *Not enough autonomy.* In some larger income-sharing communities, some members chafe at not having enough independence, or feel frustrated by too many systems or agreements.

3. *No equity, and sometimes, limited access to high-ticket items.* Other than offering the financial benefits of your labor, when you join an income-sharing commune you don't invest financially in the community, so you don't have any equity ownership in the usual sense. In a few income-sharing communities, however, you can build your own dwelling on the property and sell it to another member if

ASSET-SHARING COMMUNITIES

In asset-sharing communities, you not only pool your incomes into a common pot when you join the community, but donate your assets too. It's a huge step, and communities that ask this of incoming members know it means they cannot join lightly or frivolously. New people have to be quite sure they want to live in this community, and, given the financial implications of this requirement, to live in that community for the rest of their lives.

Many income-sharing Christian communities are also asset-sharing; few secular communities are. In many Christian communities, if a person joins, donates all their assets, and later leaves, either because they want to or because the community kicks them out, they don't get their assets back. As noted in

Chapter 9, this is the case with Hutterite and Bruderhof communities.

Alpha Farm in Oregon, although not a Christian community, is both asset-sharing and income-sharing. For this reason the community asks all residents to wait awhile and be sure they want to become a full member before committing all their assets. Full members of Alpha Farm, unlike residents, are co-owners of the community's properties and all other assets. And if a full member has debts, Alpha Farm will pay them off. Also, unlike many Christian communities, Alpha Farm gives back the assets when a full member leaves, even if they have to borrow money to do so.

you leave. With that exception, you cannot take any equity with you if you leave. If you stay for a long time and have children, they'll grow up in a wonderful environment with other close friends. However, depending on how the community functions financially, it may not provide funds to buy them braces, elective surgery, piano lessons, or a college education, unless the group can afford these expenses *and* decides to pay them. And if you live in the community for decades and retire there, you'll have your medical needs met and a comfortable home for the rest of your life. But as an elderly member you won't get special expensive operations that cost tens of thousands of dollars, or the kind of round-the-clock medical care you may need towards the end of your life. And if you someday decide to leave the community, you take nothing with you. You may have joined right after high school and worked to build and develop the community for 40 years, but if you leave, while you have experiences, skills, and wonderful memories, you have nothing material, and certainly no large chunks of cash. You arrived with the shirt on your back; you leave with the shirt on your back.

4. *Potential for inefficiency.* In the mid-1990s three recent ex-members of an income-sharing community told me about the situation which led them to leave. No one knew how to manage the community businesses effectively so that the number of hours each person worked was not too high for the amount of income the community earned. Everyone ended up toiling long, hard 60-hour work weeks but the community earned about $2 an hour. While people were aware they were working too hard, no one could quite put their finger on what was wrong. "This is just the way community is," a longtime member said. If their businesses had been well-managed, however, the group could have earned more income and its members could

have worked less hours and had more free time. Burned-out members tended not to stay long, and the unusually high turnover rate hurt the community too. And things apparently didn't change over time. Ten years later another recent ex-member told me it was extremely frustrating for him to see this community's large, fertile garden lie fallow, as members were working such long hours in the businesses that no one had the time to work in the garden too. The community didn't grow anything but bought all its food from local stores.

5. *Potential for discouraging responsible, productive members.* Sandhill Farm is a productive and well-managed working farm, and in the planting and growing seasons its members work every day, with no weekends off. It has been making money for over a decade, and is financially well-off enough to offer relatively high benefits for its members, including creating a college fund for one member's child.

However, the managers of community-owned businesses in two other communities told me that their businesses were either not well managed or the manager's methods were not backed up by the community. They felt the income-sharing model discouraged the group's most productive and responsible people. They ended up feeling demoralized by being in bed financially with those who had a more laid-back attitude towards work, paying little attention to how they used their time, for example, or treating the community's commonly owned tools and other physical resources fairly casually. The productive folks ended up believing that their energy and focus were subsidizing the people who worked less and cared less. The laid-back folks ended up feeling criticized. "Hey, what's your problem? Quit being so anal." This dynamic resulted in an ongoing, low-level field of resentment and conflict, demoralizing everyone. And while many felt demoralized, those who got so frustrated that they actually left the community were the more organized, productive folks, who took their energy and skills with them. A group in this situation can suffer from, not exactly a brain-drain, but more like an effectiveness-and focus-drain. The community members who remain tend to be more relaxed, *laissez-faire* types, and some-times its businesses tend to meander along on a just-break-even basis. In my opinion, this is more likely to happen when the community doesn't have a well-crafted membership process. See Chapter 22, "Choosing Your Community," for more on this topic.

6. *Potential for over-dependence on high-salaried members.* I've heard more than one tale of high-income professionals in income-sharing communities whose salaries contributed two or three times more to the community than anyone else's. This is fine, since everyone, including the high-salaried professionals, have agreed in advance to pooling incomes. But then the community financially *depends* on the high-salaried members. In one relatively small income-sharing community, for example, an emergency room physician wanted to quit that high-paying, stressful job and start a private practice in holistic medicine, which would mean a serious drop in his income. Unfortunately, the community had become dependent on his emergency-room salary, and would suffer immediate financial distress if he quit his job and opened a clinic. So, after several meetings in which the community agonized over this mutual dilemma, the doctor agreed to keep working in the emergency room, but only part-time. This lowered his stress, dropped his salary, and reduced the community's income, but not drastically. In the long run it wasn't a satisfying solution for any-one, though, as the doctor was still unhappy at

work and the other community members were unhappy too, because they cared about his well-being. Finally, the doctor and his family left the community altogether. In one fell swoop the group lost beloved community members *and* a major part of their annual income.

7. *Potential for high turnover.* Because income-sharing communities are easy to join financially, they are also easy to leave. For this reason, and other reasons noted above, sometimes these com-munities can have a relatively higher rate of mem-ber turnover than independent-income commu-nities. Twin Oaks, for example, has an estimated 25 percent annual member turnover (although the average Twin Oaks member lives there for 8 years).

Who Income-Sharing Works Well For

Why do groups choose income-sharing? Well, it's radical — economically, politically, and socially. It's a put-your-lifestyle-where-your-mouth-is repudi-ation of the win/lose, dog-eat-dog, competitive consumerist lifestyle we've all been taught is nor-mal. And it's compassionate. In most income-sharing communities, most of the time people's needs are taken care of, regardless of whether they worked a number of hours that "earned" the right to meet those needs.

And it's altruistic. I spoke with one commu-nity founder who started an income-sharing com-munity in the early 1990s with a handful of people with no assets and modest incomes, even though he made nearly $100,000 a year himself. When I asked why he chose income-sharing, he said it was because his co-founders were artists who didn't earn much money, and he didn't want them not to be able to join the community because of this, and income-sharing was one way they could all live in community together. I was impressed!

Income-sharing communities, then, are especially appealing to people who are:

- Inspired by egalitarian ideals, or who have a passion for social and economic justice.
- Seeking close, intimate connections with others (if it's a smaller commune).
- Flexible enough to enjoy working in many different kinds of tasks — they're happy mopping the floor, doing the accounting, facilitating a meeting, taking out the compost, etc.
- Eager to learn a wide variety of new skills.
- Comfortable with living simply and being thrifty.
- Not much concerned with issues of absolute fairness but feel a certain generosity or financial largesse.
- Not much concerned about money issues or don't have money-specific emotional issues.
- Young, or with few assets.

Income-sharing communities tend to appeal much less to people who are:

- Less interested in close, intimate connection with others, who want more personal and emotional space, and who prefer to have others a bit less "in their face."
- Interested in financial autonomy and independence; or have specific plans for their capital or projects, including projects in community, which they already want to fund.
- Interested in building financial equity in the community.
- Already in a particular profession, job, or business that they enjoy and in which they want to continue working.
- Looking for a greater degree of comfort or amenities than typically found in an income-sharing community.
- Concerned about areas of possible resentment in community, and/or issues of fairness.
- Older, and/or financially well-established.

Next, we'll look at what it costs to join most communities.

INCOME-SHARING COMMUNITIES CITED IN THIS CHAPTER

- Twin Oaks, Louisa, Virginia: *twinoaks.org*
- Sandhill Farm, Rutledge, Missouri: *sandhillfarm.org*
- Skyhouse, Dancing Rabbit Ecovillage, Rutledge, Missouri: *skyhousecommunity.org*
- Acorn, Mineral, Virginia: *ic.org/acorn*
- East Wind, Tecumseh, Missouri: *eastwind.org*
- Dandelion Co-op, Enterprise, Ontario: *dlion@kingston.net*

- Meadowdance, Walden, Vermont: *meadowdance.org*
- Ganas, Staten Island, New York: *ganas.org*
- Alpha Farm, Deadwood, Oregon: *pioneer.net/~alpha*
- Federation of Egalitarian Communities (FEC): *thefec.org*

≈ SECTION 2 ≈

Researching

Chapter 11

What Does It Cost?

WHILE IT USUALLY costs nothing to join an income-sharing community, or an urban community where you rent, joining most communities means buying into shared property ownership. I've met many people with such romantic notions about intentional communities that they don't realize this, and they're shocked and disappointed when they find out. ("Earthaven is so into *money*," an indignant young work exchanger once blurted out in frustration. "If it was really community it wouldn't *cost* anything.") Living in community also often involves monthly payments, or annual dues and fees. So let's look at some basic principles of community costs:

1. People who can afford to buy their own home can afford to join a community.

2. People who cannot afford to buy a home often cannot afford to join a community unless the group offers a payment plan or sweat equity. (This doesn't apply to income-sharing communes and those in which you rent). Also, costs can be lower in rural areas, so some city dwellers with modest savings can feel well off in a rural community.

3. In some communities you purchase property directly, with a deed to a lot, house and lot, or housing unit. Having an individual deed can sometimes also include having shared ownership in the rest of the community's commonly owned property.

4. In other communities all members share ownership of the community's property. The joining fee or buy-in fee either pays back the community founders who originally purchased and developed the property, goes toward the mortgage, or (if the founders are already paid back or the property is paid for) goes towards future capital development.

5. Most communities also have annual (or quarterly) dues and fees.

6. The basic annual expenses of most communities are: loan repayments (principal and interest) on the purchase and development of the property; property taxes; property insurance; repair and maintenance of roads, buildings, vehicles, equipment, etc. One-time expenses can include new building construction, buying a tractor or excavator, creating gardens (clearing, fencing, water systems, soil amendments, etc.), setting up a community-owned business, and other as-needed expenses such as legal fees, hosting celebrations, buying back equity from a departing member, and so on.

7. Sources of income for a community (not for individual community members) can include annual dues and fees, new-member joining fees, membership fees, site lease fees, and so on; the sale of a lot, house, or housing unit; rent from renting housing to members; lease fees from leasing a portion of their property (sometimes to their own affiliated nonprofit organization); income from any community-

owned businesses; and interest from members making payments towards their joining fees or site lease fees, etc.

Factors in the Cost to Join

Joining a community can either (1) cost just as much or even slightly more than buying a home anywhere, or (2) cost less (and sometimes far less) than market-rate housing, or (3) cost nothing at all. If it's not an income-sharing commune, what it costs depends on the following factors:

1. Is the community one in which everyone buys into the property, everyone rents, or some people own and some people rent?

2. Are the property values in the area low, medium, high, or off-the-charts-exorbitant? In the rural South or rural areas of some Mid-western states and provinces, land prices are relatively low and you'll pay less to join. In California, the Pacific Northwest, the Gulf Islands of British Columbia, both coasts, large cities, or progressive college towns, land costs are higher, and you'll probably pay more.

3. What's the relationship between the size of the community's land area and the number of members who will be splitting its land purchase and development costs? If it's a large property and/or has fewer members, you'll probably pay more. If it's a smaller property and/or has a larger number of members, you'll probably pay less.

4. Local zoning regulations determine "population density" — how many people can live on a site. If the property is in a county or region which has zoning regulations, these regulations may not allow as many people per acre as the community founders might have wished. With fewer community members to split the property purchase and development costs, you'll pay more to join.

5. If the community is in a city or town it will probably cost much more than if it were in a semi-rural or rural area — not only because land usually costs more in a city or town than in rural or semi-rural areas, but also because of strict urban development standards. A city zoning board might hold a forming intentional community to the same standards required of commercial developers in exchange for OK'ing a higher-than-normal population density. This could include, for example, re-quiring some of the property to be deeded to the city for public parking, a city park, or a pro-tected land along a creek, or requiring that a certain percentage of the housing units be affordable housing, offered at below-market rates. All of these requirements come out of the community founders' pockets, and they have to spread this higher expense among all potential members — which raises your cost to buy in.

6. Is the community well-established and its land already developed, with roads, utilities, com-munity buildings and dwellings? If so, the cost of joining can be higher than joining a compa-rable newly forming community. (At the same time, fully developed communities established years ago may have paid so much less for their land at the time that they are relatively inex-pensive to join now.)

7. If the community is newly forming, with raw, undeveloped land, you could pay less to start with. But keep in mind that you and future in-coming members will have the shared costs of building roads and buildings, and probably the costs of building your own home. At Earth-aven, it was cheaper to join in the early days when it was just forest, streams, and a few rudi-mentary buildings. The founders raised the site lease fee $500 every year, and later added a

joining fee, because with each passing year the community's physical and administrative infrastructure was more developed than it had been the year before.

8. If you're purchasing a lot, or a house and lot, you'll probably pay the community founders a down payment and monthly payments. If it's just an undeveloped lot, add in the cost of temporary shelter and/or building your own home.

9. If you purchase a housing unit on a deeded footprint of land, as in a cohousing community, you will most likely get a mortgage, paying a down payment and monthly payments.

10. If you're buying in to cohousing, as you'll recall from Chapter 5, the cost can seem slightly higher than comparable market-rate housing for similar-sized local housing units, but it's really not any higher since the cost of the common house and other shared facilities are taken into account in the asking price. Paradoxically, the up-front costs of joining a cohousing community can be more affordable than some non-cohousing communities in which everyone owns all the land, since in cohousing you will most likely get a mortgage.

11. If the community is in a rural area with little-to-no zoning or enforced building regulations, "building a home" can be as cheap as putting up a canvas yurt or bringing on a travel trailer or mobile home. If not, you'll have the full-on expenses of building a house — at a time of ever-escalating labor, lumber, and building materials costs. (If you plan to build a smaller-than-normal home of natural materials such as straw bale or cob, do zoning regulations permit smaller-than-normal structures? Do building regulations allow straw bale or cob structures?)

12. If you plan a natural-built home, do you have the funds to pay the unusually high amount of labor just to put up the walls and roof? If you're building your home yourself, do you have the time and energy to work at your job and build a house on the weekends? Or can you afford to quit your job and build it?

13. If you're joining a community which is off the grid and you must build your own dwelling on a homesite, add the cost of your renewable energy system. Whether microhydro, photovoltaic panels, or a wind generator, you'll also need a battery bank, inverter, and other necessary devices. Depending on the size of your system, this can range from $5,000 or more to several tens of thousands.

14. As you will learn in Chapter 14, "Your Criteria for Communities to Visit," if the community property is owned as a 501(c)3 nonprofit (or nonprofit cooperative or society in Canada), the joining fee may be much lower than if the property were owned through a different legal entity, or there may be no joining fee at all. However, while you may hold equity in any home you build or buy in this community, you will not have equity in the land. As you will learn, if the community ever disbands, the land cannot be sold and its profits divvied up among its members, as in most communities. Rather, the property or the funds from its sale would need to be donated to another 501(c)3 nonprofit.

15. As you may also recall from the last chapter, if you're joining an income-sharing community you probably will pay nothing to join, however, you usually won't have equity in the community's property either.

16. A few secular income-sharing communities and many Christian income-sharing communities are asset-sharing as well, and would require you to contribute all of your assets to the

group when you joined. If you later left the community your original assets would most likely not be returned.

For one couple's common-sense assessment of these issues, see "Community Affordability: Elusive and Necessary," in Chapter 19, "Seriously Seeking Community."

"If I have no funds can I still join a community?"

You can. Your choices will be limited to income-sharing communities, or communities in which people rent, such as urban shared group households, or cohousing communities with rental units.

You could also join a well-established community in which the land was paid off and all the buildings paid for decades earlier. When a group of newcomers joined Light Morning in Virginia in the late 1990s, for example, it was a community whose land and buildings were completely paid for, and the new members paid no joining fee. Or you could join a rural community with relatively low land-purchase costs, a land trust ownership structure, and leased, not purchased, homesites. Residents of Dancing Rabbit Ecovillage in Missouri, for example, pay no joining fee. They pay two percent of their annual income to the overall nonprofit organization, and a lease fee of one cent a square foot a month for a suggested 50-foot by 50-foot leased plot, which comes out to $300 a year, plus the costs of building or renting their own off-grid home.

You could also join a buy-in community with special provisions for young people or others with few assets. Yarrow Ecovillage in British Columbia, for example, allows members to rent community-owned housing before they buy, and offers a limited number of housing units at five percent down ($7,500 Canadian) instead of their normally re-

quired 15 percent down ($22,500 Canadian), and some of this fee can be paid off by sweat equity. Similarly, Earthaven Ecovillage allows people with little money to pay the $4,000 joining fee in monthly installments. Once that's paid off, they can begin paying the site lease fee in payments of $150 a month for several years. Up to four community members may go in together on leasing a quarter-acre homesite and two people can go together on leasing an eighth-acre site, which further reduces the site lease fee. Earthaven also offers a sweat equity trade. New members can clear forested land for agriculture in exchange for all or part of the joining fee and site lease fees. So it is possible for young people or people with few assets to join communities like these that have property buy-in fees.

Many communities offer intern or work exchange positions, in which a person trades room and board for labor in the community. This is a great way for someone to "try on" a community before committing. In fact, it's theoretically possible that if you're a responsible, hardworking, skilled person you could "live in community" for years on end at no cost, moving from one community to another in a series of internships or work-exchange positions, contributing labor, enjoying life, and never paying actual cash for the experience. This would most likely work for people with good references and experience and the kinds of skills communities want, which can include cooking, gardening, farming, carpentry, and maintenance and repair.

Cohousing, Housing Co-ops, Conference Centers, Spiritual Communities, Communes...

As you probably realize by now, different kinds of intentional communities have quite different financial considerations.

In cohousing communities, for example, you don't pay a joining fee as such, but buy a housing unit (which you own outright with a deed) and share ownership of the rest of the property. Most cohousing units are market rate, though some, with government assistance, are less. In most cases, people pay a down payment, get a mortgage from a local lending institution, and make monthly payments.

In housing co-ops, and here I mean limited equity co-ops, you also buy in (sometimes with a down payment; sometimes with a smaller fee), and make monthly payments. While housing co-ops can all be structured somewhat differently, you often own shares in the property and, through a lease, have the right to occupy one housing unit, or in a large house, to occupy one or more rooms and have use of the whole house. Sometimes co-ops are rural, such as Spirit Dance Cooperative Community, and Yarrow Ecovillage, both in British Columbia, in which you purchase shares in the whole property, and have the right to build a home on a particular footprint of land. Also, in many urban communities which are not housing co-ops, you don't pay a joining fee, but do pay monthly rent.

In retreat and conference centers, you may or may not pay a joining fee, depending on how the center is organized. At Lost Valley Educational Center in Oregon, you pay a joining fee of $1,000 and then rent housing from the community or supply your own temporary housing.

Spiritual communities also vary widely in terms of costs for new members. In many, the property and buildings have been paid off for many years, and you don't buy in, but may exchange work for room and board, pay rent, or build your own living quarters on the property.

Christian communities are often similar. At Nada Hermitage in Colorado, and many Catholic Worker communities, you exchange work for room and board. Protestant intentional communities are often organized as income-sharing communes.

In income-sharing communities you usually pay no joining fee. You either work at a community business, at an outside job, or at a job at home, and all profits from community businesses, or from private wages or salaries, are pooled in a common pot. In exchange you get room, board, and either a stipend, like at Twin Oaks, or the community pays for your basic needs, like at Emma Goldman Finishing School in Seattle.

In communities which are both income-sharing and asset-sharing, the "joining fee" is to donate all or most of your assets to the community. In most Christian income-sharing communities organized this way, your assets are not returned if you leave. However, at Alpha Farm in Oregon, an asset-sharing community, your assets are returned if you leave.

Do Communities Tell You What It Costs?

Mostly yes. When I emailed communities to ask what it cost to join their community I got back friendly, straightforward answers right away. Most communities are happy to tell you up front, so as not to waste your time (and theirs) if the costs might be out of your range. They offer this information in handouts to visitors, in handbooks for potential new members, and/or on their website.

However, some communities don't tell you until they get to know you. I know the founders of one community who prefer to share cost information only after people have visited many times or lived at the community for several months. Joining a community and sharing land ownership is an intimate kind of relationship, and I can see why a community would want to proceed cautiously. At the same time, I think most people would want to know if they could afford to join a community first, before investing time off work and travel costs to visit the community several times before they found out whether it was even in their ball park.

Sample Costs: What It Costs to Join a Community

In order to convey a sense of the wide range of costs, I surveyed communities in one bioregion of North America, the Pacific Northwest. I chose this area because it includes both Canada and the US, and many intentional communities are located there. (Many more communities exist in the Pacific Northwest than the ones noted in this chart — these are just examples!)

You'll find basically three kinds of communities and joining fees in the chart:

1. Urban communities, including group households in which people rent, urban housing co-ops with minimal buy-in fees and monthly payments, and one income-sharing community.

2. Rural or semi-rural communities with a wide range of joining fees, including rural land co-operatives, conference centers, and one income-sharing community.

3. Cohousing communities — urban, suburban, and semi-rural.

Please note — most of the costs in this chart are accurate as of July, 2006. So this chart is not to tell you what these communities cost now, as you read this chapter. Rather, it's just to demonstrate to you that, yep, the cost of joining communities varies widely.

Members have equity in all communities listed below unless it says "No equity."

Sample Communities in the Pacific Northwest	
British Columbia **Rural or Semi-Rural Communities**	
Cougar Hill, Grand Forks	$40,000 for one of 10 title shares and right to build a housing unit, either as an outright purchase or lease-to-own.
EcoReality Cooperative, Salt Spring Island	Buy-in fees are, first, a co-op member share for $1,000 (required as the first stage in membership), and second, a minimum of $10,000 in investment shares (required to live on the property), with total fee at $100,000 to $150,000 per household, which includes community-owned natural-built house. Investment shares capitalize land, buildings, and infrastructure. Members with fewer assets can borrow investment shares from more affluent members with nominal interest payments.
Spirit Dance Cooperative Community, Quesnel	$7,000 per person or per two-person household for membership share in land co-op, plus monthly "land fee," which over time purchases additional shares in the co-op (and share costs are redeemable if the member leaves). The cost of building a dwelling, or purchasing an existing dwelling from another member is additional.
Next Step Integral, Winlaw	Buy-in fee is $30,000 to $65,000 (which can sometimes be reduced by sweat equity) for membership and right to build on a footprint of land. The cost of building a dwelling, or buying a dwelling from another member, is additional.

Yarrow Ecovillage, Chilliwack	$1,000 per person or per two-person household for membership share in land co-op, plus cost to purchase community-owned housing. To purchase a housing unit requires a 15 percent down payment ($22,500) plus monthly payments ($700–$800). A limited number of housing units can be purchased on a rent-to-own basis with a five percent down payment. Rental units are $200–$300. (All fees other than housing down payments can be reduced by sweat equity.) Members may also acquire investment shares which can earn a return, and which can be applied toward the purchase of a residence.
100 Mile Lodge, 100 Mile House	Rental costs range from $400 plus utilities for a one-bedroom house to $775 plus utilities for a four-bedroom apartment. No equity, although the community is considering buy-in and ownership equity options for the future.

Cohousing Communities

Quayside Village, Vancouver	$400 per square foot: from a 449 square foot studio at $179,600 to a 1063 square foot 3-bedroom unit at $425,200, plus four 80 percent-market-rate units, and one below-market-rate rental unit. Plus monthly maintenance assessment. Housing units can be purchased with a down payment and a mortgage.

Washington
Urban Communities

Apex Belltown Co-op, Seattle	$2,100 for a member share in this limited equity housing co-op (which can be paid with 25 percent down and payments over 7 months) gives the right to one living space and a share of the commons. Members also pay a monthly "carrying charge" — each member's share of the mortgage, utilities, taxes, maintenance, etc. (based on those fluctuating yearly costs and the size of one's living space) — ranging from $389 for a 110 square foot room to $527 to 350 square foot room. Only one person in a couple sharing a room may be a co-op member; the other person has "roommate" status and also pays a small fee.
Bob, the House, Seattle	$480 covers rent ($300) and other monthly expenses ($180), plus $300 deposit, which can be paid off over time, to live in this urban group household. No equity.
Bright Morning Star, Seattle	Depending on whether there are 6 members or 7, the cost per person per month for sharing expenses ranges from $509 to $579 respectively in this urban group household, which includes food ($166/month) and utilities. No equity.
Emma Goldman Finishing School, Seattle	At this urban income-sharing commune, each member contributes around 100 hours of labor per month through work around the property and at their paid job. No equity.
Tacoma Catholic Worker, Tacoma	Community members do service work (offering shelter and hospitality) in exchange for room and board in the Tacoma Catholic Worker's seven houses. No equity

Rural or Semi-Rural Communities

Windward Farm, Klikitat	$400 monthly dues plus 2 hours labor daily in exchange for room and board. Full members can build a dwelling, which they donate to the community if they leave the community. No equity.

Port Townsend Ecovillage, Port Townsend	Buy-in fee might range from around $65,000 to $85,000 for each of 25 "household member-ships," with at least $32,000 of that in a contract option at 6 percent interest. This does not include the cost of an individual's dwelling, which may range from a room in a cooperative house to a cabin, cottage, or multiplex. Annual assessments for shared spaces and facilities will be over $1,000 per household, in part depending on number of adults. Rental fees range from about $400 to $575 plus utilities.
To Honor Community, Ione	Joining fee of $2,500, plus costs of building a standard-sized strawbale home with full amenities, at an estimated cost of $80,000 per home, with community providing water hook-ups and milled lumber, for 5 to 8 homes total. No equity, but a lifetime lease.

Cohousing Communities

Bartimaeus Cohousing, Bremerton	Housing unit costs range from $217,000 for a two-bedroom 1,091 square foot unit to $235,000 for a 1,293 square foot 3-bedroom unit. and $326,000 for a 4-bedroom 1,800 square foot unit. Plus monthly fees for maintenance, etc. Housing units can be purchased with a down payment and a mortgage.
Jackson Place Cohousing, Seattle	The community's 27 housing units range from 2-bedroom flats to 2-story 2-bedroom and 3-bedroom apartments, and town homes with from 2 to 5 bedrooms, with prices ranging from $220,000 to $350,000. Plus monthly utilities and maintenance fees. Housing units can be purchased with a down payment and a mortgage. Rental units range from $800 a month for a room in a housing unit, to $1,200 a month for an apartment.
Sharingwood Cohousing, Snohomish County	Houses are on separate lots; new members buy the house, lot, and a share of common land. Houses have sold for $175,000 for a 2-bedroom house to $480,000 for a 5,000 square foot triplex. Rents range from $500 a month for a studio apartment within a house to $3,000 a month for a whole house. Plus monthly utilities and maintenance fees. Housing units can be purchased with a down payment and a mortgage.
Songaia Cohousing, Bothel	Duplex units range from $200,000 for a 1-bedroom unit to $250,000 for 2-bedroom unit and $300,000 for 3-bedroom unit. Plus monthly utilities and maintenance fees. Housing units can be purchased with a down payment and a mortgage. Daylight basement studio apartment rentals are $550 a month.
Winslow Cohousing, Bainbridge Island	A 700 square foot studio sold for $200,000 and a three-bedroom unit for $340,000 (compared to average price in local area of $550,000 per house). Plus monthly utilities and maintenance fees. Housing units can be purchased with a down payment and a mortgage.

Oregon
Urban Communities

Du-ma, Eugene	Buy in cost of $65,000 per member, which is a portion of the remaining debt owed on this 10-bedroom house (if each member paid a portion of the market value it would be close to $120,000 per person). Financing options are also available. Some rooms available for rent at $330 a month, plus utilities.
Maitreya Ecovil-lage, Eugene	About 25 to 30 people rent houses and apartments in this community of owners and ten-ants on 4 adjacent city lots. Below-market rents range from $100 to $400 per month, and $900 a month for a 3-bedroom home, plus a triplex (three 2-story housing units) and straw-bale cottage with sale price of $500,000. No equity, except for triplex.

Walnut Street Co-op, Eugene	Members buy in with a nonrefundable joining fee of $1,000 per person. Members and renters both pay $325 per month; for members, one-third of that fee goes into an equity account, which appreciates at three percent a year. Members who leave after three years are reimbursed their equity portion, if the co-op can afford it. Members and renters also pay $80 a month for utilities and $130 a month for food, for a monthly total of $535 per person.

Rural or Semi-Rural Communities

Alpha Farm, Deadwood	Residents and members exchange work for room, board, and all expenses paid in this income-sharing and asset-sharing community. Members, who must be residents first, donate all their assets to the community when they join. They have equity, since the monetary value of their assets is returned, in monthly payments, if they leave. If the community ever disbanded each member would receive a share of the income from the property sale in proportion to the amount of their donated assets, relative to everyone else's.
Lost Valley Educational Center, Dexter	Joining fee of $1,000. Members either pay rent for community-owned housing units ($40 to $220 a month) based on square footage and amenities, or live in their own mobile homes or other temporary structures and pay a site lease fee ($30 to $70) based on the amount of square feet their dwelling occupies and the degree of utilities and infrastructure services they use. All members and provisional members also pay a $250 monthly community support fee, and $100 a month for food. No equity (except departing members can sell their privately owned dwellings to other community members.)

Cohousing Communities

Cascadia Commons, Portland	Purchase fees of $175,000 to $225,000 for housing units ranging from 1 to 3 bedrooms. Plus monthly utilities and maintenance fees. Housing units can be purchased with a down payment and a mortgage.
Downtown Eugene Cohousing, Eugene	Purchase fees range from about $185,000 for a 2-bedroom unit to $300,000 for a 4-bedroom unit, plus monthly utilities and maintenance fees. Housing units can be purchased with a down payment and a mortgage.
Fordyce St. Cohousing, Ashland	Purchase fees range from $210,000 for 1,000 square foot unit to $323,400 for 1,630 square foot unit, plus 2 affordable housing units based on buyer's income, in range of $135,000 to $165,000. All units are equity-limited if they are sold to new buyers, since property was purchased at below-market rates. Plus monthly utilities and maintenance fees. Housing units can be purchased with a down payment and a mortgage.

Now that you've got a sense of what it can cost, what else does it take to join a community? In the next chapter we'll consider the qualities that enable people to thrive in the community lifestyle.

Chapter 12

What Does It Take to Live in Community?

Not for the Faint of Heart

While living in community can be wonderfully rich and fulfilling, it takes time, money, and willingness to learn a new way of life. It means being able to meet the community's requirements for contributing labor and money, attending meetings, and abiding by the group's agreements. It may also mean that you change personally in ways you never imagined. And researching, visiting, and joining a community is a major project, not unlike taking a long and complex overseas trip, moving across the country, or getting married. It's not as significant a project as starting your own community from scratch — but it's close.

"Community isn't for the faint of heart," declares Larry Kaplowitz in his humorous essay "Community on a Bad Day," which first appeared in *Permaculture Activist* magazine in 1999, and is reprinted in Chapter 27 of this book. I agree! Many people who live in community will tell you it's one of the best things they've ever done, and also one of the hardest. Living in community can require a steep learning curve and the patience to simultaneously live upstream and downstream from everyone else — meaning, to consistently pay attention to the potential effects of your actions on your fellow community members, and to be continuously vulnerable to the effects of their actions on you. It can take patience to learn your community's self-governance process, which will probably include small committee meetings and

community-wide business meetings and, quite likely, consensus decision-making. While the consensus process generates wider and more enthusiastic compliance with decisions than, say, majority-rule voting, consensus takes longer to come to a decision than majority-rule voting, and certainly a lot longer than when one person makes a management decision. Making decisions by consensus can seem glacially slow to new community members — especially for impatient Type A folks and executives used to being in charge.

Just like living in mainstream culture, living in community can also take good time-management skills — there's always a work party, a committee meeting, something more that needs to be done. One must really learn to balance one's own needs with the needs of the group, which sometimes means saying no.

Living in community is certainly emotionally enriching; it can also be emotionally challenging, for several reasons. First, because people usually co-own property and are financially and legally connected, and because they often live relatively closer together, they can affect one another far more than when living in mainstream culture. People often need to speak up and tell someone else how their actions are affecting them. Besides all the positive feedback you'll get in community, and all the new skills and talents you might discover and be appreciated and acknowledged for, you might get critical feedback too. "I'm upset that you didn't clean the common house yesterday; I had to do it myself." "When you whine like that it's really annoying." "I think you're doing that 'power-over' thing again." Getting critical feedback can be mighty uncomfortable. So community members are often forced to look at and deal with some of the most hidden and least functional aspects of their psyches — and this can be painful.

Living in community can be emotionally challenging in other ways, too. You might find yourself wanting to criticize others — those who don't understand things as quickly as you do, or who don't seem as responsible as you think people should be, or who don't clean up after themselves in ways you expect, or who seem terminally wrong-headed about most things most of the time. This takes patience! And patience takes energy. A person can end up feeling drained by the simple act of extending patience and tolerance to someone whose actions they'd normally want to just get away from. But in community you can't get away — these folks are still your fellow community members the next day.

Then there are the people who want to explore difficult interpersonal interactions in more detail than you do, or who want to do what is sometimes called "processing" with you — exploring what's hidden, and what's going on emotionally for each of you. For some people this is a way of gaining better clarity, patience, and understanding, and is valued in community as it helps build bonds of friendship and harmony. New people often don't see processing this way, however, and would prefer to just get on with their tasks without examining the underbrush. Some people consider being asked for more depth and clarity about what they're feeling in the moment, especially when they're upset, an act of friendship and caring. However, others, especially if they're new to community, can interpret this as pushy, prying, or invasive.

Or what if you want to feel "a sense of community" — being surrounded by the acceptance, inclusion, and friendship of others — but this community-connection feeling is not happening for you yet. All those other people know and like each other, and you're just an outsider, a newcomer. They're having lots of warm, friendly connections with each other, so why don't you feel included? The answer is, of course, that you haven't been there long enough to establish those bonds of community friendship. This will come! But waiting for the "sense of community" to arise between a newcomer and existing community members can be challenging for shy or timid people, or those who feel socially awkward or who don't make friends easily — or those who expected that the feeling of community inclusion would happen right away. (In smaller communities one can feel a sense of community sooner; in larger ones it can take more time before feeling this.)

Living in community can be exciting and rewarding, as I hope you can tell from accounts in previous chapters, but it does take an adjustment to shift from the lifestyle that most of us are used to. So, what qualities make it easier to live in community?

What Works Well in Community?

Here's what seems to work well in community:

- Confidence, self-acceptance, self-esteem.
- Assertiveness.
- Humility, willingness to listen and learn.
- Willingness to serve, to contribute to something larger than yourself.

By "confidence" and "self-esteem," I don't mean egotism or self-importance, but the simple appreciation of one's own worth, which usually results in an innate willingness to extend respect and good will to others. People who feel fairly good about themselves tend to treat other people well, and to enjoy living in community. However, people at the lower end of the self-worth spectrum — both those who behave as if they feel worthless and inferior, and those who behave in ways that are prideful or dismissive, or who put on superior airs — seem to have difficulty adjusting to community. Sometimes these folks have trouble with other people's feedback hitting them too hard. Sometimes these folks don't know how to take their fair sense of responsibility for things they have done. They either take too much responsibility — "Oh, I'm a terrible person!" — or too little — "I do *not* do that! *You're* the one with the problem."

Assertiveness often accompanies self-confidence, but not always. By "assertive" I sure don't mean "aggressive," but rather the ability to speak up, ask questions, ask for what you want (sensitively and respectfully, of course), to patiently persist, and to take the initiative. Sometimes it simply means having enough initiative, patience, and persistence to deal intelligently with something in the community that really needs help.

Once, for example, a retired woman joined a community in which minutes had been taken at community business meetings, but the minutes were stored in different places throughout the community: sometimes in file folders, sometimes in people's computer files, and many minutes had been lost. People couldn't look things up easily (or at all), and many past agreements existed only in the memories of various long-time members — with all the accompanying conflict that happens when people remember things differently. Frustrated by this situation, but unwilling to let it get her down, she searched out all the old minutes she could find, and created a series of three-ring binders with minutes and a decision log for each year of the community's existence. *That's* assertive.

A third important quality for living in community, in my opinion, is humility. I certainly don't mean self-deprecation or groveling, but a simple willingness to assume that we may not know many things, we may not have all the answers, and we may learn something new. This kind of humility is a simple kind of gentle gratitude and respect for ourselves and others. It also means not assuming we know more than other people, but can learn new things. It's what Zen Buddhists call "beginner's mind" — being open and willing every day to be surprised and delighted, informed and reformed.

Lastly, it helps to take genuine pleasure in working with others to create something that is much larger than our own small selves. Think of a time when you worked with friends or colleagues on a project that benefited others, or one which you could never have done alone. If you enjoyed the experience, you'll know what I mean. I often view living in my community as a lifelong ecological art project. It's a lot bigger than anything I could ever do by myself — it takes collaborating shoulder-to-shoulder with others. It feels great!

For examples of people who have this combination of qualities, see "The 'Great Guests' Hall of Fame" in Chapter 18.

Who Does Well in Community?

Coming at this from a different angle, here are the kinds of people who seem to do well in community.

1. Someone who doesn't "need" it.

People who are fulfilled and effective in the world and doing well in their lives are more likely to thrive in community.

Paradoxically, the more anxious or desperate a person is to find community, or the more difficult a person finds living outside community, the less likely it is he or she will be invited to join one, and the less likely he or she will do well or feel comfortable living in one.

2. Someone with a healthy sense of self.

As mentioned earlier, this includes people with self-esteem and a certain kind of self-awareness. They know what they want, know their strengths and limitations, and are on a program of personal growth for themselves. These are people who are secure enough to seldom feel the need to defend, protect, or prove themselves.

Can people who sometimes or often feel insecure or unconfident live in community? Certainly. However, they will generally find themselves facing the same issues as they always have. In a small to medium group of very caring individuals — who have excellent group process skills, well-trained consensus decision-making skills, and a desire to see every member shine — a person with less confidence can benefit enormously from community. But it depends on the level of patience and compassion in the community. And on the new person's willingness to change and grow.

3. Someone who is open and flexible, and able to hear and consider other points of view.

The rigid person; the aggressive, competent loner who knows best; or the person who's never worked cooperatively with others before, either don't do well in community or change and grow enormously. If you're a CEO of a large and successful company, or the indomitable matriarch of a large extended family, for example, community may be difficult for you.

4. Someone who has a sense of connection to people, an interest in the well-being of others, and well-defined boundaries.

People who feel an innate sense of connection to others tend to thrive in community. However, people who have been hurt deeply, especially at an early age, tend not to feel trusting of or connected to others. They can be insensitive toward or uninterested in others — and have no idea that something isn't right. Yet it also helps to not feel too sensitive and open to others. In those community situations which involve living closely with others, for example, in sharing a house, each person will be affected by other people's lives and their challenges. Sometimes this can seem like an overwhelming drama if one doesn't have the ability to "put up their shields" and *not* take on other people's issues.

5. Someone willing to abide by group agreements.

Some people believe that an aggressive sense of autonomy and independence protects their freedom and safety. These folks can tend to bristle when someone else asks them to do something. "Don't tell me what to do!" They resent authority figures, or they see "authority" in people who aren't in that role at all. The idea of cooperation or interdependence with others annoys this kind of person; they believe they might lose themselves.

A person who realizes that their identity remains intact no matter how they may cooperate with a group can move from "I" to "we" without losing their sense of self. It feels good to be interdependent with others; however, it takes a certain amount of self-esteem and trust even to try it.

6. Someone willing to find a balance between community goals and personal goals.

Many people are happy to give their time and energy to the needs of the larger group. While it's healthy to do it in moderation, it's also healthy to know when to say no, and create balance between community needs and personal needs.

7. Someone willing to speak up ...

As noted earlier, this kind of person is assertive,

willing to risk taking the initiative, and when called for, to disagree, or ask for what they want.

8. ...And to listen.

The person who is dynamic, assertive, and full of ideas may sometimes need to tone down that energy in group meetings so that others feel like they have the space to speak. Such a person may need to practice managing their energy so that other people don't resent them for seeming pushy, or like know-it-alls.

9. Someone willing to learn and practice good communication skills and fair and empowering decision-making skills.

This often takes actual training and mentoring, as, again, it goes against the grain of our typically competitive, aggressive, isolated way of life in North America.

10. Someone with a desire to see themselves as they really are.

This is really difficult — and painful — but exceedingly worth it. A person with this attitude can grow, in terms of self-awareness and emotional maturity, far faster and more effectively than they ever thought possible.

11. Someone willing to stick with it.

For community to succeed, its members need to be willing to persevere through conflict, changing individual needs, and higher-than-normal demands on your time.

OK, do all people who live in community have all the positive qualities listed above? Not at all. They're just regular folks like you and me, with the whole tumult of beneficial and annoying qualities that arise at various times. But that key quality of *willingness* goes a long way. Willingness to take a

look at oneself (even at those dark corners — yuck); willingness to be open to new experiences; willingness to revise many of one's lifelong habits in favor of a more cooperative lifestyle with others. If you often feel self-confident, and can be assertive when you need to, can often remember to listen and learn from others, and take delight in working with others to create something larger than yourselves, I believe your life in community will be much easier. Even wonderful.

Who Does Not Do So Well?

People who behave as if they feel deeply ashamed of themselves or who feel wretched much of the time, will tend to feel ashamed and wretched when living in community too. Neither does community seem to fit for people who are angry and impatient much of the time, or those used to getting their own way, being the boss, or having their orders followed without question. Community living would never satisfy such folks. Marine drill sergeants, maharajahs, and pouting princesses need not apply!

Neither does community seem to work very well for people with strong opinions about what community "should" be. In my years as editor of *Communities* magazine I've met several individuals who are passionate and opinionated about community and what it "should" be but who don't actually seem to get along with other human beings. They love the idea of community but can't actually live in one.

Preparing for Community

I firmly believe that the successful community seeker can't know too much about community. That is, your ability to choose the community you'll one day enjoy living in depends upon your ability to know *what you're seeing* when you visit different communities, and how to compare one to another — to have a context for assessing each community wisely. Studying the *Communities Directory*, the Online Directory (*directory.ic.org*), and scoping out community websites will give you a broad, overview perspective. It's like looking over the wide plains from a tall peak, so to speak, as you'll see in the next chapter, "The *Communities Directory*, the Internet, and You."

You'll need a deep perspective as well as a broad one. Deep perspectives can come from extended community visits, but before doing that, a simpler (and much cheaper) way to gain depth on the subject is through videos and books about specific individual communities or a handful of specific communities. See "Learning Broad, Learning Deep" in the next chapter.

But books and videos pale in comparison to actually being there. While I consider the *Communities Directory*, *Communities* magazine, the Online Directory, and Geoph Kozeny's *Visions of Utopia* videos must-see reading and viewing for anyone who wants to live in community, I think it's *equally* valuable to create your own "Community Living 101" course by experiencing various Community Experience Weekends or Weeks, Visitor Programs, and work-exchange or internship programs — even in communities you already know you're not interested in joining. These are all valuable ways to get a general overview of what it's like to live in community. We'll look at these opportunities more closely in Chapter 16, "Planning Your Visit."

And we'll go into much more depth about focusing in on your values and needs for community in Chapter 14, "Your Criteria for Communities to Visit."

Another kind of preparation is to experience living with other people in a shared living situation for awhile, and take workshops in process and communication techniques such as consensus decision-making, Nonviolent Communication, Arnie Mindell's Process Work, and so on.

What Do Communities Want from You?

You should also find out what communities will want from *you*.

This is fairly easy to learn. Communities will tell you what they're seeking in new members. Some will tell you on their websites. Twin Oaks' website reads: "Basically...a person needs to be willing to abide by the agreements of the community. They also need to be able to fit into our social norms which, because we live so closely together, are quite particular (e.g. being sensitive to people's 'personal space,' being able to pick up on social cues, being able to be cooperative and share control, etc.)."

"We have to be better off with you than without you," declares the website of Windward Farm, a rural homesteading community in Washington State.

"You operate well in a busy environment," reads the online ad for new housemates in an urban community. "You're able to declare what is important to you so the people around you can honor your journey. Bring your passion: lukewarm people will not fare too well here. You are happy to contribute a little time to keeping up the shared spaces. You are respectful of other people's hot-button issues and celebrate the incredible diversity all around us. If exploring is more fun for you than judging, then you're a good fit."

Many communities will tell you what they're looking for in their membership literature. And most will tell you if you e-mail and ask them.

Here, for example, are excerpts from the Selection Criteria document of Mariposa Grove, a social-justice activist and arts community in Oakland, California:

Future Mariposa Grove members:

+ Are enthusiastic about living collectively with a diverse group of people.
+ Have the ability and willingness to commit

time for and share equally in household activities: house meetings, chores, shared meals, maintenance/renovation/repair of the land and houses, creating new legal and organizational systems and fun/social time with members.

+ Show initiative to add beauty and inspiration to the community.

+ Are dedicated to a socially and environmentally responsible lifestyle.

+ Are able to communicate openly and honestly on a one-to-one basis as well as within a group setting.

+ Are capable of participating in and contributing to consensus decision-making.

+ Respect personal boundaries and those defined by the group as a whole.

+ Have skills in dealing with conflicts.

+ Are able to make a commitment to the financial responsibilities of living at Mariposa Grove.

+ Are truthful in their public and personal affairs.

+ Have the ability and willingness to remain free of addictive/destructive behaviors.

+ Have enthusiasm for life and a good sense of humor.

"We're looking for people who will contribute considerably more energy and benefit to Earthaven than they may require of the community in return," states one of Earthaven's membership documents. "That is, you will give Earthaven more energy (such as skills, good ideas, good will) than the energy you may require in return (such as needing more than the usual amount of time required for Heartshares, mediations with other members, or support by the Care Team)."

Another good source of information about what a particular community wants in new members are their criteria for interns and work exchangers. Often, they are looking for interns or work exchangers who are eager to learn, flexible, energetic, comfortable in groups, hard-working, self-motivated, have good communication skills, and are "able to manage a broad diversity of challenges at once."

That just about sums up what *every* community is looking for in members, in my experience. However, being able to work hard is not an absolute requirement in most communities, since not all community seekers are young, energetic, and strong. Most communities also appreciate the wisdom and experience of older or less physically able people, as well as the financial assets they may bring in terms of being able to afford the buy-in fee, or even loan the community money on friendly terms.

You can also get a sense of what communities want — and don't want — by the questions they ask of people who want to visit, intern, or become a resident or a full member. You can see some of these community questionnaires in Appendix A, "Sample Community Membership Documents."

What About Young People Just Out of School?

"I'm going to join an ecovillage," inspired and visionary people often tell me, fresh from high school or just out of college with a degree in environmental education or eco-spirituality. "And I've prepared myself well already," they continue. "I've learned how to garden organically and save open-pollinated seeds, and I've taken the permaculture design certificate course and workshops on cob and strawbale building. Next I'm learning off-grid power."

If only it were this easy! I take a deep breath and try, with as much kindness as I can muster, to tell them that, in fact, while it's great that they've learned these good things, it's often not enough. For most, but not all, ecovillages, what new members need besides their values and interests, is cold, hard cash. As you know from the last chapter, most rural communities involve property ownership, and many have hefty joining or buy-in fees.

What do I advise these folks? Not something nice and ecologically sustainable, I'm afraid. Instead I suggest that if they want to join a community with a joining fee they have two choices, both of them difficult. One is to get the best job they can find, two jobs even (with values and practices they can live with), and earn and save as much as they can over a few years, especially if they're young and still have that youthful visionary drive and seemingly endless energy. I believe that most people can work for a few years and save enough to have a much easier time getting started in community, although this may not be true for those who are systematically oppressed in our culture based on race, class, etc. If they are able to work steadily, live frugally, and save up $10,000, $20,000, or $30,000, they'll most likely have their community buy-in fee and a head-start on the costs of building their home in community. Then they can pick the ecovillage or sustainable community of their choice, without financial considerations hindering them. In addition to becoming a provisional member in this community, with this plan the young person would hold off actually moving to the community, but would work and save *now*, outside of community, in mainstream culture, while jobs and cash flow are still relatively available — given the ever-escalating economic effects of Peak Oil. They'd save up a bundle, then move into their community.

The other choice is to move to the community without much money, and work hard while living there, which could mean living in substandard conditions for a long time. Many determined members at communities all over North America have joined community and lived onsite without funds, working their way slowly through time into full membership and a decent place to live. And if we asked them, many would tell us this was exactly the right move for them, and they wouldn't have it any other way. They got to live with like-minded friends and colleagues right away. They got to live out their sustainability values right away. They got to reduce their ecological footprint right away. But it's *hard*.

I recommend the first choice — work and save now; move into the community later. I don't want young people, or anyone with few assets for that matter, to become subsistence-existence, working-poor community residents, forced to eke out a living at low-paying part-time or occasional jobs, while paying off their joining or buy-in fees slowly over time. Or to live in primitive conditions in substandard housing — moldy tents or canvas yurts, hot tin-box camper shells or falling-apart travel trailers — while they work and save for years just to start building a permanent home with actual insulation, running water, and real windows and doors. Many energetic, well-educated young people with fine college degrees and a great grasp of many sustainable systems have shown up at Earthaven's gate, only to learn that it can be a long, hard road to become co-owners of a large, developed million-dollar-plus property without having the funds up front.

If you're a person in this situation who wants to live in a sustainable community, I'd like it to be a lot easier for you than this!

In the next chapter we'll explore the first major step in joining a community — researching what communities are out there.

≈ Chapter 13 ≈

The *Communities Directory*, the Internet, and You — Researching Communities

By now you've learned about why people enjoy living in intentional communities, and about the many different kinds of communities that exist. You also have a fairly good idea of the wide range of costs to join a community (including no cost at all), and the personal qualities that help make it easier to live in community. The next steps are to learn about the specific communities that are out there, come up with your own personal criteria for what kinds of communities you'd like to visit, and then visit them. It's exciting!

Print and Internet Resources

The ways to find out what communities are out there include *Communities Directory*, an invaluable reference book about intentional communities in North America and worldwide; the "Communities Seeking Members" classified ads in *Communities* magazine; and the hundreds of community listings (with links to their websites) on several different online communities directories, including the Online Communities Directory of the Fellowship for Intentional Community: *directory.ic.org*.

Associations of specific kinds of communities — ecovillages, cohousing, and others — also provide online directories of their member communities or search functions for finding specific communities. These include Ecovillage Network of the Americas (ENA), Canadian Cohousing Association (CCA), Cohousing Association of the US (Coho US), Federation of Egalitarian Communi-

ties (FEC), Camphill Communities, Catholic Worker Communities, L'Arche Communities in Canada, and North American Students of Cooperation (NASCO).

For Europe or Down Under, print resources include *Diggers & Dreamers*, a directory of communities in Great Britain; *Eurotopia*, a directory of communities in Europe; *Eco-Villages and Communities in Australia and New Zealand*; and *Utopianz: A Guide to Intentional Communities and Communal Living in Aotearoa New Zealand*. On the Internet, you can find websites of ecovillage networks in Canada, Europe, Australia, and New Zealand. The world is rich in communities directories!

Communities Directories and the Internet

One way to begin your research is to get a copy of the latest *Communities Directory* (available from bookstores, libraries, and *store.ic.org*) and leaf through it to get a sense of the wide range of communities out there. You can do this online as well, but I suggest starting with an actual physical book you can hold in your hand, because getting information from pages of a book will give you a whole different sense of the subject than reading online, and my hope is that you'll utilize both. A new, updated version of the *Directory* is published about every 18 months.

The *Communities Directory* lists intentional communities alphabetically, both in North Amer-

PRINT AND ONLINE COMMUNITY DIRECTORIES

Print Directories

- *Communities Directory,* Fellowship for Intentional Community (new editions every 18 months): bookstores, libraries, *store.ic.org*
- *Diggers & Dreamers: The Guide to Communal Living, 2006-2007,* (Great Britain), Sarah Bunker, Chris Coates and Jonathan How, ed., Diggers & Dreamers Publications, 2006. *diggersanddreamers.org.uk*
- *Eurotopia: Directory of Intentional Communities and Ecovillages in Europe, 2006–2007,* Volker Peters, Martin Stengel, ed., Volker Peters Verlag, 2005. (English and German editions.) *eurotopia.de/englindex*
- *Directory of Ecovillages in Europe,* Barbro Grindheim and Declan Kennedy, *gen-europe.org*
- *Communi, Communia, ed Ecovillaggi in Italia,* Manuel Olivares, Malatempora, 2003. *manueloliveras@liberto.it* (In Italian)
- *Eco-Villages and Communities in Australia and New Zealand,* Barbara Knudsen and Morag Gamble, GEN-Oceania/Asia, 2000. Available in the US from Ecovillage Training Center, *ecovillage@thefarm.org*
- *Utopianz: A Guide to Intentional Communities and Communal Living in Aotearoa New Zealand,* R. Greenaway, et. al., ed., Umbrella Trust, 2004. *straw@paradise.net.nz*

Online Directories

- Fellowship for Intentional Community: *directory.ic.org*
- Intentional Communities Database: *icdb.org*
- WikiPedia, Intentional Communities: *en.wikipedia.org/wiki/communities*
- Ecovillage Network of the Americas (ENA): *ena.ecovillage.org*
- Ecovillage Network of Canada: *enc.ecovillage.org*
- Urban Ecovillage Network: *urban.ecovillage.org*

- Cohousing Association of the United States (Coho/US): *cohousing.org*
- Canadian Cohousing Network: *cohousing.ca*
- Federation of Egalitarian Communities (FEC): *thefec.org*
- National Association of Housing Co-ops (NAHC): *coophousing.org*
- North American Students of Cooperation (NASCO) (Student Co-op Housing): *nasco.coop*
- Senior Cooperative Foundation (Senior Housing Co-ops): *seniorcoops.org*
- Cooperative Services, Inc. (Senior Housing Co-ops): *csi.coop*
- Camphill Communities in North America: *camphill.org*
- Catholic Worker Communities, North America: *catholicworker.org/communities/commstates.cfm*
- Queer in Community (Gay and lesbian communities): *queerincommunity.org*
- Global Ecovillage Network-Europe: *gen-europe.org*
- Eco-Village Network UK: *evnuk.org.uk*
- Global Ecovillage Network (GEN): *gen.ecovillage.org*
- Camphill Communities in the UK: *camphlil.org.uk*
- Camphill Communities in Ireland: *camphill.ie*
- L'Arche Communities, Canada: *larchecanada.org*
- L'Arche Communities, UK: *larche.org.uk*
- L'Arche Communities, international: *larch.org* (in French)
- Global Ecovillage Network-Oceania/Asia: *genoa.ecovillage.org/genoceania*
- Ecovillages and Cohousing Association-New Zealand: *www.converge.org.nz/evcnz*

Other web resources

- Economads website: *economads.com*
- Eco Tour of North America blog: *ecotourofnorthamerica.blogspot.com*

ica and internationally. Look at the maps showing where communities are located in various states and provinces. Dip into the Community Listings pages and read randomly. On any two-page spread, you might find a long-established Christian community, a Camphill community, a Catholic Worker community, a cohousing neighborhood, and a forming ecovillage. Scan the Cross Reference Charts, where you can compare at a glance the locations, founding dates, number of members, number of acres, and lifestyle issues of all the listed communities. The Communities Listings Keyword Index will show you communities associated with a wide variety of different kinds of interests and values, for example, "Homeschooling," "Homesteading," "Hospitality." Use these keywords to find names of communities associated with the topics that interest you most, then find and read about each of these communities in the alphabetical listings. An informal browse through the *Directory* will give you a fairly good sense of the kinds of communities that exist, and individual communities that catch your interest. Each community listing provides contact information, including websites, e-mail addresses, street addresses, and phone numbers. You can do the same with *Diggers and Dreamers*, *Eurotopia*, and the Australian and New Zealand directories.

Or you could start online. I suggest beginning with directory.ic.org, the online version of the *Communities Directory*, which is part of the website of the nonprofit Fellowship for Intentional Community (FIC), ic.org. The FIC also publishes the print version of the *Communities Directory* and *Communities* magazine; runs Community Bookshelf, a mail-order book service with books on intentional communities; distributes Geoph Kozeny's two "Visions of Utopia" videos; and hosts regional "Art of Community" conferences around North America.

Searching Online

At the directory.org website you'll find "Communities Listings," "Search," and "Maps." "Communities Listings" will give you alphabetized as well as geographical listings of all the North American and international communities in the print version of the *Communities Directory* — and considerably more, as communities list themselves directly on the website all the time. The site allows you to choose only already-established communities, only forming communities, or both. Its search function offers more options, including searching for a cohousing community, a non-cohousing community, or both. You can search for whether or not the community is open to visitors or has a shared common spiritual path or is open to gay and lesbian members. You can search for the number of members; whether the community is urban, suburban, or rural; the number of shared community meals per week; its decision-making style; and whether the community has independent incomes or is partially or wholly income-sharing. You can also search the text of each listing itself for key words that may lead to communities with activities that interest you; i.e., "permaculture," "food-self-reliant," "off-grid," and so on.

The advanced search option is even more specific. You can select for how the community's land is owned (by the group, by one person, by an absentee landlord, etc.); what age ranges or gender the group may be seeking or any age or gender restrictions; if they have specific dietary practices or restrictions; amount of alcohol and/or tobacco use or any restrictions; the percentage of food grown onsite; and if the community incorporates any religious or spiritual practices, and if so which ones.

Once you hit the search button you'll get a list of community names that correspond to the criteria you outlined. When you choose a name you'll get a specific listing for that community, its location, the date it was founded, contact information (including website, if they have one), perhaps an informal outline of their mission and purpose, and anything else the group may want you to know about them. Below that will be a chart with their number of members (adults and children), percentage of men and women, whether they have property yet, its acreage, number of buildings on-site, and more. If they don't have a website, at least you'll have the group's street address and phone number, and you can hit the "Send an E-mail" button to e-mail them.

The "Maps" function of the Online Directory allows you to zero in on any part of the US (or the world) where you might want to find communities. You can scroll over various parts of any regions, and zoom in close to cities or counties. Images of small map pins will show you where intentional communities are located. Click on one and you'll get the community's name and listing; clicking on their name will bring up their specific listing. You can also use the map to show all the communities with specific characteristics you select in a given search, such as, for example, the locations of all communities which are open to visitors and have more than 50 members. Very cool.

Online Listings: User Beware
Another FIC-sponsored online service which is ideal for community seekers is the "Reachbook" page of the FIC's website (ic.org), offering dozens of free short listings, like classified ads, by communities looking for new members. The listings are arranged by date order, with the most recently entered listings at the top of the page. You scroll down to see what was entered in previous days or weeks. You can also list yourself and what kind of community you're looking for, so communities looking for new members can find you, too.

As you use these online functions, please keep three things in mind.

First, anybody and their brother can go to the Online Directory's website and fill out a form, and voila! — they've got a communities listing. The website hosts can't monitor everything, nor can they verify accuracy, so they simply provide this service and count on your good judgment. This is also true of the print *Communities Directory* (which is generated from the data at the Online Directory) as well as the "Communities Seeking Members" classified ads in *Communities* magazine. So be forewarned, not every group listed is necessarily a "community"; some listings might be just a good idea someone has about a community they'd like to start. (There's more about this in Chapter 14, "Your Criteria for Communities to Visit.")

Second, even with existing, for-real communities, it's the community members themselves who write their own listings. They might describe what they *wish* their community was like instead of what it's really like. So again, be discerning. (More about this later, too.)

Third, neither the print *Communities Directory* or Online Directory include every intentional community out there; they include only those which either responded to a questionnaire sent by the *Directory's* editorial staff or which listed themselves online per the website's instructions. Several intentional communities I know of were not on the website so I located them by Googling.

Broadening Your Search
This brings us to three other online services that can boost your research: Google (or a comparable search engine), the Intentional Communities Database (icdb.org), and WikiPedia. When I can't find what I'm looking for on one of the large online community networks, I just try these.

Once, while searching the online Communities Directory for Buddhist communities and not finding many, I Googled for "intentional communities Buddhist," which got me one or two. I found considerably more, however, when I got inspired to try "dharma centers," "Tibetan Buddhism," "Zen," "Vipassana" and "Insight Meditation." I've used Google to find specific communities in England, Australia, and points in between — since while some international communities list themselves on the *directory.org* website, many do not. And while *directory.org* lists individual Camphill and L'Arche communities, it was only through Google that I found the websites of Camphill Communities in North America and L'Arche Communities worldwide. If a community has a website, and if they've ever been mentioned in a publication, Google will have them.

The home page of Intentional Communities Database (*icdb.org*) says, "icdb.org is a self-serve, open, free, multi-lingual and paperless database/directory, serving intentional communities, and their organizations, individuals, and groups searching for intentional communities." It was created by a group of young Internet-savvy community activists, with help from some FIC communities activists. As with the FIC's Online Directory, people write up their listings themselves. Similarly, you can search for the variables you want: country, kind of community, specific focus, and so on. You can also enter a description of yourself and what kind of community you're looking for, which communities looking for new members can read.

En.wikipedia.org/wiki/Intentional_community, is the intentional communities section of WikiPedia, the largest free, online encyclopedia in the world. It's written collaboratively by readers online and by experts in their field, and hosted by the nonprofit WikiMedia Foundation in St. Petersburg, Florida. Encyclopedia entries are available in English and many other languages, including Asian languages.

Another good way to get a sense of communities is to talk with other community seekers and ask what they've found out in their community-visiting travels. You can also read the website journals or blogs of people who record their impressions of community visits online. Two of my favorites are the Economads website (*economads.com*), in which two young people from Palestine, Ofek and Erika, record the sustainable homesteads and communities they've visited in the Middle East, North Africa, Europe, and North America. Another is Eco Tour of North America (*ecotourofnorthamerica.blogspot.com*), in which Shane Snell from Whole Village Ecovillage in Ontario visited sustainable homesteads, education centers, and communities in the southeastern and southwestern US, recording his adventures along the way with photos and text.

Searching More Specifically

Are you looking for ecovillages specifically? While *directory.ic.org* lists ecovillages, you'll find websites specifically for ecovillages at Ecovillage Network of the Americas (ENA): *ena.ecovillage.org*; Ecovillage Network of Canada: *enc.ecovillage.org*; and Global Ecovillage Network: *gen.ecovillage.org*. Here's a tip: to find a list of ecovillages worldwide, go to *gen.ecovillage.org/index*, click on "find ecovillages," and when that screen comes up, click on "search" without checking any of the parameters.

If you're looking for ecovillages outside North America, try Global Ecovillage Network-Europe: *gen-europe.org*; Eco-Village Network UK: *www.evnuk.org.uk*; Global Ecovillage Network-Oceania/Asia: *genoa.ecovillage.org/genoceania*; and Ecovillages and Cohousing Association-New Zealand: *converge.org.nz/evcnz/*.

Are you looking for cohousing communities specifically? If so, check out *cohousing.org* and *cohousing.ca*, the websites of the Cohousing Association of the United States (Coho US) and the Canadian Cohousing Network (CCN), respectively. The FIC's Directory Online site, *directory.ic.org*, lists all the same cohousing communities as that of Coho/US; however, the Coho/US website decides which communities that want to list themselves are really cohousing communities, whereas the Online Directory allows communities to self-identify as "uses the cohousing model." Thus those listed on the Coho/US site are "real" cohousing communities, not just people who liked the word "cohousing."

The Coho/US site lists cohousing communities geographically by state, which shows the community name, its city or town, state, amount of acreage, and the year it was completed, or whether it's forming, seeking a site, or in construction. Like the FIC's Online Directory, this website includes a database-style search function. The Coho/US website also offers a photo gallery virtual tour of cohousing; *Cohousing*, the organization's online magazine, which you can read and subscribe to online; resources; and classified ads of interest to people seeking cohousing, with listings about homes or units for rent or for sale, community guest rooms, housemates wanted, exchanges and short-term or vacation rentals, and cohousing communities specifically seeking new members.

The Canadian Cohousing Network website offers a map of cohousing locations in Canada and a geographic listing of specific communities (noted as forming, in development, or completed); listings of housing units for rent, sale, or exchange; cohousing resources; and CCN's online newsletter, which you can read and/or subscribe to.

You can do essentially the same with the other, more specific communities websites noted above. The communities you'll find in these websites will overlap some, but the occasional redundancy won't detract from your research. (By the way, if you're specifically searching for urban housing co-ops in the *Communities Directory* or Online Directory, the word "House" in the community name often means it's a co-op.)

So, by exploring all sections of the *Communities Directory* and browsing these websites for a few hours, you'll have given yourself a broad overview of the communities movement. You'll have a sense of the communities available in your desired geographical regions, and a general idea of what they're about, how big they are, and how long they've been there.

Some communities will stand out — they'll be a close match for the mission and purpose you're seeking, or the area you'd like to live in, or the lifestyle that draws you. Drink in these websites, read every page. Look for the community's mission and purpose, their daily activities, their goals. Some describe their recent accomplishments. Some community websites offer a virtual tour, with photos of their buildings and grounds. Others show photos of their members, or offer member bios. Some include community documents and agreements, or their membership policies. Some offer downloadable community brochures. Those with e-newsletters usually have online back issues — which offer photos and articles about recent events and ongoing matters of importance to the community. Communities which offer classes and workshops have an online schedule of events, with linked pages describing each course. Download whole sections, print the parts of sections that especially interest you, read them again later. Spending an hour or so on the website of each community that interests you, and downloading and re-reading those that interest you most, can save you enormous amounts of money, time, and energy down the road. Studying community websites will tell you which ones you'll want to visit — and which ones to skip.

Communities *magazine*

Another invaluable source of information about communities is *Communities* magazine, if I do say so myself. (As mentioned earlier, it's been my privilege to edit this magazine since 1994.) *Communities* is the only print publication in North America (as of 2006) that focuses solely on intentional communities of all kinds and organized neighborhoods — "creating community where you live now." Besides its numerous "Communities Seeking Members" classifieds in every issue, *Communities* magazine has special issues on sustainability in community, elders in community, children in community, and so on, and on specific kinds of communities — cohousing, ecovillages, student co-ops. You can check out the magazine on its website, *communities.ic.org*, or read it in libraries and buy it in food co-ops, larger health food stores, or from *store.ic.org*. Back issues are available through libraries or the website. One of the best ways to learn about communities is to read the articles in this magazine (many of which are excerpted in this book), and get the back issues whose articles interest you most. The best articles from back issues are posted on the magazine's website. *Communities* magazine comes out four times a year.

Separating the Wheat from the Chaff

Of course no *Communities Directory* or online directory listing can represent a community completely. Every listing will be colored by the aspirations and prejudices of the community members who wrote it. The community's aim is to present their group in the best light. They're writing to impress. So how can you tell if their presentation is exaggerated or sugar-coated? Or if it leaves out significant facts? For example, does a website show photos of beautiful natural buildings, but they're living "under the radar" because local building codes don't actually allow that kind of construction? Or does the text glowingly portray the community they hope to become some day, but not describe what the place is actually like now?

You'll have to use discernment — and a touch of skepticism — to separate the exaggerators and prevaricators from the straightforward and the transparent. Over the years I've learned what kind of descriptions tend to be correlated with grounded, stable, successful communities. Here's what impresses me:

+ The community is at least several years old.
+ It has more than a few people.
+ It has a website.
+ The directory listing and website are clear and straightforward.
+ The website shares practical information such as what it costs to join, how decisions are made, and, if it's in a rural location, how its members make a living.
+ The website has photos.
+ In the photos, the people look happy; the physical infrastructure looks well-cared for.
+ The website seems well-designed — the links work, words are spelled correctly, the photos look good.

When I read some community listings or websites I find myself wrinkling my nose in disbelief. Here are some characteristics of directory listings that raise red flags for me:

+ **The community name is over-long, theoretical, spiritually idealistic, politically adamant, or all-encompassing.** Relatively short, down-to-Earth names such as, say, "Raccoon Hollow," "Green Prairie Village," or "Good Shepherd Commons" are credible to me. "Peace, Equality, and Justice Homestead" and "Living

Adherents of the Divine Order" are not. A community with an exceptionally positive name that sounds like an affirmation — "Acolytes of Angelic Actualization" — arouses my suspicion: I picture founders so idealistic they don't realize that such a name would deter the kind of grounded, practical people that could help their community thrive. Communities with academic-sounding or ancient Greek names (hubris alert!) conjure up for me an image of people with theoretical, probably inflexible ideas about community, and likely little practical experience or people skills.

• **The community's mission and purpose statement is also over-long, theoretical, spiritually idealistic, etc.** In my experience, theoretical, vague, flowery, new agey, idealistic, or high-falutin' community descriptions tend to be highly correlated with forming communities that never get off the ground — their founders have little practical, grounded experience or people skills — or with an imagined commu-

LEARNING BROAD, LEARNING DEEP

I firmly believe that the successful community seeker can't know enough about community. Wisely choosing the community you'll join depends on knowing what you're seeing when you visit a community, and knowing how to compare one to another. You need a *context* for assessing each community wisely. Browsing websites and reading the *Communities Directory* will give you a broad, overview perspective — like looking over the wide plains from a tall peak.

But as well as a broad perspective you'll need a deep one, which can come from extended community visits. But before doing that, a simpler and much cheaper way to gain depth on the subject is through videos and books about specific individual communities or a handful of specific communities.

Broad, overview resources
• *Visions of Utopia Videos,* Geoph Kozeny, Community Catalyst Project, 2002. Part I (2002) features an overview of communities in western culture, what seems to work well in communities, and well-crafted profiles of Camphill Special School, Breitenbush Hot Springs, Purple Rose Collective, Twin Oaks, Ananda Village, Earthaven, and Nyland Cohousing.
• Part II (forthcoming, 2007), profiles Catholic Worker House of San Antonio, Community Alternatives Society, The Farm, Fraser Common Farm, Ganas, Goodenough Community, Hearthaven, Miccosukkee Land Cooperative, N Street Cohousing, Remote Hamlet, and Sandhill Farm. This project gives an extremely good sense of what a wide variety of different communities are like — urban and rural, secular and spiritual, independent incomes and income-sharing. Available at *store.ic.org.*
• *Communities* magazine. Besides "Communities Seeking Members" classified ads from communities in North America — which you'll find invaluable — you'll find articles on joining community, starting a new community, and creating community where you are, decision-making, process and communication issues, resolving conflict, ecological sustainability, romance and love relationships in community, children in community, growing older in community, making a living in community, and so on. Also different kinds of communities — ecovillages, cohousing neighborhoods, student-housing co-ops, urban communities, spiritual communities, and more. Available in food co-ops, health food supermarket chains, and at *communities.ic.org.*
• *Cohousing Journal Online,* Cohousing Association of the US's bimonthly e-newsletter about

nity that doesn't actually exist yet. It's not that I think these folks don't have positive visions; it's that I think they're likely not to know how to start a community, and tend to repel the very kinds of folks who could help them get the place built!

Further, I assume that if the description says "our community believes this" and "our community believes that," it's a project in the early, theoretical stages, probably with just one person and most likely no property yet. I prefer

websites which tell you what the community has actually done, what they're actually doing now, and what they plan to do in the near future — not just what they believe in.

- **The listing doesn't say it's a forming community, yet it has only two members.** With only two people, they are definitely still in the forming stages. Why don't they say so?
- **They just have two people, and they've been there for years.** Why hasn't anyone joined them? Or if many people over the years join for

the cohousing movement in the US, offering an exceptionally clear introduction to cohousing for the newcomer, as well as in-depth articles about various aspects of the cohousing movement and specific cohousing communities. *cohousing.org*
- Canadian Cohousing Network's online newsletter, *cohousing.ca*
- *The Findhorn Book of Community Living*, Bill Metcalf, Findhorn Press, 2004. A great introduction to intentional communities worldwide and, unlike many community books out there, it's *not* North-America-o-centric.

Resources for diving deep
- *EcoVillage at Ithaca: Pioneering Sustainable Community*, Liz Walker, New Society Publishers, 2005. A poignant and inspiring story of one woman's journey to found and develop this unique community, and what it's like to live there now. Highly recommended.
- *Ecovillages: New Frontiers for Sustainability*, Jonathan Dawson, Green Books, London, 2006.
- *Reinventing Community: Stories from the Walkways of Cohousing*, Dave Wann, ed., Fulcrum Press, 2005. After reading these great stories about life in cohousing communities, you'll have a real good sense of life in community (including non-cohousing communities).
- *Creating a Life Together: Practical Tools to Grow Ecovillages and Intentional Communities*, Diana

Leafe Christian, New Society Publishers, 2003. Although I wrote this book for community founders, readers tell me it really helps to give a good sense of what it's like to live in community — and what to look for in one.
- *Ecovillages: A Practical Guide to Sustainable Communities*, Jan Martin Bang, New Society Publishers, 2005. An overview of sustainable living projects worldwide.
- *Senior Cohousing: A Community Approach to Independent Living*, Charles Durrett, Ten Speed Press, 2005.
- *Fire, Salt, and Peace: Intentional Christian Communities Alive in North America*, David Janzen, Shalom Mission Communities, 1996.
- *Is It Utopia Yet? An Insider's View of Twin Oaks Community in its 26th Year*, Kat Kinkade, Twin Oaks Publishing. 1994. Not only informative, but funny! *twinoaks.org*
- *Voices from the Farm: Adventures in Community Living*, Rupert Fiske, ed., Book Publishing Company, 1998. Stories about life in a classic hippie income-sharing commune in the early days — but one which has been so successful it's still going strong today (although no longer income-sharing). *thefarmcommunity.com*

a short while and leave, why is that? What's turning people off?

+ **The tone is preachy, plaintive, or bitter.** This could mean the person who wrote it was going through a rough time, but it could also reflect the general tone of the community.

+ **The website is poorly done — links are broken, words are misspelled, photos are fuzzy.** On the one hand, this could reflect the level of attention and care at the community as well. On the other hand, you can't always judge a community by its poorly done website. Tony Sirna, editor of the FIC's Online Directory, notes that since many community members are not tech-savvy, some communities may have poor-looking websites but are still fine communities — and vice versa.

Once you've got a list of communities that look promising, what then? Is there a way you can pre-screen them, just by their directory listings and websites, to know if they might be a good fit for you, and save you time visiting if they're not?

Fortunately, there is. We'll take that up next.

COMMUNITIES CONFERENCES

Another good way to get a good overview about communities in a short time is to attend communities conferences, where you'll learn from keynote speakers, workshop presenters, community members looking for people to join them, and community seekers like yourself who have researched and visited communities and can share what they've learned with you.

- **Twin Oaks Communities Conference.** Annual event in August at Twin Oaks Community in Virginia. *twinoaks.org*
- **Art of Community Gathering.** Sponsored by the FIC (Fellowship for Intentional Community) these weekend events are held every few years in different regions of North America. *ic.org*
- **NICA Gatherings.** NICA is Northwest Intentional Communities Association, which hosts annul regional communities gatherings in Washington or Oregon. *nica.org*
- **North American Cohousing Conference.** Sponsored by the Cohousing Association of the US, these weekend events are held every two or three years in different cities in the US. *cohousing.org*
- **NASCO Institute.** Sponsored by the North American Students of Cooperation (NASCO), these three-day conferences held every fall in Ann Arbor, Michigan, cover creating, managing, promoting, and enjoying life in student housing co-ops.
- **FIC Organizational Meetings.** These biannual public meetings, held in different communities across North America, also serve as gathering places and social events for communities in the region.
- **Findhorn Foundation's Ecovillage Conferences.** Held in 1995 and 2005 so far, Findhorn Foundation in Scotland is one the primary centers of ecovillage gatherings internationally. *findhorn.org/ecovillage*
- **Ecovillage Designers Conference.** Max Lingegger/EcoLogical Solutions, Queensland, Australia. *ecologicalsolutions.com.au*

⤞ Chapter 14 ⤝

Your Criteria for Communities to Visit

W HAT FACTORS should you look at when considering communities you'd like to visit? Developing your own personal criteria is important, and we'll look at that first. But other factors you might not have thought of — like a community's size, how it selects its members, how it owns its land — are equally important, and we'll spend most of this chapter looking at them.

What aspects of your life give you so much happiness and fulfillment that you wouldn't want to give them up? And are there any aspects of your life you would like to change? Creating your personal criteria for joining a community means, among other things, recognizing what you don't want to live without, and what you may most want to give up.

As you're making notes about what you want and don't want, I suggest you make three lists: (1) characteristics of community that would be mandatory: your non-negotiables; (2) strong preferences; and (3) features that would be nice to have, but which you could live without.

Where to Start

One way to start is to look first for communities that reflect your values and lifestyle, which will be reflected in a community's mission and purpose, and then narrow that group down by geographic location. To some people, location can mean "a dry climate, no humidity;" for others, "within an hour's drive of my family." The screening process might go like this:

"I want (*first*) an ecospiritual community near a college town, (*second*) within a two-hour drive of Toronto."

"I want (*first*) a cozy cohousing neighborhood where I can raise my children in a great environment, (*second*) with enough snow for cross-country skiing in winter."

"We want (*first*) a Christian Community with emphasis on service to others, (*second*) in a climate that's cool and moist, like the Northwest."

Or, the location or region of the country might be the most important factor for you, and the community's values, mission and purpose and lifestyle secondary. In that case, the search process might go like this:

"We want (*first*) to live in a region with warm weather and short winters, (*second*) in a community involved in peace and social justice activism."

"We want (*first*) to live near my mom, so no more than an hour from Albuquerque, (*second*) in an ecovillage that serves as a model demonstration site for sustainability."

Or maybe where the community is on the urban-rural spectrum is the deciding factor for you.

"I'm a city girl: I need theater and art galleries, coffee shops and bookstores."

"We hate cities and noise: we need to live where it's beautiful, peaceful, and quiet."

Or maybe your first priority is getting work.

"I'm an emergency room physician and bicycle activist: I need to live near a hospital where I can ride by bike to work."

"We're musicians: we need to live near a cosmopolitan city with clubs."

Of course, in all cases you will most likely want to know if you can afford the joining fees and/or buy-in fees and whether it's an independent-income or income-sharing community.

You get the picture. Values, mission and purpose, preferred climate and/or proximity to friends or family, community finances, and work opportunities are usually the top three factors most people consider. (See Figure 1.)

In Chapter 19, "Seriously Seeking Community," for example, Patricia Greene writes that her personal criteria include an affordable rural community in a low-population area with no zoning and non-enforcement of building codes (so she and her partner could build more cheaply), in the East Coast from Georgia to Maine, "whose members eat together, meet regularly for both business and emotional sharing, and coordinate group work projects," with group meditation, ritual, and celebration, "and some possibility of our earning our incomes on the land."

Now that you're clear about what really matters to you, there are a few other considerations you need to keep in mind. These include the size of the community, whether it can select its members, its likely amount of member turnover, and how the community works financially.

Community Size

Whether the community is large or small, and

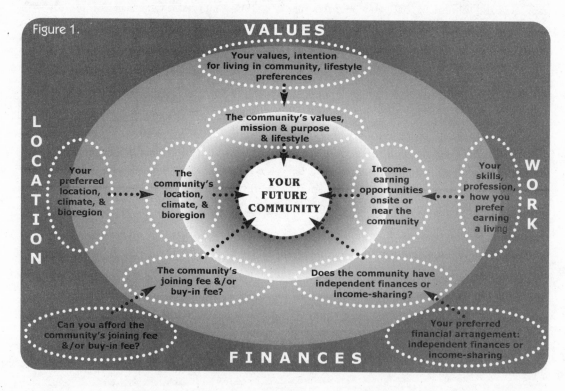

Figure 1.

VALUES

Your values, intention for living in community, lifestyle preferences

The community's values, mission & purpose & lifestyle

LOCATION

Your preferred location, climate, & bioregion

The community's location, climate, & bioregion

YOUR FUTURE COMMUNITY

Income-earning opportunities onsite or near the community

WORK

Your skills, profession, how you prefer earning a living

The community's joining fee &/or buy-in fee?

Does the community have independent finances or income-sharing?

Can you afford the community's joining fee &/or buy-in fee?

Your preferred financial arrangement: independent finances or income-sharing

FINANCES

whether its members live in close proximity or in widely spread-out housing, will also affect your experience of community. This is because a community's population size and their physical proximity totally affects its social and interpersonal dynamics. In large communities, say, with 20 to 50 or more people, with either clustered or far-flung housing, you don't need to be close to or like everyone in the community, since you won't be interacting with everyone in equal amounts. You'll have closer friends, and people you see more often and less often. If someone joins the community, their presence is usually not so impactful that it changes the energy or tone of the community. If someone leaves, while it does affect the group for awhile, it doesn't change the energy of the community substantially. With this many people you'll have many different kinds of skills, expertise, and interests among your members. Some will love good books; others will love sports; still others will love to make things in the woodshop. Some will probably play musical instruments, sing, do art, or put on plays. Socially and culturally, you'll be rich.

In a smaller community, however, with, say, less than 20 members, you'll have a different experience. Whether you live in separate dwellings or in the same building, in clustered housing or in spread-out housing, in a small community you'll probably know each community member quite well. You'll find it easier to live in a smaller community, however, if you like and get along with everyone most of the time, and much harder to live in a community of this size if there's even just one person who bothers the heck out of you. Compared to a larger community, interpersonal relationships can be intense — requiring lots of time processing and communicating when there is conflict, until the issue is resolved. A smaller community can be exceptionally rewarding, and a great school for emotional and spiritual growth. It also can be

time-consuming. Sometimes it can drive you crazy. Yet the opportunity for deep intimacy and close emotional bonding is also there, and many people love this — it's the reason they joined a community. Creating a close, intimate, known and knowing relationship with a small group of people can feel wonderful. Having bonded brothers and sisters you can count on can be one of the best things you ever experienced, as noted in Chapter 1.

Another factor is that a small number of community members in a rural area is quite different from the same number in an urban area. With, say, five members in an urban area, your social life is probably just fine even if you only see many of your housemates infrequently during the week, since you're presumably surrounded by friends and colleagues in your city or town. But with five community members in a rural setting, especially a rural area in which you're the only people like yourselves around, you can feel pretty isolated socially.

In a small community, people leaving and people joining can totally upset the applecart. When a new person joins the group, depending on how close the group's physical proximity may be, the new person can totally influence the community — calm it down, energize it, motivate it, help solve major problems for it, drain its energy, or penetrate every corner with good will or resentment and hostility. And someone leaving can leave an enormous hole — one that may not be filled for a long time. It can be disheartening to join a community, bond closely with several members, experience a group consciousness or sense of "we," only to have this all wrenched apart when one or two of your best friends leave. This is particularly traumatic for children, who tend to form extremely close, brother-and-sister relationships with other community children. If too many people leave a small community in too short a time, it can leave both adults and children feeling bereft. If this happens too frequently, both adults and children tend to withdraw and be more guarded and distant with new people who join.

So, a small community can offer you much greater intimacy and potentially greater rewards than a larger one. But it can also be more vulnerable than a larger one. When you consider communities, please take this into account.

Can the Community Choose Its Members?

As you research communities and consider which ones to visit, please take into account that there may be the potential for more conflict in those which sell individual lots or housing units than in those which don't. Being able to screen incoming members, and to evict any who may become disruptive, affects a community's level of cohesiveness and harmony. How a community owns its property greatly affects whether or not it can do this. As you research communities and consider which ones to visit, please take into account that there may be the potential for more conflict in communities in which community members own and have title to individual lots or housing units than in communities where they don't.

In the United States, when a community is set up so that all members own the whole property and no part of it is purchased with individual ownership and a deed, the community is relatively free to select who joins them. They can have criteria for membership, a provisional membership period with a process for orienting potential new members, and a careful, well-organized selection process. They can screen for people who understand and support their values, mission and purpose, lifestyle, goals, activities, financial and labor requirements, and governance system. They can say no thanks to people (or evict existing members)

who don't seem to "get it," or who raise red flags, such as people who simmer with hostility; who seem abusive, irresponsible, or dishonest; or seem to have problems with alcohol, drugs, overwhelming debt, vindictive ex-partners, and so on.

However, if the community is set up so that members buy property with a deed — either their own individual housing units (as in cohousing communities), or buy a lot and a house, or a plot of ground on which to build — the community may not be able to choose who joins them, particularly if they advertise their housing units or property for sale on the open market. Federal and most state laws governing residential real estate transactions, especially if the real estate is advertised, may restrict the community's ability to refuse to accept an offer to join the community if the buyer is willing to pay full price and meet the terms of the sale. Many states' housing laws may be even more restrictive than federal laws, and these can vary from state to state. These communities cannot evict members either, since no group of neighbors can force another neighbor to sell their house.

Communities which cannot select their membership are thus vulnerable to the potential conflicts which can arise from having members who might be clueless about community living, indifferent to community agreements, unwilling to work or participate in meetings, or are disruptive in some way. Or, the group could end up getting perfectly wonderful new members who get along well with with everyone, but who are not aligned with the group's mission and purpose, and want the community to be about something entirely different. For example, if the community is a model demonstration site for sustainable living, and the new people don't want tours and visitors coming through all the time, they could throw a monkey wrench in the gears each time there's a proposal about managing the tours better or welcoming visitors. If the community has consensus decision-making — meaning everyone must agree on a proposal for it to pass — the new people can inadvertently cause all kinds of havoc by blocking proposal after proposal that everyone else wants. (And in fact, one requirement for consensus decision-making to work well is that the group has a common mission and purpose that everyone agrees on.) Thus, communities which offer property for sale on the open market can end up having more conflict than communities that can select new members according to their own criteria. This sometimes happens in cohousing communities, for example.

Members of cohousing communities will often say that having units for sale on the open market works out fine; their members self-select, since no one would buy in to cohousing who wasn't drawn to this way of life. Thus the group does end up attracting new people who understand and support the cohousing vision, and are willing to participate in community meals, attend meetings, and take part in work days. However, a cohousing community has little to no recourse when it comes to applying consequences to people who don't participate, who frequently block proposals everyone else wants, or who consistently violate community agreements. This kind of conflict keeps process and conflict consultants busy traveling the country to help cohousers deal with these dilemmas. And exactly this kind of gut-wrenching conflict affected EcoVillage at Ithaca for several years (until the non-aligned new members moved away), as described in Liz Walker's *EcoVillage at Ithaca*.

However, some cohousing communities have been advised that if they never publicly advertised their units, houses, or lots for sale, and sold only to someone from a pre-selected waiting list of people they'd met and gotten to know already, *before* there

was any property for sale, the community in effect *would* be selecting its new members, but legally. The communities were told that if the group screened new people before there was anything for sale it would be within the law. Increasing numbers of cohousing communities are doing this with housing units which may come up for resale. In addition, the community could require attendance at orientation sessions for potential new members, which could provide another layer of informal screening.

Of course this issue isn't all black and white. A community's ability to select its own members doesn't mean the community *won't* later have conflict; it just means this particular source of conflict will be less likely. And, many communities in which members buy their own individual houses or lots often don't have — or at least not for long periods of time — the kind of values-clash, mission-and-purpose-clash conflict just described.

Age of Members and Rate of Member Turnover

Sometimes community founders who want to save on taxes, receive donations, operate an educational organization, or protect their property from certain kinds of undesirable future development or speculative gain will use a certain kind of nonprofit legal entity through which to own their property: in the US, a 501(c)3 nonprofit; in Canada, a nonprofit cooperative or society. However, this kind of property ownership can often have an unintended consequence. Communities which own their property this way tend to attract younger community members with few financial assets instead of members from a wider spectrum of ages and financial circumstances, and tend to experience a higher member turnover than other communities. Let's look at this more closely.

While many different kinds of nonprofit

organizations exist, US 501(c)3 nonprofits and the similar Canadian nonprofits specifically allow certain desirable tax breaks and are vehicles through which these organizations can receive tax-deductible donations. However, they also require that if the organization ever disbands, its assets (including its property, or income from the sale of the property) must be donated to another US 501(c)3 nonprofit or Canadian nonprofit cooperative or society, respectively.

This kind of community might be ideal if you're a young person or someone with few financial aspects and you're seeking a community which is easy to join financially, or one with a wide variety of people who stay for a relatively short time, or one which you might want to experience for awhile yourself before moving on. However, it may not be ideal if you're an older person or someone with assets to invest, or you want to sink roots deeply in a community and build larger or permanent housing, and/or you think about the long-term consequences for any money you might invest in your new community. Since the age ranges of members who live in a community as well as its turnover rate can affect your experience there, I'd like you to consider these factors in advance.

The reasons communities owned this way tend to attract younger members and experience fairly high member turnover involve several factors, all financial.

First, community joining fees and/or buy-in fees are likely to be considered by the IRS and the Canadian Revenue Agency as one-time tax-deductible donations, and thus are either not refundable or only partially refundable if a member later leaves the community. For this reason, such communities often have no or low joining or buy-in fees, and instead generate funds through monthly member fees and/or by renting living space to members, or by leasing a building "footprint" to members upon which they can erect a portable shelter or build a small, inexpensive home. These fees and rents are, of course, not refundable either if a member later leaves the community.

Also, because such communities must give away their assets away to another similarly organized nonprofit if they disband, they cannot divide the profit among its members the way other communities can. (This give-your-assets-away-if-you-disband rule may also apply to other kinds of nonprofits in a given state or province, depending on its laws.)

While this rule will most likely not affect people who only intend to live in the community a short while, or those who believe the community will exist indefinitely and never disband, it *is* a financial consideration for incoming members who do consider what might happen if the community broke up someday. Let's say this member wondered, "Well, if I lease a building footprint from the community and build a home, if the community ever disbanded, would I be reimbursed for the cost of building my home from the proceeds of the sale?" Most likely it would be considered a tax-deductible donation to the nonprofit organization, and thus not be reimbursed.

Thus, such communities tend to attract people with few assets or who don't think much about finances and the long-term consequences of current financial choices, and repel older, more financially established people. And for the above-noted reasons, people who join such communities tend to either rent housing from the community, or build small and relatively inexpensive homes, or live in inexpensive portable structures such as tipis, mobile homes, or canvas yurts. For young people right out of school this is fine; in fact, it's great. Families with children, however, and people with more assets, usually want to establish themselves in larger, more comfortable homes, and not only that, to sink equity into the community. (And expect that if they ever had to leave, they'd get it out again.) Thus, communities owned this way tend not to attract potential members with assets who want not only to feel "ownership" but literally *have* ownership in the community they join — who want plant their roots, emotionally and financially.

You can probably also see why such communities may also have relatively high member turnover. When people are young they are at their most mobile and adventurous — the time in life when they might like the experience of living in a community for awhile, before going on to other experiences. In addition, when a community is relatively easy to join financially, it's also relatively easy to leave — "easy in, easy out." Not much financial commitment is required to join, for people of any age.

High turnover can be perfectly fine, or quite undesirable, depending on how you look at it. If you think a community is mostly its property, buildings, mission and purpose, and primary activities, and/or that it's fine that many members pass through its gates and out again, then you might really enjoy living in this kind of community. But if you believe (and this is my bias) that the community is all of these things *and* the specific members who live there, then high turnover may not be enjoyable for you. If high turnover wouldn't matter, or if you'd love a community that was easy to join financially, this kind of community could be exactly right for you. However, if you'd like to sink your roots, feel a sense of stability, feel a sense of ownership, and put equity into the property, such a community may not be for you.

(Note: this discussion is only about how a community's *property* is owned. A community could own its property through a different kind of legal entity and have a separate 501(c)3 nonprofit

educational organization, for example — in which case these considerations wouldn't apply.)

Independent-Income and Income-Sharing Communities

As you'll recall from Chapter 10, whether community members have independent incomes or pool their incomes will totally affect community dynamics, and thus your experience living there, interpersonally and financially. To review these issues, in independent-income communities you'll probably pay a joining fee, membership fee, site lease fee, or property purchase cost. You'll probably have annual dues and fees. Your income, savings, investments, and other assets will remain your own, and you'll handle them however you wish, just as you do now. You'll need a job, or some source of income, just as you do now.

In an income-sharing community, you'll either work for one or more community-owned businesses, or earn money onsite or at an outside job, and pool your income into a common pot. You'll receive room, board, and either a monthly stipend or the community will pay for your other basic needs. In some income-sharing communities you'll need to put your savings, investments, and other assets in trust for the period of time you live in the community. You'll pay no fees when you join, and no annual community dues or fees.

The social and interpersonal issues are different in each kind of community. In income-sharing communities, what each community member does in terms of work style, how they treat commonly owned tools and equipment, and their level of responsibility, has much more impact on everyone else than in an independent-income community. A relatively small income-sharing community can be interpersonally warmer, closer, more connected, and more bonded than any other kind of community. Or, it can be more challenging. If community is a crucible, an income-sharing community is a mega-crucible. Your fellow community members may tend to be younger people with few assets; there may be relatively few older community members (unless it's a large, old, and well established income-sharing community, in which case there may be quite a few older people). The community may have relatively high turnover due to the minimal economic barriers to joining and leaving.

So if the communities that appeal to you are income-sharing, please keep these benefits and potential challenges in mind.

For more details on these issues about income-sharing communities, and the "why" behind them, please see Chapter 10.

Your Future Community: Ideals and Realities

Let's say you've thoroughly digested your research in the *Communities Directory*, the "Community Seeking Members" classifieds in *Communities* mag-

"HIGH DEMAND" GROUPS — GET MORE INFORMATION

As mentioned earlier, there are some high-demand groups — usually religious or spiritually oriented groups — with reputations for authoritarian leadership or coercing their members in various ways. These reputations can linger, fueled by the occasions in which formal accusations almost get to court before the cases are dropped, or fueled by the accounts of former members in news stories.

"These cases were never proven," or, "All charges were dropped against us," says the group. And while I find newspaper accounts of ex-community members fascinating, I know well to take them with a grain — maybe even a whole fistful! — of salt. Disgruntled ex-members, or community members who were asked to leave, can say all *kinds* of untrue and exaggerated things about the place. What are we to believe? As noted in Chapter 2, regardless of the dropped charges, the thrown-out court cases, and the tendencies of former members to exaggerate, if there are enough stories like these, and they keep reappearing long enough, I personally tend to believe them. With all this smoke, there's probably a fire someplace.

So I strongly recommend that if a community's literature, or their website, or their proselytizing efforts in the local café gives you even just a hint of unease — *get more information*. Please, Google around to see what other information may exist about that community. The website of one large net-

work of communities, for example, had questions on its FAQ page that really got my attention: "Are women subservient to men in our communities?" "Why do our women dress as they do?" "Do we discipline our children?" "Do we allow our members to get medical help when they need it?" "Are we racist?" "Are we anti-Semitic?" So I Googled this group and found *four* additional websites about this group. The other websites, hosted by outside researchers or former members of this group, posted excerpts from tracts written by community leaders for internal use and not shown to the public; newspaper stories about the group; and accounts of living in the communities by former members, including people who grew up there as children. What I read in these websites appalled me. Another large group has a similar reputation, and a website in which former members tell their stories and offer support and healing for one another online and in in-person gatherings. Yet, for many other large and well-known networks of communities — such as Camphill, L'Arche, and Catholic Worker communities — I found no such outside critical websites. For these community networks, there seemed to be evidence of nothing but a good reputation.

So, as noted in the last chapter about researching communities — please don't believe everything you read on a group's website. And if a place seems suspicious, by all means, check it out further.

azine, online directories and community websites. Let's assume you've considered the factors noted in this chapter too — about the effects of a community's size, and the various ways communities can be structured, financially and legally, on your future life in community. And perhaps you've been noting down what you want in three lists: non-negotiables, strongly preferred, and it-would-be-nice. Maybe you've even taken the next step of comparing the communities you've learned about with the factors that draw you (and deter you) — to create a list of those you'd like to visit.

So, is there an ideal community out there for you? And can you find it with massive amounts of print directory and online research before you go visiting?

Whew! There may be, but — I think it's much more like the question, "Is there an ideal life partner for me out there?" In other words, through your research and community visits you could very well find a community you fall in love with and become devoted to after you live there, even though, of course, you discover and learn to accept (or put up with) its various flaws.

Or, you could choose a community that looked really wonderful at first, but once you lived there you find that it's not what you expected, and you don't like it at all. You're so miserable, in fact, that you find yourself considering separation and even divorce. (This latter scenario is what this book is designed to prevent, and we'll look at many ways to get a good sense of each community ahead of time, so you don't end up having painfully unrealistic expectations.)

I think it works better not to expect an ideal match while you're researching and visiting, but rather to invest a good deal of time just learning. I suggest you consider yourself essentially on an information-gathering mission — keeping an open mind, not making any fast judgments as you read, web-browse, visit, talk with people, watch, listen, and learn. Gather information first, get a real good sense of what's out there that most closely matches your vision and values, then narrow your list, and perhaps visit your favorite communities a second time.

In the next chapter we'll meet Jane Gyhra, who planned a five-month journey to visit communities.

⁓ SECTION 3 ⁓

Visiting

≈ Chapter 15 ≈

My Marathon Tour of Communities

In 2003 community seeker Jane Gyhra undertook a 5-month journey to 16 communities. In this chapter she writes about what this taught her about communities — and about herself.

ON A BEAUTIFUL day in August, 2003, I pulled off Highway 22 in Virginia into the gravel driveway of an old farmhouse that would be my home for the next month. This was the first of 16 different communities I'd visit in my five-month marathon tour of communities — a journey that turned out to be the most thought-provoking and exhaustive road trip I've ever taken. In fact, it had far more of an impact on me than I initially anticipated.

The communities I visited ranged from some of the most conservative (a Catholic cloistered religious order) to some of the most liberal (former hippie communes), to ecological (rural ecovillages). My stay at each place ranged from a two-hour visitors' tour to month-long visits.

My itinerary:

- *Little Flower Catholic Worker Farm*, Trevilians, Virginia. A rural farm and peace activist community comprised of a nuclear family and ongoing volunteers who promote living simply, nonviolence, and hospitality.
- *Twin Oaks*, Louisa, Virginia. A 90-member rural income-sharing community which manages gardening, dairy cattle, and tofu-making,

book indexing, and hammock-making businesses on about 465 acres.
- *Acorn*, Mineral, Virginia. A 15-member rural income-sharing community which operates organic seed-saving and tinnery crafts businesses.
- *Innisfree Village*, Crozet, Virginia. A 550-acre farm community of 60 people, where everyone, including their large population of developmentally disabled adults, works in various task areas such as livestock care, gardening, cooking, cleaning, baking, and making craft items for sale in their woodshop or pottery.
- *Moonshadow*, Whitwell, Tennessee. A rural community of an extended family and ongoing volunteers who practice permaculture and teach classes on sustainable living.
- *The Farm*, Summertown, Tennessee. A well-known former hippie commune on 1750 acres, currently with 157 members. Member-owned and community-owned businesses include mushroom-production supplies, video services, and books, an alternative school, as well as midwifery services and teaching midwifery, and teaching permaculture and ecovillage

design, and nonprofits like Plenty, an aid organization.

+ *Little Portion Hermitage*, Eureka Springs, Arkansas. A 20-member rural Catholic monastic community of lay members and vowed celibates who garden organically, raise livestock, teach classes in spirituality and living simply, and run a small school.

+ *Sandhill Farm*, Rutledge, Missouri. A five-member rural income-sharing homesteading community and working farm.

+ *Dancing Rabbit Ecovillage*, Rutledge, Missouri. A rural aspiring ecovillage of 20 members on 280 acres in the prairie, intending to be a village of 1,000 with many smaller subcommunities.

+ *Our Lady of the Mississippi Abbey*, Dubuque, Iowa. A cloistered Catholic Cistercian order of 30 sisters who farm organically, offer retreats, and operate a candy factory on 550 acres.

+ *Michaela Farm*, Oldenburg, Indiana. A Catholic religious community, the Franciscan Sisters of Oldenburg, whose 350 sisters run an 300-acre organic CSA farm, growing produce, raising beefalo and other livestock, and offer classes in organic farming.

+ *Humility of Mary*, (two locations) Cincinnati, Ohio, and Villa Marie, Pennsylvania. A Catholic religious community of 223 sisters whose ministry includes education, health care, and social services. They also operate an organic CSA farm, raise sheep, and operate an Earth Spirituality center.

+ *Earthaven Ecovillage*, Black Mountain, North Carolina. A rural aspiring ecovillage on 320 forested mountain acres. Currently with 59 members, they intend to be a village of 150 with 10 neighborhoods.

+ *Mt. Tabor Benedictines*, Martin, Kentucky. A rural Catholic community of five Benedictine sisters who operate a retreat house and serve the needs of the poor in the Appalachian Mountains.

+ *Christian Appalachia Project*, McKee, Kentucky. An inter-denominational human service organization serving low-income people in the Appalachian region with mostly volunteers who live together family-style.

+ *Sacred Heart Monastery*, Yankton, South Dakota. A Catholic community of 145 Benedictine sisters who run a liberal arts college and a hospital, and offer other social service work as needed.

I suggest visitors ask which rules and regulations are truly enforced, which will give an idea of what that community truly values.

The first thing I noticed about every community I visited was how they looked and what that told me about them. Some, usually older communities, were landscaped beautifully, even with a professional-looking sign at the entrance. Others, usually newer ones, looked like their buildings had just dropped from the sky, with piles of construction materials everywhere. But most were in the middle, with normal-looking residential dwellings. I got the impression that communities that made an effort to make their entrances attractive had more of a sense of pride in their place. Little Portion Hermitage in Arkansas, for example, had both a beautiful entrance and a prayer garden tucked between their chapel and commons/kitchen area complete with fountains and pools, trellises and vines, a deck, a gazebo, sculptures, and decorative grasses and flowers. Moonshadow in Tennessee, while not landscaped extensively, had artistic designs on every building. Seeing touches of tasteful artwork around a community really lifted my spirits and gave a whole different impression of the place that I wouldn't have had without it.

Once at a community, I would quickly start learning about their methods of communication, process, and decision-making. It was at Sandhill Farm in Missouri where I first experienced "check-ins," where people around the circle take turns telling the group how they are doing. I thought this was great — until I experienced a check-in at a larger community that took so much time it made their weekly meeting drag on longer than I liked. Different decision-making methods also intrigued me. I observed the Planner-Manager system of Twin Oaks, where people volunteer to manage various ongoing processes such as cooking or hammock making or oversee operations of the whole community. I also got to experience the widely popular consensus decision-making method as well as the hierarchical, leader-decides method used in most Catholic communities. Some seemed to combine consensus, voting, and hierarchical methods. For example, at Sacred Heart Monastery in South Dakota, the leader (the Abbess), and a nine-member council are established by democratic vote of all 145 permanent members. Goals are set by consensus, with a trained facilitator brought in. (One member of this monastery mentioned how, by using a facilitator, they successfully reduced the 120 goals they'd selected down to four manageable goals.) The council advises the Abbess on major decisions, while she makes minor daily decisions alone.

Our Lady of the Mississippi Abbey in Iowa had a unique decision-making method. Similar to

A helpful question I learned to ask was, "What do you like the least about this community?"

the combination method used by Sacred Heart Monastery, it also included a private communication process with the Abbess. All 30 members must sign up to meet with her once a month to discuss how they are doing and to offer any observations or suggestions for the community. I was told if they don't sign up for a scheduled time, the Abbess will go looking for them, since not signing up often indicates the member is going through a rough time. The current Abbess is so loved by the members that she got voted in for her fourth six-year term. Also, in order to stop harmful gossip, this community had the policy that secrets are not allowed and everyone has the right to mention anything they have heard to the Abbess who can then use the information as she sees fit!

One big difference I noticed between secular and Catholic religious communities was the length of temporary or provisional membership. While it's usually a year or less in most secular communities, it can be six to eight years in Catholic religious orders. Of course this is really comparing apples and oranges, since in the latter people don't simply join an intentional community, but take vows for a lifetime religious commitment. However, even those in which members take annual vows have a provisional membership period of two years.

In addition to the usual long trial period, Our Lady of the Mississippi Abbey has a feedback and evaluation process in which for the first two years a potential member meets monthly with several permanent members who affirm her positive traits and discuss areas she needs to work on to help the community. For the last four years, these meetings are only once a year but involve all community members. A temporary member of this community who doesn't show an effort to make any requested behavioral changes is asked to leave. No wonder some of these religious orders have lasted nearly 1500 years!

One thing I liked about a few of the larger communities was when groups of members lived in small groups eating dinner together once a week or more, and doing other activities together such as celebrating birthdays, cleaning house, and of course having recreation and fun. Two communities I visited even had *mandatory* recreation time: one once a week and the other five times a week!

One community I visited seemed a little less welcoming than the others. For example, when I emailed requesting permission to visit, their short reply said I must first read three of their founder's books, which described their values, and only if I agreed with these values and was still interested, could I visit. I didn't have time to read the books, but was determined, and asked to visit anyway. They allowed this but put me in a retreat house six miles away from the community center. I had to do quite a bit of persuading, in fact, to be able to meet some of the other members and join them for a meal and a work party. This left me with quite a negative impression!

Some of the communities I visited allowed public nudity on their property, and I quickly discovered this was a turn-off for me. One community tour guide told me nudity was allowed only at the swimming hole, but after talking with other members, I learned that this was not enforced at all and "public" nudity — meaning, being nude anywhere in the community — occurred regularly. Therefore, I suggest that visitors to communities ask which rules and regulations are truly enforced (and may have consequences), which will give an idea of what that community truly values.

A helpful question I learned to ask at each community was, "What do you like the least about this community?" The answers sometimes surprised me and made me wonder whether I'd want to join them after all. Some answers I received were:

- "Filth"
- "Strong-willed members"
- "Lack of guidance when wanting to join"
- "Construction mess"
- "Having to support myself financially" (!)
- "Disliking the decision-making method"
- "Allowing questionable people to join the community"
- "Gossip"
- "Communication problems between managers and workers"

But it was the deep soul searching I experienced which perhaps surprised me the most on this journey. The various issues communities were wrestling with swirled around in my head as I drove from place to place.

"What does it really mean to live sustainably?"

"Is dumpster diving for food really living simply?"

"Can some protest marches cause more harm than good, and how does one determine this ahead of time?"

"Can a pet policy be created that satisfies both members who like pets and members who extremely dislike them?"

Traveling through the state of Kentucky caused my mind to work overtime! It started by seeing some of the Appalachian mountains blown apart in the zeal to mine coal. Then I heard the stories of black lung disease, and people's lives or whole towns uprooted when coal companies bought up mountain property and started mining there. Passing through these mountains made me realize that any community that claims to have environmental values needs to consider limiting the amount of electric power generated by such an Earth-destroying practice. This led me to start figuring out what other indicators I would look for in communities which claim environmental values and practices. Does the community:

+ Reduce electricity from nonrenewable sources?
+ Grow or buy locally grown organic food?
+ Use biodegradable chemicals?
+ Reduce fossil fuel use?
+ Recycle, even human waste if possible?
+ Reduce excessive materialism? (Every item we purchase has an impact on the Earth through harvesting of raw materials, the manufacturing process, transportation, storage, and display.)

The insights and new ideas I gained on this community journey affected me deeply; in fact, it turned out to be as much a spiritual journey as a physical one. For one thing, what I value in life became more clear to me. Also, the exciting but complex interaction of community members with different kinds of personalities and the cooperation required to make community living work, will provide food for thought for many years. Most importantly, the journey helped me realize that my moral and religious beliefs are number one for me when looking for a community. It became apparent that, for me, all community issues and problems eventually distill down to this sooner or later. Therefore, I found I couldn't consider a community that had an eco-friendly vision that wasn't accompanied by spiritual beliefs to morally guide its actions. To me, it is just as important *how* and *why* something is done as it is that it just *is* done. So, thanks to my marathon tour. I decided to join a religious community. So although I'm no longer turning into gravel driveways that lead to yet another community, this experience will be forever very precious to me, for it helped clarify who I am and what I believe in.

Reprinted with permission from *Communities* magazine, Spring, 2004.

Next we'll look at how to set up, get ready for, and have a rewarding time during your first round of community visits.

≈ Chapter 16 ≈

Planning Your Visits

By now you've probably got a pretty good sense of how to research communities through the *Communities Directory* and the "Communities Seeking Members" classified ads in *Communities* magazine, and through online communities listings, books, videos, and communities conferences. If so, you've almost certainly got a good idea of what you want in your community home in terms of:

+ climate and location, whether urban, rural, or in-between;
+ kind of community (cohousing, rural homestead, ecovillage, spiritual community, urban group household, etc.);
+ community values, and mission and purpose, and lifestyle;
+ what you can afford in terms of buy-in fees and ongoing fees;
+ and how you might make a living there.

You've probably considered whether you want a community that's smaller and more intimate or larger and more village-like (or in-between), and looked at the other factors we examined in Chapter 14. You've made your list of non-negotiables, strong preferences, and aspects of community that would be nice but which you could live without.

Maybe you've even taken the next step, comparing the factors that draw you with the communities you've learned about, to create a list of those you'd like to visit.

The next part of your project to join the community of your dreams is visiting and evaluating communities — the most exciting, illuminating, adventure-rich phase of the process. Visiting communities can be time-consuming. And depending on how you do it, and how much time you have, it can also be expensive.

Like Jane Gyhra's marathon tour described in the last chapter, you can visit many communities in one or more longer trips of several months' duration, or you can take many different weekend or weeklong trips, visiting one community at a time, like Geoff and Sue Stone did (as you'll see in Chapter 17). Whichever way you do it, it's a huge undertaking, comparable to looking for a new job, moving a long distance (physically or culturally), and going on a series of dates — with lot of people at once! And whichever way you do it, it's a fairly major, if not difficult project.

If you spend more time on your community visits — for example scheduling visits during a time when you've got some savings and are not working at a job — it will take less cash, particularly if you catch rides with friends, bicycle or take public transportation, do work exchanges for room and board at the communities you visit, and plan an itinerary that takes you to different communities along a logical route of travel from your home and back again. If, however, you have less time for visits — because, for example, you've got a job — it can cost more in terms of cash outlay, since you'll be packing your visits into long week-ends, vacation time, or any days off your workplace might owe you. You'll probably visit only one, or maybe two communities at a time, and most likely will fly and rent a car to get there and back quickly, saving most your time off for actually visiting the community.

Be that as it may, community visits will help you understand more deeply what you do and do not want in your future community home. And because you'll be exposed to a series of unique situations and people, you'll learn lots more about yourself, too. Visiting communities can be as much a journey to discover Self as it is an exploration of the community lifestyle.

There are at least two ways to visit communities. One is to visit only those you're actually considering joining, given what you know at this point. Another way to visit communities, which I highly recommend, is to visit those you know you're interested in *plus* other communities along your route, or in the same area as the ones you're interested in, or which would otherwise expand your knowledge of communities in general. Better yet, sign up for the Community Experience Weeks or Weekends, and/or three-week Visitor Programs at various communities, in order to get an immersion style education about community living in general. The first is more the laser beam mode: "I'm interested in joining A, B, or C community, so I'll visit each and choose between the three." The second is the information-gathering mode: "I'm most interested in A, B, and C right now, but I *also* want to learn as much as I can about community living before I make this huge decision, so I'll also visit, D, E, F, G, and so on before I decide anything." If you visit communities which are different from the ones you think you'd like to live in — immersing yourself in a relatively wide variety of community circumstances — you'll further clarify what you do

and do not want. Knowing what you don't want can be helpful in honing your choices about what you *do* want. If you recall, this is what Jane Gyhra did, and as you'll see in Chapter 17, that's what Sue and Geoff Stone do too. (Some communities, however, prefer visitors who are really interested in their community and not just "on tour." Dancing Rabbit member Tony Sirna notes, "We strongly filter our visitors for serious member potential.")

I suggest that when you visit communities, in *either* scenario, you psychically place yourself in "information-gathering mode," rather than in "oh-my-god-I-have-to-decide-this-right-away!" mode. The latter mode, can to make you feel fairly tense, which communicates itself to the communities you visit, which affects their opinion of you (and your opinion of them), which can affect how the whole community-choosing process turns out. The information-gathering mode, however, if you can psych yourself into it, can take the pressure off both you and the community, allowing you to feel more relaxed (after all, you're just making observations and taking notes), which will communicate itself to the communities you visit, which will affect their opinion of you, and so on.

Whichever way you do it, you'll need to plan your visits carefully.

(This chapter, by the way, only covers planning visits. Chapter 18 is about the experience of visiting communities, and Chapter 20 is about evaluating what you learned in your visits and taking the next steps.)

Setting Up Your Own "Marathon Tour" (or Multiple Shorter Visits)

One way to start is to look at the communities you might most want to visit in any one region, and look at a map to pick out an obvious route between one and another. Are there other communities in the general area, or close to the route you'd take, which you can also visit? Or, if you want to primarily visit one community in an area, and you might get there by plane, train, or bus, are there any other communities nearby you could also visit once you're there, perhaps by bicycle or rental car?

However you plan to travel to communities, there's one inviolable rule about community visits — *don't just show up*. Arrange your visit ahead of time; make sure you're invited first. Communities are people's homes, not pit stops for the road-weary traveler who might like to drop in unannounced. Just as in your own home, sometimes community members are open to visitors, and other times they simply want to enjoy their lives without the stimulation and extra work of hosting company.

Please don't assume that every community welcomes visitors, as some don't. And those that do host visitors may do so for reasons other than seeking new members. They might like meeting new people or count on the labor and skills of visitors to finish work projects. They might use guest fees as a source of community income, or it might be part of their mission to demonstrate ecologically sustainable living or their particular spiritual path, economic system, or lifestyle choice. Finding out *why* a community welcomes visitors — by asking them before you visit — can help you plan a mutually enjoyable experience.

How long should you visit each group? In her communities tour, *Communities* magazine guest editor Julie Pennington planned at least five days at each place, which she found worked well for her. She also recommends visiting at least two communities on any given trip:

It will help your perspective and make the most efficient use of your travel time. If you find one or two communities that you definitely want to visit, find out which other communities may be

roughly near the route. Even if you had no interest in some of these groups during your original research, consider them again. Every group of people living intentionally together has something to teach the community seeker. You might want to use communities along your route as rest stops in which to reflect on the previous community visit and prepare for the next. A spiritual retreat community with hot springs among cozy cabins would make for a great rest stop!

Communities, Spring 2004.

Jane Gyhra, on the other hand, stayed longer than five days at each community, in some cases up to a month. Sue and Geoff Stone, whom you'll meet in the next chapter, stayed from a weekend to several days at each community, returning to some for longer follow-up visits.

Some community members find they have lower energy for visitors late in the season, in September and October. "I often think our April or May visitors get better attention and energy," notes Tony Sirna at Dancing Rabbit. Often winter is a slower time in rural communities, which can sometimes allow time for long talks with members by a cozy fire, but often does not offer much in the way of quality outdoor work parties.

Larger communities can take more time to get a sense of, so consider staying longer at communities with a lot of property and a relatively high population.

So the second step in planning your journey, after figuring out which communities you'd like to visit and when you'd like to visit them, is to check their websites or e-mail them to find out when they welcome visitors (and if, in fact, they *do* welcome visitors), and what their visitor policy may be. Many communities have specific three-week Visitor Programs throughout the calendar year, or special Community Experience Weeks, or Weekends. Other communities welcome visitors only on weekends, or only during the warmer months.

You'll need to figure out how much time you can spend on your visit or visits (including how much time you can take off work, if that's a factor), and coordinate the times you may be free to travel with the times communities are available to visit. And, ideally, if ecological sustainability is part of why you want to live in community, plan your trips to use the least fossil-fuel-intensive way of getting there.

The third step is to get each community's OK to visit — specifically, an invitation. Contact communities several months in advance, if possible. Generally, arranging visits is handled by e-mail rather than by telephone calls or written correspondence, since this is often less time-consuming for the community.

Websites can be invaluable for letting you know about the group's visitor policy, who to contact, and the community's visitor guidelines for when you get there. Some communities will ask you to fill out an online questionnaire and go through a series of e-mails with their visitor manager or visitor committee; others ask you to e-mail a letter of introduction about yourself. Some charge visitors for accommodations and food; others don't. Some larger communities charge for community tours. In any case, follow the guidelines on their website. Even if they don't ask for an e-mail or snail-mail letter of introduction, it's a good idea to briefly introduce yourself and tell why you'd like to visit, for example, because you're seeking a community to join or you're doing preliminary research for living in community later. (By the way, please don't send them your views on what a real community "should" be doing. It won't endear you to them as a potential visitor and it might just stop them from inviting you at all.) If you already know someone who lives there, or even a

friend of a friend, let them know this, as it can help smooth the way. It's even better if this person is willing to recommend you to the group as a visitor. Describe your interests, experience, or skills. If you have any special needs, mention them. If you can provide your own sleeping accommodations, such as a tent, van, truck and camper shell, or RV, tell them this too, as it helps make you a more desirable guest. If you will be traveling by public transportation and will need to be picked up (which can be a plus for communities which value ecological sustainability), tell them you'll try to arrange a convenient time and place of arrival, and will reimburse their travel costs if they can pick you up. They may ask you to coordinate your travel with other trips they make to town so be flexible. Be prepared to wait, if need be. Ask about their expectations of visitors, possible visiting dates, and possible length of stay. You might also let the community know how you heard about them (which will help their promotions team). Provide contact information so they can get back to you. If you are under 18, the community may also require legal consent from your parent or guardian in order for you to visit. If you write a snail-mail letter, include a self-addressed stamped envelope.

Some communities get many requests from potential visitors or answer e-mails or letters infrequently, so you may not hear back right away. Sometimes not getting an answer means the community is not that interested in having you visit, but other times it may only mean they haven't gotten around to answering their e-mails, so don't be too discouraged unless the lack of response drags on too long. A good rule of thumb is if you don't hear back in two to three weeks, try again, or contact them in a different way. If you've e-mailed, try sending a letter, or another e-mail, or calling on the phone. (A good time to call is in early evening, or around dinner time, rather than late at night or first thing in the morning when people might be busy getting ready for work.)

When the community responds, they may or may not tell you what to expect and what you should bring with you. If they don't provide this information on their website or in their e-mail response, go ahead and ask them. Can they send directions to get there? What are the parking rules? What might the weather be like at that time of year, and what do they recommend you bring in the way of extra layers, rain gear, or footwear? Do visitors stay indoors or should you bring a tent or sleeping bag? What else do they suggest you bring? Does the community have a preferred diet? Are children welcome? Are several visitors at once welcome, such as you and some of your friends traveling together? What's their policy regarding visitors' dogs or cats? If you have special dietary needs, can you put your food in their refrigerator and perhaps use their kitchen? What is a suggested amount of money to cover your expenses? If you have further questions, who would be the right person to ask? Who should you ask to see, or who will be your host when you arrive?

If this is a spiritual community, will they expect you to participate in shared spiritual practices? If it's a Christian community, do they prefer that you are a member of the same denomination or otherwise share their beliefs and practices? If the community values group process sessions, such as talking-stick circles, heartshares, check-ins, "shadow-work" sessions, Arnie Mindell's "Process Work" sessions, or ZEGG Forum-like sharing circles, will they explain these processes and how one participates? Will you be welcome (or expected) to sit in or take part?

If the group has a particular lifestyle related to their environmental or economic values, you may be expected to live the same way while you're there, and you can ask about this. If it's a community with off-grid power, composting toilets, or constructed wetlands, for example, you will most likely be expected to conserve electricity and water, learn the basics of using composting toilets, and use biodegradable soaps and shampoos.

Another really good source of information about how to visit communities, what to bring, and what to expect, is to ask experienced community members you know, and friends who have made community journeys of their own. What do they advise?

If you should need to alter your dates or cancel the visit, inform the community as soon as possible. They may have scheduled specific activities for your visit or turned away other visitors in order to accommodate you.

Last, but not least, it will help your visit immeasurably if you know as much as possible about the community before you ever set foot on the place. Here's why:

- Having this information ahead of time can help you feel more grounded, relaxed, and at ease during your visit. If you know little about the community it can make you feel uncertain or disoriented at first, particularly if you're the kind of person who enjoys first having a context for what you're seeing and experiencing.
- It can save you time when talking with community members. Instead of asking them the basics, you can spend your time finding ways to make personal connections — which is far more satisfying for you and for them.
- It will make you look good in their eyes — a visitor who has taken the time to find out a lot about them first. All *right!*

In addition, if you know as much as possible about your own values, interests, ideal community lifestyle and so on — and can discuss these with community members — you will be in a much better position to make connections with people, not to mention saving both you and the community all kinds of time.

What to Pack

If the community is in a rural area, you may need a sleeping bag, a tent, and camping gear (or, with indoor accommodations, perhaps your own sheets and bedding), a towel, bug spray, rain gear, sturdy outdoor shoes, and perhaps a bathing suit. (Or not: in some rural communities wearing a bathing suit in the swimming hole is considered overdressed. Ask them.) At rural communities you will almost certainly need a flashlight; bring extra batteries too.

As noted earlier, if the community is ecologically oriented, and especially if it has graywater recycling or constructed wetlands, make sure any soaps, shampoos, or other personal-care items you bring are biodegradable.

"COMMUNITY LIVING 101" OR: VISITOR PROGRAMS, COMMUNITY EXPERIENCE WEEKS, AND INTERNSHIPS

You sometimes hear stories of how visitors to larger rural communities found their visit disappointing (although they may have enjoyed the guided tour). While community members may have been courteous enough, they were often too busy to spend much time with visitors, maybe didn't seem open to answering many questions, spoke mostly with one another at mealtimes, and didn't often go out of their way to include newcomers or explain things. The guests, frankly, were often lonely or bored, and didn't learn all that much about the group.

This is understandable from a rural community's point of view, given that its members are simultaneously trying to earn a living, grow food, raise children, and live their lives, often in an ecologically sustainable way. While I don't think this happens often, it's much more likely to happen if you visit when a community is not running a special program for visitors. Guests can have quite different experiences visiting during Community Experience Weeks or Weekends, Visitor Programs, or by taking other programs, such as internships or work exchange positions, which are specifically designed to orient visitors to the community and foster interactions with its members.

Several communities, such as Twin Oaks Community in Virginia, offer three-week Visitor Programs throughout the year. Their Visitor Program is designed to give an in-depth experience of living there, and is a prerequisite to applying for membership (although anyone is welcome to do it, whether or not they are applying for membership). The program is designed as a kind of total immersion experience to help visitors learn what it's like to live there. Visitors attend meetings, take community tours, and participate in orientations with members who share various aspects of Twin Oaks' financial, legal, health, labor and self-governance structures.

Other communities offer Community Experience Weeks or Weekend Programs, providing a range of activities in which visitors learn about the community's culture, history, governance, economics, and sustainable systems, often accompanied by plenty of music, entertainment, and opportunities to interact with its members. Still other communities offer more structured educational programs which serve the same purpose and offer many of the same activities, along with formal classroom and hands-on instruction in subjects ranging from sustainable education to yoga.

Another way to learn about communities in general or try on a specific community, is to become a community intern or work exchanger for a few weeks to a few months, depending on what you arrange. In

To be as self-reliant as possible and not draw too heavily on the community's resources if you catch a cold or get poison oak or sustain a minor injury, consider bringing your own Vitamin C, a first aid kit, and other likely supplements and remedies.

Be prepared to take care of your own special needs, including dietary needs. Don't expect the community to accommodate you especially.

For those times when you might want to entertain yourself, bring books, CDs, perhaps a journal. In fact, keeping a journal of your community-visiting experiences is a great way to record your impressions, and have something tangible to help you remember and reflect on them later. (See Chapter 17, "Excerpts from a Community Seeker's Journal.") A journal can also serve as kind of silent friend and confidant, in case you need an outlet for feelings if you sometime find parts of your visit delightful, inspiring, astonishing,

---

these programs you can not only learn even more about community living, but you also might pick up new skills such as biodynamic gardening, strawbale building, or cooking for 50.

Communities use different terms for these temporary residencies including "intern," "apprentice," "work exchanger," "work-trade resident," and so on. In some communities labor is traded for room and board. In others, the temporary resident also pays a small fee, especially when personal instruction and onsite workshops are also included. Interns get days off. Some communities offer vacation time as well, depending on the length of stay. In some communities interns do many different jobs and projects; in others, they have a specific role: garden intern, natural building conference center intern, childcare intern, and so on. Interns are often expected to bring their own tents, or sometimes live in rustic dorm-style or individual cabin accommodations, depending on their length of stay. The community provides meals, often vegetarian. Communities seek interns and work exchangers who have "an eagerness to learn, and to work hard" (Emerald Earth, California) or are "flexible, energetic, comfortable in groups of people, and able to manage a broad diversity of challenges at once" (Occidental Arts and Ecology Center, California).

To find intern, apprentice, and work exchanger positions, you can use the Online Directory (*directory .ic.org*) to select for rural communities which are not cohousing, have been in existence for awhile, have more than just a few members, and have websites, since communities like these might be most likely to have intern and work exchange programs. Then in the communities' websites look for pages called "Interns," "Apprentices," "Work Exchangers," or "How to Get Involved."

In my opinion, you can't know too much about communities — both to make a really good decision about which one to join, and to thrive once you live there. That's why my ideal orientation to community living would include participating in several of these Visitor Programs and Community Experience Weeks, even if the host communities were not on your list of communities you'd like to join or even similar to them. My own fantasy "Community Living 101" experiential education program would start with, say, Twin Oaks' three-week visitor program, followed perhaps by EcoVillage at Ithaca's week-long course, "Creating Sustainable Communities: The Ecological Dimension," or Lost Valley's two-month "Ecovillage and Permaculture Certificate Program," because of all the hands-on education on sustainable systems you'd get in each community. Community Living 101 would continue with your choice of one or more Community Experience Weeks, Visitor Programs, or intern or work exchange positions at any one of the other communities offering them. What a great way to learn about communities!

overwhelming, discouraging, or upsetting, or even if you just need a silent "listener" to share things with sometimes.

If it's a small community, consider bringing a "guest gift"...a bag of tangerines, organic ice cream, gourmet coffee, and so on. However, you'll need to be sensitive to the community's culture when deciding what to bring; don't present steaks to a vegetarian community or exotic cheeses to a vegan community, for example.

If you play music, bring your musical instrument. Most communities are mighty fond of guests who bring music, and more often than not there will be people to jam with and other musicians to relate to and play along with. Making music together is an excellent way to get to know people and trigger those community-connected moments, but if you're a musician, you already know this!

Sometimes visitors' guidelines will tell you what not to bring, and if not, you can always ask. The don't-bring list usually includes pets, guns, drugs, sometimes liquor, sometimes candles (for fire safety), and if it's a vegetarian community, meat.

Bring Work Gloves

Last but not least, bring old clothes, sturdy shoes, and work gloves. Communities love it when visitors pitch in and help with work tasks, from doing dishes to weeding to digging ditches to hauling firewood. If you're don't have the energy or stamina to offer physical labor, you can always help out in the kitchen, or with clerical tasks, or with childcare — which will also be welcome. Some communities expect visitors to work and assign them work tasks; in other communities it's not expected but gratefully received.

Working together with community members is one of the very best ways to get to know a community and vice-versa — and it sure does put you in a good light. There's probably no better way to simultaneously get a sense of the other people, experience those "community-connected moments," contribute to the group, and impress people, than working alongside community members.

Don't Bring Fido

While a few communities do welcome visitors' pets, most ask you to leave them at home. Why would a community insist that we leave Fluffy, Fido, Whiskers, or Rascal at home when visiting their community? Especially since Fluffy, Fido, et. al. are far more loyal, smart, clean, and affectionate than many humans we know?

The don't-bring-pets rule is not personal, and communities are not animal-haters. In some cases, it's because the community already has dogs and cats, and they don't want to upset the balance of power, start a fur-war, or end up with a spontaneous, adventurous dog pack that hunts. In other cases, the community doesn't have dogs and cats (or just a well-managed few), in order not to frighten away or kill wildlife. Other times it's simply that the group has learned through experience that it's demanding enough to host visitors, not to mention the visitors' small friends who might bark, yowl, pounce, scratch, bite, pee, or defecate where the community least wants it.

Sometimes leaving your dog or cat at home is not possible, however. If you have no choice but to bring your dog or cat on your journey and the community says yes, keep your animal in a pen, dog run, or vehicle. (And please don't assume that your dog will be considered well-behaved by other people's standards.)

When You Arrive

You will most likely be met by someone whose role it is to welcome and orient visitors, and you'll probably be shown a campground, dorm space, or room where you will sleep, where the bathrooms are (or composting toilets and solar showers), where meals are served, and when to arrive for the next meal. You may also be told when and where various community activities will take place during your stay — work parties or any already scheduled tasks you'll be assigned to, community meetings, campfire circles, and so on. You may be given a run-down on what is expected of visitors in terms of behavioral norms, for example, kitchen use, ecological guidelines, members' private spaces, quiet hours, smoking, drugs, nudity near a sauna or swimming hole, etc. You'll probably also get advice on things to know about that part of the country, which could include how to deal with or avoid snakes, ticks, mosquitoes, and so on. The welcoming person may give you a tour of the community, or tell you when and where to meet for any regularly scheduled tours.

Once you're settled in and comfortable at this new community, all that's left is to meet its people and find out what it's like to live there. What can you learn from this place? Will this community be the one you'll someday join?

In Chapter 17 we'll get another perspective of the community journey, as we'll follow Sue and Geoph Stone's community visits through entries in Sue's journal.

In Chapter 18, we'll explore how to make the most of your own community visits, and how to be that prized community visitor — a "great guest."

FROM THE COMMUNITY'S POINT OF VIEW

Valerie Renwick-Porter, who is a member of Twin Oaks' Community Visitor Program, makes the following observations:

We have a relatively structured visitor program, and do some amount of screening, people have to send letters that include certain types of information, etc. We are not casual about who we invite for three-week visits. Our screening process is fairly straightforward — we receive the person's Letter of Introduction (as outlined on the 'Visiting Twin Oaks' page of our website), and make sure all the information is there. Sometimes there is something significant about the letter — some information is missing, the letter is extremely short or extremely long, and sometimes there are red flags. If that happens, and we want to find out more before inviting them to visit, then we'll have more of a conversation with the person, either by email or telephone, asking them to explain more about whatever the issue is. Sometimes these issues are about actual events or difficulties; other times it's more of an intuitive feeling about the person's situation.

Believe me, once you've read a couple of hundred visitor letters, you develop a sixth sense about it. Once we've asked more questions about whatever is concerning us and the person has responded, we'll either decide that it seems fine, and invite them to visit, or we'll decide it doesn't make sense for them to visit the community based on the information we received, and ask them not to visit. In these cases, we will tell them why we are not inviting them to visit, so they have that information/feedback. But most visitor applications are fairly straightforward. It's amazing, though, the number of people who have interest in visiting us (or visiting any community), but who can't quite get focused enough to write a Letter of Introduction. For us, this is the first filter—if they can't even do that, it likely isn't going to work well for them in a community environment as highly structured as ours is at Twin Oaks.

Chapter 17

Excerpts from a Community Seeker's Journal

Sue and Geoff Stone, a couple nearing retirement age, had lived in Ozark, Arkansas, for 14 years. Geoff worked as a chemical engineer for a large company in the area. Sue was the musical director of the local church. From 1994 through 1998 they visited dozens of communities looking for one to join. Here are excerpts from Sue's journal, with her personal observations and insights into the sometimes inspiring, sometimes arduous, community-seeking process. The names of people they met, and several of the communities, have been changed.

December, 1994, Missouri.

On Winter Solstice weekend in December Geoff and I visited Warm Springs, a small community on 75 acres in Missouri. We felt comfortable there soon after we arrived. The couple who'd invited us, Sam and Debra, seemed genuinely interested in us and our ideas and experiences. It was easy to talk with them and we seemed to have a lot in common.

When we first arrived, I was surprised to see just an ordinary little house. We had tea with Sam and their two boys, who were making pumpkin pies in a toaster oven. The boys took us on a tour. It was pretty land, but there wasn't much there in terms of physical infrastructure: a shed for outdoor cooking, a teepee, a sweat lodge, a children's fort. The home-schooled boys were impressive: mature, knowledgeable, serious.

Saturday I helped Debra fix up the teepee and Geoff helped Sam prepare the sweat lodge. Debra took me on a short hike to a spring. She told me about the women's group that meets there, and showed me the women's altar. She told me about how they had lived in a teepee when the boys were small.

Saturday night was what community is about for me. Other people arrived, including another couple, Roger and Sarah, and their son, and two men from St. Louis. We had a potluck dinner, talked, and played drums. Geoff and I talked a lot with Roger, who actually owns the land. He had lived at Ananda Village in California, and told us about that community. He was excited to learn about Geoff's greenhouse, and I got the feeling that we would really be an asset to their community, if we chose to go there.

The solstice ceremony was held around a fire. We lit candles and spoke of our feelings about the past fall and the coming of the winter and the new year. We went into the teepee and talked and played drums. That night Geoff and I slept in our tent, at least tried to, as it was really too cold to sleep well. The moon was full, and we were beside the creek and I could hear it all night.

The weekend was hard in a lot of ways. The bathroom situation was a problem, a choice between an indoor toilet which didn't flush or a long walk to a cold outhouse. I was tired from not getting enough sleep, and felt grubby and uncomfortable and cold much of the time. And there was also the unknown: What is going to happen next, and when, and what will it be like?

A new guest came the next day for the sweat lodge ceremony to be held that afternoon. I liked hanging around inside near the stove that morning, talking and drinking coffee. One visitor was a musician, a drummer; the other was a young man from Syria. The third was a storyteller, very interesting and personable. They were all so nice — friendly, warm, interested in us and seemingly glad to have us there.

I kept crying at the ceremonies. It all felt so right to me. I felt awkward and uncomfortable and apprehensive, and yet like it was where I wanted and needed to be. Even though Geoff and I couldn't stay for the entire sweat lodge ceremony, I loved it and I felt wonderful afterwards, and I felt so loved and appreciated. They thanked us for being there!

The bathroom was a choice between an indoor toilet which didn't flush or a long walk to a cold outhouse.

What I really appreciated about these people was their dedication and commitment to the land. Sam wants to respect the land as the Native Americans do, and do the celebrations and ceremonies to honor it and work with it. Sarah worked with Starhawk and does rituals with women's groups. The group also wants to have a garden and passive solar houses. And they have already worked hard to build good relationships with the local community.

They'd like to buy more land adjacent to their property. I could see us being part of that, and helping to buy that land. The problems I could see with this community are that there doesn't seem to be much opportunity for getting jobs outside, and the land is pretty isolated. Also, it would be a small community. They are only two hours from St.

Louis, so that is a resource for people and a market for products or services. What I liked best about it was the people, the Earth ceremonies, and their dedication to the land. It seemed like a definite possibility.

January, 1995, Arkansas.

A few weeks later we visited Thomas, who plans to start a community on his small parcel of land in the crystal-mining area of Arkansas outside of Hot Springs. We were there to take his workshop on ferro-cement construction and attend his birthday party.

His land is really pretty, and has a nice, year-round stream. I found Thomas a kind, interesting, and talented guy. I enjoyed walking in the hills, learning to do ferro-cement work, and talking with him and his friends. The party was another taste of how I imagine community would be: good music, really interesting conversation, and especially drumming by candlelight. I felt so good after that weekend, energized yet relaxed.

Yet, Thomas doesn't have much land, so his future community would be small, and there aren't many good sites for passive solar construction, or even for a garden really. He has had a lot of experience with communities, though. Geoff likes him and works well with him, and I certainly like him, too. Also it would be really easy, comparatively, to get started there, certainly much easier than moving somewhere farther away. But "easy" is not what the community search is about. It's about what we want, whatever that is!

February, 1995, Massachusetts.

First day. We're here at Sirius Community in Massachusetts, and it's beautiful! The main community building is made with all this hand-hewn natural wood. The guest area is like a sort of rustic cabin, but really comfortable. Separate rooms lead off a hallway sitting area, with a wood stove and a place to fix tea. Best of all: three showers, several toilets and a bathtub! We've had a shower and a rest and I feel normal again, more or less.

We have pretty much concluded that a nearby community we just visited, Gaia, is too activist-oriented for us. They love their land but otherwise seem so focused on saving the world that organizing and maintaining their own community seem to be neglected. And I really didn't sense the central focus.

I kept crying at the ceremonies. It all felt so right to me.

I expect Sirius to be different. It is much more physically comfortable, of course, but it is 16 years old, so they've had more time to get it together. Anyway, it is nice to be here, finally. I expect I'll want to join and already I'm trying to figure out how it could be done. I guess I should just "be here now" for the present.

Second day, morning. Dinner last night felt like my concept of what community is all about: people sitting around a table after a meal, talking and sharing, then working together to clean up afterwards. Dinner began with everyone standing silently in a circle holding hands. Everything here starts that way. We saw a slide show about Sirius and introduced ourselves, met some members and had an orientation.

I slept really well and feel pretty good today. I still think I'd prefer my own bathroom, but I guess I might eventually get used to this down-the-hall set-up. Other members besides the guests use the bathrooms here, and there is no gender designation, so you might be washing up or showering or using the toilet next to someone of the opposite sex. Of course, the toilets and showers have doors,

and usually there isn't anyone else there, but it still seems strange.

In some ways Sirius doesn't fit my concept of a community, as most of its members don't live here. It seems more like a church. You pay dues to belong and donate eight hours of work a week. You might rent living space here, or get it somewhere nearby. You have to earn your own living somehow. There are shared meals, but you have to subscribe to them, and take your turn supplying and cooking a meal. You can pay $25 a month for a share of garden produce, and $20 to use community bulk foods. It's not like the sort of community where everyone lives together. But they are, nevertheless, working toward goals which are similar to ours.

Second day, afternoon. So far I feel really good here. Right now I'd love to stay forever. After breakfast we had a tour. Breakfast (and meals in general) are in the farmhouse, the original building here. There's a kitchen and a living/dining room with a wood stove, a few chairs and couches, and three long tables, with windows looking out over the garden. It's cozy and neat, though well-used. Also, there is a library and a bulletin board. People hang out there before and after meals. Before meals and before going off to work projects everyone stands and holds hands in silence for a few minutes, to "realize oneness." There's a short blessing before meals, sometimes announcements, and the menu. After meals, they discuss what work needs to be done.

After the tour we spent two hours in a meeting where we were told how Sirius operates. I got the feeling that the only way to get here would be to move to the area and find some way to live, and meanwhile spend months or years working through the membership process. I was told later that "exploring members" can rent space here, assuming it's available and that you have enough income. Anyway, it's not as hard as I thought it would be. The people are so nice — warm, friendly, helpful. I'm sure there are problems at times, but they all seem happy and relaxed. I haven't noticed anyone rushing around or looking stressed.

Again at lunch it was relaxed and congenial, lots of interesting conversation. People just pitch in and help clean up, and it seems to go quickly and smoothly. After lunch, I helped with a mailing at the farmhouse, and Geoff helped with firewood. I went for a walk on the trail through the woods.

Every place I've been so far I can imagine myself living, so I guess I can't be sure my feelings at this point are a reliable gauge. After one day, how can I really have enough information? This is really the first operational community I've experienced. I just keep thinking how good it would be to live here. But there are disadvantages; for example, housing costs seem double those in Arkansas, and there aren't many jobs close by. It would be a half-hour commute to get to work, most likely. And part of the reason for community living is to get away from that stuff! There's a possibility of a job here in the community, perhaps, or a business operating out of the community eventually. So it might work out, if we really wanted to be here.

Third day, evening. Geoff and I spent the time before dinner discussing pros and cons and possibilities. We just go around and around and back and forth. I am already tired of the uncertainty, but I guess it will go on anyway!

Last night one of the founding members, Bruce, gave a talk on the role of community in the modern world. He said there is typically a break-

> *"Easy" is not what the community search is about. It's about what we want, whatever that is!*

down of the forms and structures in society, then a period of chaos. Then comes a time of creation of a multitude of possibilities for new forms and structures, after which there is suddenly a "quantum leap" to a new form, a new level. He talked about how it is easier to grow and evolve and expand one's consciousness in a supportive and energized environment such as Sirius. He talked about how living outside is oppressive and can tend to hold one down and prevent this expansion, unless the person is very strong and evolved. This struck such a chord with me — that is exactly how living in Ozark feels to me!

After breakfast I had a massage with a woman who lives here, and it felt so good! Then I joined in for part of the circle dancing, in the new octagonal meeting hall. I kept looking around the room, at the people, the beautiful building, the woods outside, thinking, "I'm really here! I'm dancing at Sirius!"

There was a meditation before lunch. There was one yesterday, too, a half-hour "meditation for planetary healing." At lunch there were several visitors, as today was Open House, and the dining area was really crowded. Everyone managed to get fed and find a seat and there were several shifts for the dish-washing and cleanup. After lunch we had a closing meeting, where everyone, including the leaders from the guest department, shared their thoughts and feelings about the weekend. I said I was impressed by the care everyone seems to take with everything — people, buildings, dishes, etc. — and that it feels very good being here.

It really does. I'm sitting here by this fire, curled up in a chair, feeling right at home. An occasional person walks through, and I can hear people moving around upstairs. It's peaceful, comfortable, safe and secure; no need to lock doors or worry about other people. Everyone is a friend. It's hard for me being in this situation, feeling like I need to be in a place like this. But our search is about what Geoff and I both want, not just about what I want. If it were just me I'd try to find a way to be here at Sirius, but it's not just me. It could be another four years before Geoff is ready to do this. I hope it doesn't take that long! I wish we could just stay here.

I kept thinking, "I'm really here! I'm dancing at Sirius!"

I know I can't know enough in two days to be sure this would be the right place. I may visit others that are as good, or better. But I've spent 14 years of my life in Ozark and I'm tired of it! While there have been good times and I've grown and learned a lot, sometimes I think about what it could have been like all this time, somewhere like this, and I feel sad. Sometimes it seems like such a waste of time to not live in community, and how much do I have left? I don't want to waste any more time.

Fourth day, morning. Geoff has gone with the Sirius building crew to do some logging. He'll be coming back early to help fix lunch and I'll help with that. I decided to stay here and go for a walk, then take it easy.

Last night's dinner was very good, but there wasn't much conversation for us. The members sat together, and we were with the interns. It was comfortable and homey there, though. I was thinking about how it would be if we joined a community, wondering how long it would be before we really had friends and felt included. It seems easy for me to feel left out and not part of things. I know people enjoy being with friends and carrying on their relationships, and it's not the same when new people are there, so I understood the situation. But I expect it might be hard at first in a community, like moving anywhere.

It's probably been good being here the extra days. On the weekend the guest department people were here for us, and there were four of them and six of us, so they'd be around at meals, etc., to talk to us and answer questions. Now people are going about their normal business, and there aren't many of them. Most work outside, and only a few work here, so it's pretty deserted and quiet. If the building crew were working today on the conference center there would be lots of noise next door, but they are out logging. We have to find our own ways of being, which is more real.

I love this place, and I long to be part of something like this. Being here, though, would probably involve working outside the community, at least for several years. I have been feeling that I'd prefer a place where more people actually lived and worked in the community. That may happen here eventually. There is talk of building more member housing, community businesses, a larger greenhouse, and expanded guest housing. Right now, though, it would be more like moving to a new town in the ordinary way. You'd have to find a job, locate housing, and so forth. But you'd live here, or near here, and participate in the activities, work and meals and food sharing. It would be a good life, a large improvement on Ozark. But I'm not sure it is what we were picturing when we came up with this idea to live in community. We'll see, I guess, when we visit East Wind, what it's like to live in a community where people live and work all the time.

They talk here sometimes about how you can "create community" anywhere you live, and that community is not necessarily living with other people. Someone also said it's not so important what is accomplished in a physical sense in community but how it's done — the relationships and growth and learning of people. It's respect for your tools and your surroundings. It's your own growth and learning, peace of mind and spiritual focus that is important. It's the journey that matters, not the destination.

Fourth day, afternoon. I ended up making most of lunch, mixed together a few batches of leftover beans, made some cornbread, and found some apples. Geoff made some salad with the apples, raisins, and sunflower seeds when he got back. Another member was there, fortunately, to find a recipe and give suggestions. It gave me another taste of what community life would be like. Geoff went back to help with the logging again. I guess he is doing my four hours of work for today. Most of what is going on today is with the apprentices and a couple of members only. It seems like most of the work on the building and in the garden gets done by apprentices, as the members usually work only eight hours a week. I have decided to spend my last afternoon taking it easy, reading and writing. Hauling brush might be more fun, but this is my last day of vacation — might as well re-create!

New members, a family from the West Coast, live near us in this building, The father does carpentry, so he can earn a living anywhere. They have two young children and have been here five months. They probably aren't going to stay. They have decided they want a community where people mainly live together, that being the main focus

> *Sometimes it seems like such a waste of time to not live in community, and how much do I have left?*

and purpose, rather than as it is at Sirius, with the focus on the ecovillage, gardening, and conference center. This place doesn't suit them. Too much energy goes into the various projects, they said, rather than into real community living. In a way, I agree. It all seems quite scattered here. It's a nice place, but where is the community? I do understand the idea that "community" takes different forms, and this is a community in many ways, somewhat like a church is, but more so, because of the gardening and meal-sharing. But I think Geoff and I are looking for more than this in terms of people living together. Though we also want the gardening and sustainable living parts, too. Maybe we just won't find exactly what we want. Maybe we will have to create it ourselves ultimately, somehow. I'm sorry what I'm seeking isn't here. But I guess it's still a possibility. It'll be awhile before we are ready, and Sirius is still evolving.

Sue and Geoff Stone eventually found their community home at Earthaven Ecovillage in North Carolina, which they joined in 1999, and where they built a partially underground Earthship home.

Reprinted with permission from *Communities* magazine, Spring, 2004.

Next — how to get the most out of your community visits, and be remembered as...a "great guest."

Chapter 18

How to Be A Great Guest
(and Make the Most of your Experience)

AS YOU VISIT a community you enter a fertile, cross-pollination point — where the needs of both community and community seeker come together — a time ripe with possibilities.

The community is most likely seeking people to help enrich its community culture, build its physical infrastructure, and accomplish its mission and goals. They may also need cash. You might have exactly the right energy, skills, experience, and/or financial assets to help the community. It could be a perfect fit. You might see the question in their eyes: "Are you who we're looking for?"

Likewise, you might be considering this place as the community you might join. "Will I feel at home here? Is this my tribe? Are they doing the things I want to be doing too?"

Depending on the community's situation, and yours, these unspoken issues may hang potently in the air. Thus, as wonderful as it is to start manifesting your dreams by visiting communities, these visits can involve some ambivalence and anxiety. In some ways, for both you and the community, it's like going on a blind date, or applying for a job, or being a new kid in school. It would be difficult for you *not* to be wondering from the moment you first get to the gate and look around, "Will *this* be the place?"

Of course, the community's circumstances and your own reasons for visiting can modify this mutual assessment period. If the community is small,

say, ten members or less, or still in its early stages, with its founders only recently having moved to the property, the process will be more intense for both of you. Moreover, if the community is brand-new, and the group needs (perhaps desperately) more members to meet its mortgage payments or its upcoming balloon payment for the purchase of their land, and if you are keeping abreast of Peak Oil developments and feeling kind of desperate to get out of the city and into a rural location — whew! — it can put everyone fairly on edge. So much is riding on this visit! If, however, the community is relatively well-established, or large, with say 50 people or more (meaning you won't be establishing one-on-one relationships with every member), or in any case not seeking new members at the time, your visit can feel a lot more like a simple vacation where you have new experiences and meet new friends. The same is true if you're visiting the community because you're simply in information-gathering mode and it's not one you're interested in joining, or because it's near a community you're really interested in and is simply part of your community-education process.

In any case, regardless of your reasons for visiting and the group's situation regarding new members, certain points of etiquette and mutual commitment can help make your time there more enjoyable for you as well as the community.

By saying yes to your request to visit, the

community has made an implicit commitment to host you, orient you, show you around, answer your questions, and help you get a sense of what they're doing and why they're doing it. They have an obligation to treat you courteously and come up with a way get your questions answered, whether it's a tour, handouts, orientation sessions, or assigning various people as visitor liaison.

And by arranging to visit the community, you're making certain implicit commitments to them as well — to arrive when you say you will or else let them know if you cannot; to pay the agreed-on fees, if fees are required; to bring what they ask you to bring and not what they don't; to abide by their community agreements and their specific requests of visitors; and to treat them with the same consideration as you'd treat any host in whose home you're staying.

These commitments apply to every kind of community you might visit, large or small, secular or spiritual, rural or urban.

Let's look at some of these "rules of the game" more closely.

Community Etiquette:
What Hosts Would Like from Visitors

If you've followed the suggestions in the previous chapters, you will have prepared yourself by learning as much as you can about the community before you arrive, from their website, correspondence, handouts, or information packets. Ideally, you already know about the group's values, vision, mission and purpose, lifestyle, economic set-up, activities, number of members, and how long they've been there.

Knowing as much as you can about the community ahead of time will really help you feel more grounded during the visit. Beyond that, here are three things to remember:

- Follow the rules.

- Be socially sensitive. "Ask if you can ask questions."
- Work.

Agreements:

- Absolutely keep the group's agreements — follow the rules. Follow their requests as to where you might wander and explore and what places might be off-limits, such as members' private homes, and about noise and quiet hours, about the use of their kitchen or bathroom facilities, about if or where you might smoke or the use of alcohol or drugs. Find out whether saunas, swimming holes, or sweat lodges require bathing suits or are clothing optional, and when and where nudity may be appropriate or not. Do they have any requests about how you interact with them, their work exchangers, their children, or other visitors? Do they have requests about how you might treat their equipment, bicycles, vehicles, tools, gardens, pets, or livestock? The old saying about "when in Rome" definitely applies here.

- One rule of thumb is to consider the group's whole property — all its roads, buildings, parking areas, paths, trees, fields, gardens, or outbuildings — as someone's private home (because it is), and to use the same consideration and courtesy all over their property as you would to visit long-ago acquaintances or relatives you barely know. In other words, be *more* courteous and respectful, even, than if you were visiting good friends.

- Ask questions about how to do things properly, about systems you might need to understand before working with them. These can range from kitchen agreements, such as where the compost goes, the preferred way to operate the blender, whether the community air-dries or towel-dries the dishes, where clean dishes are stored, and so on, to agreements about outside chores, such as where the kindling is kept, where to stack logs, or where to hang up the hatchet and axe.

Energy Awareness:

If you are sensitive to your own and other people's energies and you make good personal connections, most likely community members will enjoy your visit. If you grow needy or anxious, however, hosting you could become a chore for them.

+ Be sensitive to a community member's needs for privacy and quiet time. Don't assume someone is necessarily available for conversation when they're sitting quietly by themselves, even if you do feel really curious about something or want your questions answered. Feel it out first.

+ If someone looks busy and you want to engage with them, check in first to see if they'd like to spend some time talking with you. Notice what they're already doing: are they trying to finish a task or are they on their way to meet someone?

+ Pay attention to what kind of energy you're putting out. Are you feeling anxious, needy, impatient, or burning with curiosity? Are you critical of or annoyed by their ways of doing things? Lower the volume on these energies, if you can. Just watch, listen, and bide your time. Put yourself in learning mode — you don't have to decide anything yet.

+ As mentioned earlier, humility is an appropriate attitude to take when visiting a community. The people who live there know a whole lot more about how their community functions and the background and nuances of the issues they're dealing with, than any visitor could ever know. An attitude of knowing what's best for the community, or how they might do things better, no matter how well-meaning, tends to irritate community members and makes the visitor look hopelessly uninformed and insensitive. Not to mention arrogant.

+ If someone is distant or grumpy, don't take it personally; it may have nothing to do with you. But sometimes, in fact, people might withdraw somewhat if you've stumbled a bit in your attempts to get to know the group. If you suspect this is the case, please don't assume it means you could not join this community. Once new people begin seriously considering membership and enter into a preliminary membership-exploring phase, most community members will cut them lots of slack and allow them time for learning the nuances of community etiquette. After all, unless they were community founders, they were once community seekers themselves!

Questions:

+ A golden rule of community visits is "asking to ask." The community is the group's home, and often also their workplace, and they might have other things on their minds besides hosting you. Before asking your list of questions while someone is pouring their first cup of morning coffee, ease into conversation by saying something like, "Would this be a good time to ask you a question about your pet policy?" This way you give the person a graceful way to say no thanks if it is not a good time, or if the person doesn't want to be a community spokesperson right then. You can apply this approach in many ways:

+ "Is this a good time to ask you a question about the community?"

+ "Can you tell me how I could find out more about X?"

+ "Is there someone here I could ask about X?"

+ "Is there a time when I could meet with you to learn about X?"

+ "Would this be a good time to visit so I could ask you about X?"

+ All of these ways of "asking to ask" demonstrate that you're respecting the person's time and energy, and gives him or her space to say, "No, not now," or "Later," etc. And it gives *you* a reputation in the community for being a considerate and respectful guest.

+ Don't be offended if the honest answer is no when you ask if you might speak with someone. The person is paying you the courtesy of being real with you. You could always reply, "OK, thanks. Would you tell me when a better time might be?"

+ If you're visiting for several days or longer, don't ask all your questions on the first day. Let yourself sink into the experience for awhile.

+ Leave a little quiet space in between your questions, instead of asking them one on top of the other. Be sensitive as whether the other person seems open to answering more. We once had a community visitor whose rather intense presence tended to irritate people, even though he seemed bright, well-meaning, and always willing to help. Community members took him aside various times and tried to explain that something about his way of approaching them didn't feel good, as if his energy was too penetrating.

+ "The real secret is to make personal connections," advises community activist Geoph Kozeny in his article about visiting communities, "Red Carpets and Slammed Doors" (*Communities Directory*, 2005). "Let people see that you're not an information sponge, but an interesting person who is sensitive to their needs: someone who wants to contribute and help but who isn't pushy about it."

+ Work times are excellent opportunities to ask questions. Helping someone wash dishes, peel potatoes, or weed the garden can also be a great time to ask questions about the community, if the person is willing to do so.

The Kindly Gift of Work:

Another golden rule of community visits is to bring your work gloves. Giving the gift of labor is one of the most fruitful ways you can spend time during a visit. Your work benefits the community. It benefits your reputation with community members, since it shows them that, yes, you are someone who is willing to contribute. If the work is slow-paced and quiet enough it can be the perfect time to ask questions and learn more about the community. And working together is one of the very best ways you and community members can get to know one another. "Shared work opens doors to friendship and mutual confidence that no amount of conversation can open. Most people know this intuitively," writes Twin Oaks co-founder Kat Kinkade. (*Communities Directory*, 1995.)

If you recall, when Sue and Geoff Stone visited Sirius Community, Sue helped prepare a large meal and Geoff helped with a logging project. Visitors help with gardening, landscaping, farm tasks, and construction projects. If you're not able to do physically demanding work you can always offer equally appreciated labor such as helping with cooking, kitchen clean-up, bulk mailings, or childcare. As you'll see in the next chapter, when community seekers Patricia and John visited one community, Patricia helped organize an Equinox celebration and John helped repair the group's photovoltaic system

Professional skills like John's electrical skills are especially valuable. Communities can often use help with graphic design, desktop publishing, advertising copywriting, appliance or tool repair, and electrical wiring, plumbing, and carpentry. Also, offering something special is always a delight, such as cooking gourmet meals, offering massage, Reiki healing, or chiropractic adjustments; painting a mural or carving a dead tree into a sculpture; playing music, juggling, storytelling, or doing magic tricks. Offering to focalize relatively short projects that demonstrate permaculture principles, appropriate technologies, or natural building methods, such as building an herb spiral, solar oven, composting toilet, cob bench, or horno oven can be especially valued and memorable contributions to a community. So can more esoteric skills. Among Twin Oaks' most memorable visitors, for example, were a hypnotist who did past-life regressions, including, he said, psychically communicating with a dolphin, and a clairvoyant who read people's auras. "News of these guests' talents spread like wildfire throughout the community," Twin Oaker Valerie Renwick-Porter recalls. "At every meal, it was all people could talk about — what colors their auras were, and what the dolphin may have said to them."

Sometimes the most appreciated gift, however, is just your simple willingness to pitch in and help with whatever chore needs doing at the moment.

In some communities, the visitor coordinator will routinely schedule you and other visitors for work tasks, chore rotations, or work parties. If not, volunteer. Some communities, though, aren't well-enough organized to take advantage of guests' labor, and your desire to pitch in may be perceived as yet one more problem to deal with, rather than a help. (In other situations, their work may simply be too specialized for most guests, such as woodworking or skilled computer tasks.) Be sensitive to such situations. "Make suggestions, offer — but don't push too hard," advises Geoph Kozeny. "If

they aren't able to involve you in the work and don't have much time to spend with you, be prepared to entertain yourself." (*Communities Directory*, 2005.)

Meetings:
- Attending community meetings is an excellent way to learn more about the community, but always ask first. Don't assume you are welcome to sit in on meetings, especially interpersonal processing meetings, unless you get permission first, or are specifically invited to attend.
- When you are attending meetings, don't comment or offer suggestions, unless you are specifically invited to do so.
- Sometimes you might have practical information that would truly help the group: they're dealing with a legal issue and you're an attorney who specializes in that kind of law; they've got computer problems and you're a computer consultant; their dairy cows have got mastitis and you're a large-animal vet. In that case, please do speak up. Note that the kind of information they can use from visitors is practical, not theoretical.

Love Relationships with Community Members: Be sensitive to sexual and relationship etiquette in the community. Many communities prefer that guests don't form sexual liaisons with community members or with their interns or work exchangers (even if these people come on to *you*). Most community members prefer that guests wait for a later, longer visit, or at least until they know the guest fairly well and trust in his or her integrity. Also, as you'll learn in Chapter 24 on joining a community, it's highly recommended that before leaping into a romance with someone whose recent former partner also lives there, you check in with the former partner first. Would they feel all right if you got together with their ex? And if they say "No, it's too soon," do the community-right thing — don't pursue the relationship. *Not* the kind of courtesy people usually extend one another in mainstream life, but one of the many nuances of community culture that you might as well learn now.

What happens if you go ahead and have affairs without paying attention to this etiquette? Doing so could give the community the impression you're mostly interested in gettin' some of that '60s-era "free love." "Usually you'll alienate the community members who sense you're on the prowl for romance rather than looking for community," observes Geoph Kozeny. "What you're most likely to get in those situations is the hot seat, the cold shoulder, or an invitation to leave." (*Communities Directory*, 2005.) For more on this topic, see "Sexual Etiquette for New Members," in Chapter 24.

Follow-up:

After you leave the community, consider sending a thank you note. Thank you notes make community members feel good about your visit and may help them remember you kindly if you ask to visit again.

If you decide to leave earlier than you've planned, let the visitor coordinator know, and officially end your visit, thank them for their hospitality, and say goodbye. If that's not possible, leave a note saying goodbye, etc., so the community doesn't worry that something's happened to you (and send out a search party) or wonder if you stole something.

How to Get What *You* Want from Your Visit

Of course you'll want to get every bit of what you came for at each place you visit. You'll want to get a sense of the community's culture, its lifestyle, its "vibe." You'll want to experience a good personal connection with as many members as you can, or at least a few.

You'll also want your questions answered. You'll want to make sure to resolve any major concerns about the community before you leave or have someone you can correspond with later.

What kinds of questions will most help you open the door to personal connections with community members? Once you feel people might have gotten to know you a bit (or at least, have gotten used to seeing you around), consider asking different kinds of open-ended questions. Some examples:

"How did you come to be a part of this community?"

"What do you see as the community's highest priorities?"

"What are community members most proud of?"

"How has living here contributed to your personal growth and happiness?"

"What are your highest hopes and dreams for the community?"

These kinds of questions will help you learn even more about the community itself:

"What do people tend to find most challenging about living here?

(Or Jane Gyhra's question: "What do you like the least about the community?")

"What are some of the most difficult issues the community has had to deal with in the last year?" "Or in the last five years?"

"What are some of the challenges the community is facing right now?"

"How do you resolve challenges when they come up?"

"How do you handle interpersonal conflict?"

"How many members have left in the past year or two? Why did they leave?"

"How has the community changed over the years?"

"How would you like to see the community change in the future?"

While you'll most likely have learned the following before you visit, if not, be sure to ask:

"Who makes the decisions? How do you make them?"

"How do people join your community? Do you have a membership policy?"

If you're thinking about Peak Oil issues:

"Is the community making plans for dealing with the effects of energy decline? What do you plan to do?"

And last, but certainly not least:

"Who owns the land?"

If controversy is swirling through the community during your visit, and you hear about it in meetings, it's best to not ask questions during the meeting (remember, you're going to remain silent in meetings until or unless you have useful information for the group), but to speak to the people you know best later, outside of meeting time. Again, frame your question or suggestions in a neutral form, such as "Why is it so important to the community that…?" or "What would happen if the community tried X to solve the problem?"

In asking questions, be careful to distinguish between longtime members and provisional members or short-term work exchangers. This doesn't matter if you want to know where the bathroom is, but becomes relevant if you want to know the community's priorities or recent challenges. So find out first whether the person is a full community member, and ideally, a relatively longer-term member, before you ask the more significant questions. However, work exchangers and interns can certainly offer perspectives you wouldn't get from any community member, such as "beginner's mind" observations and inside-scoop insights on the community's doings — as long as you take these with a grain of salt. Often work exchangers and interns don't know the whole story.

If people get the sense that you are genuinely interested, open-minded, and respectful of the community, they will probably be willing to spend time with you in thoughtful conversation. However, if they sense that you've already made up your mind about them and are even somewhat critical, they'll be more likely to act distant and clam up.

It's also a good idea to not project onto the group any expectations of what a community *should* be like. Don't assume the community will be off the grid, or grow every morsel of their own food, or eat or garden solely organically, or home school their children. Don't presume they will live only in natural-built homes, only car pool and ride bikes, only buy fair-trade coffee or biodegradable soaps, have a common spiritual practice, have wheelchair accessible ramps, always celebrate the Solstices and Equinoxes, have a racially/multi-culturally/socio-economically diverse membership, or only do some other politically, spiritually, or ecologically correct thing. Don't let yourself sound like that particular kind of pain-in-the-ass visitor, the ecologically correct know-it-all. Community members are only human, and starting a new community from scratch is hard. They can't do everything; they have to pick and choose what they *can* do, over time, as they can make time to do it.

If you feel critical of the way the community does things, keep it to yourself at this point. "Being outspoken or opinionated about what you think the group 'should' be doing is an easy way to wear out your welcome, fast," cautions Geoph Kozeny. "If something you value highly seems to be missing, ask them about it. Would they be open to it in the future? Would there be room and support for you to introduce it? Present your concern as, 'Is it likely the group would be open to this?' rather than 'I couldn't live here unless…'." (*Communities Directory*, 2005.)

What do you do if something uncomfortable happens? You can run into a cultural or lifestyle difference, for example, such as you're a vegetarian and they serve up Texas barbeque, or when you light up to smoke they look at you funny, or they express their feelings directly and passionately in the moment while you look around for cover. Issues like these can be worked out with a bit of conversation and mutual understanding. (If you've followed the advice of earlier chapters, you will have found out about their values and lifestyle before arranging a visit.) Or, it could be something more disturbing. For example, someone gets sloppy drunk, or persistently makes unwanted sexual advances. One option is to ask the community's visitor coordinator to intervene. If this doesn't help (or if there is no such role at this community), it's probably best to end the visit and leave. Again, do it officially, saying goodbye and thanking them first.

If not just one or two socially inept people, but the whole community does things you *really* don't like, or the place is downright giving you the creeps, absolutely leave. Don't point out the error of their ways; hightail it out of there. (But still, leave a note saying goodbye and thanking them for their hospitality. You need to lay a trail of graciousness behind you during your community visits, since, after all, your reputation as a visitor can follow you to the community you'll later want to join.)

That Elusive "Sense of Community": Don't Count on It Yet

Besides getting a feel for the place and what it might be like to live there, what most visitors want most is to feel a part of the group, that "sense of community." "It's a warm and wonderful feeling to be included by the group and to experience a sense of 'being in community' during your first visit," observes Geoph Kozeny, "but don't count on it. Deep connections often take time, and sometimes come only after mutual trust and friendship have been solidly established." (*Communities Directory*, 2005.)

Geoph and other community activists note that certain activities tend to trigger the "sense of community" among people who live in them. These include shared meals, working together, playing together, honest and self-revealing communication, making music together, and singing, dancing, celebration, and ritual. So the degree to which you might experience a sense of community during any given visit depends upon whether and to what extent you may participate in activities like these with community members during your stay. Such community-building activities are often built in to programs which welcome and orient visitors, such as Community Experience Weeks and weekend visitor programs. You'll be much more likely to experience this sought-after experience if the group is small, and you're participating in one of these programs instead of visiting during one of the non-program times. Consider, for example, how Emerald Earth, a small rural community in northern California, cultivates this sense of community through weekend work parties for visitors.

Emerald Earth member Michael G. Smith writes:

In the morning circle, after introductions and announcements, it's time to talk about the morning's activities. Various Emerald Earth members describe the projects they're leading and how many helpers they want. Before it gets too hot, Sara will take a group to finish digging swales on the south-facing meadow that we're developing as a new garden and food forest. Darryl wants four people to dig a small constructed wetlands and some connecting trenches for a graywater treatment system. Mitch and I are ready to start installing the adobe floor in the new cabin with three or four people. Gary will take anyone who's left to finish clipping the fence and do some sheet mulching.

In mid-afternoon the bell rings again to mark the end of the work period. Tools are gathered and returned to the shed and muddy visitors head to the pond for a quick swim before dinner. Swales have been dug; the fence has been clipped; the graywater pond is a couple of feet deeper. The adobe floor is finished, spread out like a pan of unbaked brownies in the redwood foundation.

The group gathers around the dinner laid out on the outdoor serving table. There is polenta, ratatouille, salad from the garden, and garlic bread. The community that has come together for this rich but brief time joins hands in a circle one final time. We close our eyes in silent gratitude for the food which is about to fill us, the nurturing land that holds us, the tiredness in our bodies, and the new thoughts in our heads and new people in our hearts.

Our visitors often tell us they feel a sense of empowerment. Because some people return year after year, and many thank us profusely for the opportunity to sweat and get blisters, we know that we're providing a service. We take the time to answer questions, give detailed tours, and sometimes do a little informal consulting. Visitors leave inspired by seeing so many interrelated sustainable systems being developed and by visiting a vibrant intentional community. They feel good about having contributed to a valuable demonstration project. And they feel supported by the confluence of like-minded people working together toward a common goal. Besides all that, our work parties are fun! We spend about six hours each day working. The rest of the time is spent swimming in the pond, playing games, hiking, talking, singing in the sauna or playing music around the campfire. People make new friends and, if they return, eventually feel like part of an extended family. (*Communities*, Summer, 2002.)

This sounds like an exceptionally fulfilling "sense of community" experience, and I would wish you many like these on your community journey. But it's not very likely — unless you mostly participate in programs like this (perhaps taking the fantasy "Community Living 101" course noted in Chapter 16) rather than visiting during non-program times.

Let's say you not only don't feel much sense of connection at the communities you visit, but sometimes your hosts even seem, kind of remote, or even ambivalent about having guests. Are you imagining this?

"Come Here, Go Away"

"Am in the right place?" or "Where's the visitor kiosk?" asks the earnest, hopeful visitor I meet on the road. Most of the time I'm glad to help. But occasionally I grow weary of answering questions or giving directions and wish visitors would leave me be. What is this — "Come here, go away?"

Yes, it is, and I'm afraid it's pretty common in larger communities, or those with a steady stream of visitors.

Like individuals, communities can get burnt out from not scheduling enough down time in between rounds of guests, or by having too many painful encounters with difficult visitors. Members of communities in this state can seem withdrawn or ambivalent, with their guests ending up feeling ignored, dismissed, or otherwise left to fend for themselves. This can also happen when a community hasn't yet developed a functioning visitor program, or if the group is going through a period of demoralization and disorganization — the social and psychological equivalent of having a flu. Individual members within a community, too, can experience these states, so visitors might encounter some people who are warm and welcoming, and others who seem withdrawn, disinterested, or downright testy. "Even under stress, many overloaded communities will agree to the idea of hosting more visitors, usually due to a sense of mission or obligation, but beware: often it is only the visitor coordinator and a few others who are enthusiastic about the idea," advises Geoph Kozeny. "Some community members, typically acting from instinct rather than clarity, will go about their daily lives while keeping a low profile and acting distant in a weary, mostly unconscious attempt to minimize interactions with the newest batch of 'tourists' — which might turn out to be you. Try not to take it personally." (*Communities Directory*, 2005.)

Recognizing this, some communities have a "quiet table" in the dining room for people who don't want to interact with visitors that day, or they create a visitor committee to interact with guests so other community members don't have to.

When communities don't recognize or deal with these issues, however, it can get mighty unpleasant.

Frank Beaty writes about his visit to a community he calls "Maplewood," though that's not its real name:

I hated it. I felt unwelcome from the first five minutes. They plugged me in immediately with the dinner crew, but for hours I chopped onions alone, failing to connect positively with anyone (I guess the newbie always gets onion duty). Some of the people were particularly ragged and, if not actually drunk, then two steps away. A woman brought a 12-pack of Budweiser to dinner and dropped it loudly on the front porch. The men vaguely glowered in my direction.

The next morning I managed to gain the favorable attention of one lone angel, Mary Beth (not her real name), who introduced herself at breakfast and offered to give me a tour of the land. I almost wept in appreciation and relief. We walked and talked, around the pottery shed and through the cow pasture and down near the river. I was full of questions and she was ready to confide some inside scoops, certainly feeling some frustrations of her own.

It seemed Maplewood had been having a hard time keeping some residents in line — and keeping newcomers at all. They had a music and rec room, which I think they re-named the "wreck" room, since the evenings unfailingly ended in drunken brawling. In a vicious cycle, Maplewood became gun-shy from hosting a series of uninterested visitors — thus the cold reception for anyone not bubbling over to join the community, and thus more uninterested visitors.

(*Communities*, Fall 2006.)

One community visitor told me she wanted to write a humorous article, "The Loneliness of the Long-Distance Community Seeker," a take-off on *The Loneliness of the Long-Distance Runner*. But it really wasn't funny. She had visited several communities, she told me — at considerable time and expense, considering plane fare and car rental, not to mention losing income from taking off work — only to find she was crying herself to sleep in her tent each night. The places she visited were certainly seeking members and encouraging visitors. And she had gotten permission to come. But these groups didn't really have a way to help guests meet community members or get a sense of their daily life. At mealtimes she was often politely acknowledged and then ignored, the conversation swirling around her on in-group topics. She was often scheduled to do community work — but by herself, or only with other visitors — still not interacting with the community members she'd come to meet. She was seldom given handouts about the community, and didn't know whom to ask questions, or when it was appropriate to ask. When she did summon the courage to ask about the community's vision and purpose, or how decisions were made, or who owned the land, the people she approached often told her to talk to someone else, or they didn't know the answers, or they were slightly annoyed to be interrupted, even intimating that she was being pushy. Ouch!

Sometimes these demoralizing encounters can be turned around. One couple visited a community they were considering joining. While they took the morning tour, they hadn't yet seen all of the property, and decided to drive around the unexplored parts that afternoon in their car. They mentioned this to one of the community members. This member didn't know that the husband, a man in his early seventies, had a physical condition that prevented him from walking more than a short distance without pain. In a well-meaning attempt to convey her view of the community's values, this community member told the couple how ecologically unsustainable it was to drive a car and that they should walk instead. Her tone was so stern, however, and the couple so unused to being spoken to in that manner, that they determined on the spot to not only drive their car, but drive it right out the gate and never return. On the road out, though, they happened to meet a second community member who stopped to say hello. His friendly manner and willingness to tell them

more about the community somewhat compensated for the sharp reprimand. Cautiously accepting his invitation to see his unusual natural-built house, they ended up visiting with him for the rest of the afternoon. His simple kindness and willingness to extend himself to others helped restore their faith in the group, which they began reconsidering as a possible future home. Later they did join the community.

I truly hope you don't end up having experiences like these, but if you do, please keep in mind that (1) this is not true of all communities, and (2) it may not even be true of any one community all the time! And, as you can see from this story, some members might be unwelcoming or "off" on a particular day, and others exceptionally welcoming.

Sometimes visitors themselves contribute to having experiences like this. And sometimes it has to do with the community's size, because it's often a lot harder to make connections with people in larger communities. "People aren't friendly here," one visitor to my own community complained. She had been hoping to feel that "sense of community," but had only taken the tour, ate meals only with other visitors at the guest quarters, and hadn't yet plugged into a work party. She was also described as "needy" by some of the community members who met her. Two other visitors — more savvy about the protocol of community visits — found ways to make connections in the same community. They asked if they could ask questions, found out how to join work parties and worked, asked permission to eat in the various neighborhood kitchens so they could meet more people, and sat in on committee meetings. These visitors were proactive: they found out what they needed to know to get what they wanted. The first visitor, unfortunately, was waiting for things to happen *to* her. I believe the be-proactive-or-miss-out strategy may be required for visitors to larger communities if they come during "normal" times, rather than during times when the community hosts special visitor programs.

Other times the community's own issues are entirely the cause of the problem — the group is inexperienced at the visitor-hosting business, or has somehow landed in a community-wide funk. If this is the case, patience, persistence, and applying visitor etiquette can sometimes improve the situation, particularly if you are open to meeting additional community members, who, as in the story above, might help you see the group in a different light. If not, well, move on. You'll most likely have a better visit at the next place.

Did You Hear About the Visitor Who…?

To be a great guest, it might help you to hear some stories about guests who were not so great. These stories might also explain why some community members you meet on your travels seem just a bit crazed and cross-eyed. They might be in recovery from guests like the visitor who:

1. Shows up unannounced; insists on directions, tours, or accommodations.
One afternoon a woman called a community and spoke to a young woman whom I'll call Iris. The caller said she had looked up the community's address on MapQuest, had just arrived in the area, was coming over that afternoon, wanted to set up camp and get a tour, and could she get driving directions. "We don't have tours on Wednesday afternoons," Iris told her. "And we don't have camping facilities for visitors after November; it's too cold." An increasingly heated conversation ensued between Iris and the caller, who insisted that if the place was any kind of community at all, it would offer hospitality; it would be welcoming; it would go out of its way to help an inquirer get there, camp

there, and take a tour. Iris tried unsuccessfully to get the caller to understand that they weren't open, didn't have a tour that day, and would she please come back on the morning of the regularly scheduled tours. But the woman kept insisting. Finally Iris got fed up. "Listen," she said heatedly, "I'm going to look up your address on MapQuest, come over to your house tomorrow afternoon with five of my friends, and walk in your back door and insist on a tour of your kitchen!"

2. Treats the community like a tourist attraction or amusement park.
1960s-era communes used to be popular travel destinations, not only for countercultural folk who'd hitchhike across the country to join them, but also for local "straight people," tantalized by all the media coverage of those colorful, tie-dyed (or possibly naked) people gamboling in the fields and meadows. In his book, *The 60s Communes*, Tim Miller recounts a story about how Sunday afternoons the local townspeople in one part of western Pennsylvania would pack their kids into the family car and drive by to gape at Oz, a local commune. A slow procession of cars would drive past the place, sometimes more than a thousand in an afternoon, so that state police had to direct traffic and post "no parking" signs along the road.

"A mistake to be avoided is treating communities like a sort of Disney World, put there for the interest of the public," cautions Kat Kinkade. "For the most part, intentional communities are not showcases, are not kept up to impress outsiders, and are not particularly interested in being looked at by casual tourists." (*Communities Directory*, 1995.)

While contemporary communities are nothing like Disney World, or Oz and other '60s communes, some people haven't gotten the message, and still think community members are some form of interesting species to be gawked at, commented on, and photographed like pandas in the zoo. For example: In order to share the benefits of cohousing with others, regional cohousing networks often organize bus tours in which people can visit several cohousing communities in one day. At two different communities where I lived," notes Betsy Morris of East Bay Cohousing Network, "visitors from the tour began videotaping the residents and the buildings without checking with anyone first. "I understand that people want to take pictures. But they should ask permission of anyone they want to photograph, especially with videotape, as well as ask general permission of the community host, in case the community has a policy in place about photos." It made many of the community residents quite uncomfortable that people would just step off a bus and start videotaping them without even speaking to anyone. "We are not tourist attractions!" Betsy says. "Please treat us as you would wish to be treated — or even better!"

3. Brings Fido

Or cats, or a ferret ("Don't worry, he's very tame."), or a gerbil, or a parakeet, or your pet tarantula ("She's really quite affectionate."), or an ant farm ("Don't worry, they can't get out.").

Once I was out in my yard when a young woman pulled up on the road in front of my homesite in a station wagon full of luggage. She looked exhausted. Her large and handsome German shepherd sat in the passenger seat, held in by a kind of dog-harness seat belt. "Is this Earthaven?" she wailed, rolling down her window. "I've been driving for hours. I couldn't find the place! Why don't you have better directions!" The dog gave a low growl. I could see that she was stressed and frazzled from the trip and the uncertainty of finding the place. I've felt like that myself. But I said

what she didn't want to hear: "I'm sorry, but do you have a reservation? Were you able to call the visitor line and make arrangements first?"

"A reservation! What kind of place is this? I thought it was a *community*. I've been driving, for hours; I'm exhausted and hungry, and I need a place to sleep. Where can I go unpack and get settled?" Disturbed that his owner was upset, the dog began to growl louder and bark at me. I explained that I was sorry but she couldn't stay; she'd need to find another place to sleep and call the visitor line from there and make arrangements; visitors had to be expected and invited, etc., and unfortunately she couldn't bring her dog when she visited.

"Not bring my dog?! What kind of people *are* you?" By this time the German shepherd was not only growling but began lunging at me across the woman's chest, held back, I realized with some dismay, by only a few thin straps. The woman was on the edge of tears with frustration. I felt sorry for her, and wanted to help her understand she needed to take a few steps back first and start again with her attempt to visit. Then I realized I might actually be in danger myself. "Er, how strong is that seat belt?" I asked. "Can your dog, um, leap out through this window and, er, you know, tear out my throat or something?" Wrong thing to say. Now the visitor was furious; I'd insulted her *dog*, who by this time was quivering with rage, slavering, snarling, and lunging repeatedly across the visitor in the direction of my, er, throat. The situation was hopeless, a no-win for any of us. With the woman in tears and calling me names and her protector convinced that I'd harmed her, there was no way I could explain that we'd be happy to host her visit if she would just do what we asked and call the visitor coordinator first, and she could only during the period when we welcomed visitors, with White Fang comfortably settled elsewhere while she took the tour. She left, cursing and crying, all three of us feeling awful.

4. Brings Johnny Walker.

One time an inquirer told Twin Oaks in his letter of introduction he was a recovering alcoholic. This was fine, since various Twin Oaks members are in recovery, so he was invited to visit. Unfortunately, on the day his visitor period started he arrived already drunk. His behavior became more difficult as the evening progressed, and he ended up harassing several of the women visitors. Finally one of the members of Twin Oaks' Community Visitor Program simply drove him to the bus station in town and paid for a bus ticket to send him back home. Several years later the man wrote and apologized for his behavior. "It felt good to receive that closure," observes Twin Oaker Valerie Renwick-Porter. "The experience was also a 'gratefulness exercise' — reminding us that considering the very large number of visitors we host here every year, instances like this are very rare, and we're doing a good job of attracting people who match our values and drawing appropriate energetic boundaries for ourselves as a community."

5. Brings a moving van!

Community members can muster up the welcoming energy to host visitors regularly *because* they come on a strictly temporary basis and then go home again. But if a visitor looks as if they're coming to stay, and even worse, as if they expect the community to provide them housing — that's another story! There's nothing that makes our blood run cold like the sight of someone we've never met pulling up in an immense truck or van with the word "U-Haul" on the side.

Please know, however, that most visitors are a pleasure to host. These hair-raising tales only stand out in community memory because they're exceptions.

The "Great Guests" Hall of Fame

Communities have their favorite guests too.

"Once we had a visitor from South Korea who was the secretary general for the Buddhist Academy for Ecological Awakening in Korea," recalls Valerie from Twin Oaks. "He was in his 40s or 50s, and his English was very limited, which normally doesn't work very well for our information-rich visitor orientation meetings and work trainings. However, in his case, he carried a certain something within him — a quiet centeredness — and it would often feel that the language barrier just melted away. He also connected with a wide range of different people at Twin Oaks, which doesn't always happen with visitors — usually they find their 'people niche' and stay there. Even today, if someone mentions his name, immediately big smiles spread across the faces of people who were there, and someone tells a story of an interesting interaction they had with him."

Earthaven had a visitor with a similar effect. He was nothing like a serene ecological Buddhist, but a brilliant young New York-based investigative reporter for a radical "government-dirty-tricks" muckraking magazine, as well as an experienced guitarist, hip hop musician, and owner of a recording studio. He not only didn't have English language limitations — he spoke the language rapidly, relatively loudly, and with a definite New York accent. He was super-energetic, laser-beam focused, in your face. You might think these characteristics would put off rural communitarians living a much slower-paced, laid-back lifestyle a thousand miles from Manhattan, but in fact this young man made friends here everywhere he went. It wasn't just that he leapt in and did community labor vigorously and well (I'll not forget the sight of him pressing cow manure into place bare-handed for my sheet-mulch project). It wasn't just that he was interested in everyone and wanted to learn what he could from them about off-grid power usage and ecovillage life. And it wasn't just that he jammed with the musicians in our coffee-house, and did amazing hip hop songs on renewable energy or foul government cover-ups. It was that he was genuinely interested in meeting each of us and delighted to learn everything he could about us and about the community — from my 7-year-old neighbor and my 90-year-old mom, to the 2 builder/farmer/renewable-energy innovators he'd come all this way to interview. He liked people; he was warm; he was genuine. Many different people living here, from little kids to the young and hip and to older folks in their sixties, told me how much they enjoyed this man's company. And… was he interested in membership?

A third visitor story involves a quiet, unassuming couple who over several months paid a series of visits to a large, rural community. They were genteel Southern folk: the woman a lawyer, the man a retired librarian, in their middle and elder years respectively. They were committed environmental activists, and each had a subtle, slightly wicked sense of humor. In their visits they were pro-active in learning all they could about the community: sitting in on committee meetings, joining work parties as they were able, and asking if they might read community documents and agreements. Even though they stood out as much more refined and "mainstream" than the group was used to, many people found something compelling and likeable about each of them. It wasn't just that they were unfailingly considerate, asking permission before assuming they could do anything or asking how they might best plug into service for the com-

munity. It wasn't just that they were always willing to work, or to offer the group skills and experience from their specialized professions. I think what most made them so memorable was their quiet kindness and genuine interest in each person they met, and their obvious respect for the community and its culture.

What did these "great guests" from widely different cultures have in common? I believe they each demonstrated an appealing mix of self-confidence, assertiveness, respect for the community and a genuine desire to learn from it, understand it, and a willingness to help the group in any way they could.

"Any community's favorite visitor is the cheerful, helpful one who is genuinely impressed with the community and not very critical of its shortcomings," observes Kat Kinkade. (*Communities Directory*, 1995.)

"Nothing makes so much difference in opening my heart to a guest," says community veteran Lee Warren, who has lived at East Wind, Acorn, and Earthaven, "than if they are genuinely impressed with our vision and with what we've done."

While mastering the nuts and bolts of visitor etiquette is good, even more important is what you make of your experiences at each community — how you interpret what you saw, heard, and felt. What does this mean for your choice of communities to visit again and consider for membership? We'll examine this at length in Chapter 20, "Evaluating Your Visits." But first, in Chapter 19, we'll meet Patricia and John, who reflect on the pleasures and challenges of their many community visits, and the trade-offs community seekers often face when they consider each community they've visited.

Seriously Seeking Community

by Patricia Greene
Massachusetts, 2001.

MY PARTNER JOHN and I sit at the table in the kitchen of our old farmhouse, sunlight streaming in the windows with a view of the Berkshire hills. Only nine months since we moved here, yet this morning we are both feeling the restless desire to hit the road again to seek a cooperative, ecospiritual lifestyle in community.

Our friends think we're crazy. Why not settle down and be satisfied with the good life we have here? They've seen us do this before. In fact, we've been visiting communities off and on for six years, all the while preparing for this move — getting the kids through college, saving money, simplifying our lives, developing skills, deepening our relationship.

Yearning for Our Tribe

While we love our friends dearly, we keep dreaming of our tribe. It seems we have this persistent, racial memory of tribal living — of being an integral part of a self-sustaining circle that includes humans and other beings, as well as the piece of Earth they call home.

Living here we see our friends every couple of weeks if we're lucky. That's not tribe. I'm greedier than that. I want to wake up and see them at breakfast, weed the garden later elbow to elbow while we talk, stop by to help them build their house, participate in meetings where we plan our lives together. I want to know them deep in where the hurt lies and offer little bits of healing daily.

And most of all I want to be on land we share 'til we die and are scattered there, mixing and mingling ashes, as we did our lives.

The tribe we dream of are those who are really trying to walk their talk about connecting with the Earth and each other, the ones who are willing to get in deep on a daily basis about transforming our society. Here it's too easy for us to think that we're doing our part just because we dutifully compost, recycle, heat with wood, avoid TV, and eat healthy.

We know that moving to an intentional community is not like stepping into utopia. It will take some massive adjustments that will demand all the awareness and attention we can give. It will involve letting go of things that we cling to — some comfort, privacy, and free time; some illusions about ourselves, some of our defenses; some pockets of cynicism; maybe our current livelihood.

On the Way to Find Out

We found searching for community to be an exciting, epic adventure, one that can also turn into a humbling challenge at any moment. It calls for unusual amounts of awareness, discernment, intuition, passion, and persistence. It should not be attempted without first gaining a basic knowledge of how communities work. Highly useful items: a flexible job that allows you to take time off, and a chunk of money, not just for joining but for the transition (unless you are joining an income-sharing community).

Several years ago we paid extended visits to some likely communities in North and South Carolina. One in particular attracted us and we went back for a three-week stay, excited about the possibility that our search might actually be coming to an end.

Purposefully we slipped into the daily routine there, which included morning meditation, helping prepare and sharing all meals, working in the garden, and participating in community work projects such as cleaning the common house, getting in the wood, and harvesting the first rice crop, as well as attending meetings and celebrating birthdays. We took time to wander the land, visiting with members individually and getting a feel for the direction of the community. I organized an Equinox celebration and John expanded the community's solar system. As we drove home, we felt we wanted to seriously explore living there.

We continued our communications with the community by email for several months, trying to iron out all our questions and theirs, as we considered moving there to begin the six-month exploring-member process. Then one day a Realtor walked up our driveway out of the blue and offered to sell our home, and we made a big *Seriously Seeking Community* mistake. In that season of hope, we decided to go ahead and put our house on the market. The idea of having our equity in liquid cash to make the transition was alluring. If we didn't join the community, we could just keep traveling and visiting other communities, we told ourselves.

Well, as fate and the fickle fortunes of the community-search process would have it, our house sold to the first people who looked at it, and we ultimately decided it was not right for us to join this community. (Take it from us: Don't give up the safety net of your old life until your new life in community is solidly established!)

The decision to this time follow our unproved intuition — that the community we were considering might not really be our long-sought tribe — was agonizing. So many things about it were perfect, yet nagging doubts about some aspects of the community kept us from getting that 80 percent *Yes!* We went back and forth, thinking maybe we were just afraid of making an actual commitment, or maybe we were too picky, or maybe we were afraid of dealing openly with the community members about some of the problems we foresaw. But in the end, whether it was us, or the community, was irrelevant. It just didn't feel right. So no matter how inconvenient, given our circumstances, we just couldn't go.

At least we were making friends with the unknown. We moved in with a friend for a few months, as we mulled over our new direction, and dealt with a lingering sense of trauma and serious loss of confidence.

After harboring sweet visions of selling all our possessions and taking off in a camper to travel the country visiting communities, we decided to follow a safer course and buy another home, settle down for a little while longer — and here we are in the farmhouse on the hill, mortgaged again.

What Do We Really Want?

Which brings us back to John and me at the kitchen table in our new house, re-opening the search. We're a little older now, maybe a little wiser. We're now in the process of weeding out the field. I sit with pen in hand as we attempt to put on paper a clear description of what we've come, over all these years, to feel would be our ideal community. We're no fools. We know that being part of a community takes much more time than living a mainstream life. With meetings, work parties, the rigors of sustainable living, more conscious communication and processing issues with other community members, being an engaged community member is like having a part-time job. And we're looking for a community with a sense of purpose that involves more than creating a beautiful place to live with like-minded neighbors.

First, we're looking for an internally bonded community whose members eat together, meet regularly for both business and emotional sharing, and coordinate group work projects. Group meditation, ritual, celebration, and resource sharing are also important, as is some possibility of our earning our incomes on the land (or at least intent to develop this).

Second, we want a community with a common dream that extends beyond just living together. It might be outreach through education or retreats, being a model and demonstration site, or volunteering service to the local community. Whatever this larger purpose might be, it means the community would have a sense of connection to the bigger picture.

Out of the Mainstream

Our ideal life has gotten farther and farther from the mainstream, as we've gone from very frustrated to terminally dissatisfied with hard work at jobs that don't thrill us, costly mortgages, the pressure to consume, and the complication, busyness, and isolation imposed by our lifestyle — which is actually fairly simple. We figured out a while ago that when we really get down to it, the only way out of this endless cycle is *out* — a radical lifestyle change. Living in a common-land, ecospiritual community has always seemed the most decisive and sane step we can take to leave the mainstream.

What we really want is to be able to do what we love — whether it's making furniture or serving on a community membership committee. If we can keep our living expenses low, we can be free to spend less time earning money, allowing us the freedom to be ourselves and become cultural evolutionaries.

However, as we've looked around at a variety of communities, we've begun to understand that living in community won't magically insulate us from mainstream attitudes or the expensiveness of society.

Once we spent a few days at a wonderful community that was establishing a retreat center with cabins, one of which we stayed in while we joined in community activities, including gladly doing lots of labor and special projects. When it came time to say good-bye and pay up, we found they were charging us $100 a night for meals and lodging. I gently said that it seemed like a lot for community visitors to pay, especially given that they had received value from us as well. Their reply: "Well, you could never get three meals and a motel room for that." We wrote out our check, glad that it was at least going to a good cause, but were left with a feeling of frustration — not so much because of the money, but because of their attitude.

We've realized that if we have to pay too much to join and live in a particular community, either through land fees, monthly dues, or the cost of building a home there, then we'll be right back where we are now — working at steady jobs to pay off loans. (Income-sharing communities have no joining fees or annual dues, but we rejected these because their shared group housing and required 30–40 hours a week of labor wouldn't allow us to have the lifestyle we're seeking.)

A few communities we've visited, usually well-established ones where land and buildings have long been paid for, held a refreshingly radical and cooperative attitude about new-member costs. One simply charged members a nominal monthly fee for room and board. Everyone lived in small, rustic cabins without water or electricity, and shared common meals in their large community building with cooking/eating/bathing facilities. Since they have few members, they were realistic about the community work requirement of about 18 hours a week, that included tasks like cooking and attending meetings. They clearly stated that they wanted to make it possible for members to live on the land without having substantial outside jobs. When we asked about their new member policy regarding joining fees, they said at first there weren't any joining fees.

"Nothing?" we asked incredulously.

Then one member said, "Oh, well people have been telling us we should have a joining fee, so we've been talking about charging $10,000, then giving that back to the member when it comes time for them to build their house." Now there's a radical and workable idea, we thought. Of course it's only possible if the land is already paid for or was bought cheaply. If you leave this community, they told us, the cabin you built remains so the next new member can use it. This is also radical in its supposition that one makes a commitment to stay for good, and if not — well, you've only lost $10,000 and you pass on housing to future community members.

Less Money, More Freedom

Visiting this community brought us to an important realization about community fees and freedom.

From what we've seen, John and I are financially fairly unusual among those seriously seeking community, many of whom are good people who've been pursuing better things than money and therefore haven't accumulated a lot of savings. While we're not wealthy or trust-funders, we have worked at saving up a substantial chunk

of money and have equity in our house. When we sell our farmhouse, we'll be debt-free, and can carry our old jobs with us if we want. We are the people communities are looking for financially because we can afford to join them — or can we?

What we've been dreaming about is financial sustainability. So we asked ourselves what our formula would be for financial sustainability in community. We'd start by being able to live on less than half of what we live on now. We'd be bank-free and interest-free — building a very simple house we could pay for without a mortgage or loans. We'd have extra money to invest (could be revolving loans to other community members), to provide some of our monthly income and relieve financial pressures, thus allowing us to transition into earning what we need from things we love doing without leaving the land. Another essential: we'd have extra money set aside for the first year to take care of temporary shelter and getting established (since most communities require six months to a year of prospective membership on or near the land before one can become a full member). Throw in the ability to freely barter, thus not having to use money as the means of exchange at all.

We like this picture! The key to making it a reality is finding an affordable community in a low-population area with no zoning and which doesn't enforce building codes (this means we can build more cheaply), within our targeted geographical region (at this point the rural East Coast from Georgia to Maine), that is currently accepting members and that we feel is a match for us. Sometimes, I must confess, we think it's a tall order.

How do we define "affordable"? Of course the formula is different for everyone, but for us to realize financial sustainability, we can afford to pay

$10–15,000 to join and have the right to lease a piece of land. Take $40,000 or so to put into a house, which we expect to build mostly ourselves, including the substantial costs of a solar system, roads, water, septic system, and other necessary improvements. Or better yet, take the kitchen and bathroom out of our house and put it in a common building. We'd still have some to invest and get over the hump of the first year.

Community Affordability: Elusive and Necessary

We know it's much harder to start a community today than when John joined a commune back in 1969. With the escalating cost of real estate, the newly formed communities we've visited have had to pass the high cost of land along to members. These members are caught needing a large chunk of money up front, because they can't get a mortgage from a bank unless they actually own (and are not leasing) the land under their house.

Some communities help out by offering a little sweat equity, a little paying over time, and sharing of house sites with others to defray costs. But if a community depends on joining fees or site lease fees to survive, offering new members the option to pay over time can strain its finances and force it to put off needed improvements — improvements which, paradoxically, would make the community comfortable enough to attract the new members with money to invest that it so desperately needs! And we've seen community members who can't afford to build their own house yet get so tired of living in cold, moldy canvas yurts after a few winters that they leave.

Joining fees in the communities we've been interested in have varied from nothing at all to $80,000. One well-thought-out community we liked had a $4,000 joining fee per person, a site lease fee of $16,000 for a homesite, and a land improvement fee (to pay for roads and water) of about $10,000. This would bring our cost, before we got to building our house, to $34,000. Add on the cost of the house and you've got about $75,000. Still pretty cheap, and we acknowledge that this would include an interest in the community center and access to the whole large parcel of land, but it would squeeze us so much financially that we'd have to get jobs in the nearby town — which was too far away.

Another community we considered had a very reasonable joining fee of about $5,000. The original founding couple was holding the mortgage and everyone was paying into it at $250 a month. If we joined, John and I would be paying $500 per month to live there, which added up to $60,000 over ten years. Plus, of course, the cost of building our house on the land, which would have been smaller and cheaper in this community as we would have shared their common kitchen, bath, and laundry facilities. Over ten years it would have cost us about $85,000, although initially only about $30,000.

Another important factor that plays into the how-cheaply-can-we-build equation is local zoning regulations and building codes. We have become much more conscious of asking communities about these. One community had built a dozen or so tiny, inexpensive dwellings with no plumbing, with members sharing a central bath and kitchen facility. They had slipped under the permitting process when the sympathetic local building inspector agreed to call the dwellings "storage sheds." Up here in Massachusetts, however, local regulations would never allow anyone to live in a house without plumbing or smaller than 1,000 sq. ft., or without 200 feet of frontage per house on a town-accepted road, and any road you built into your community would have to be 30 feet wide and paved!

Community Accessibility

So how can communities be made more accessible and affordable? We're always on the lookout for the answer to this because it seems affordability is the key that will allow us to live our ideal, unpressured, balanced life — and we've come to think this should be an inalienable right.

What about wealthy people helping out directly? We visited a community where one of the founders, a former corporate executive, raised the money to buy the land and then devoted himself to helping build the community. My sister is joining a women's community where the founders had enough cash to buy land in a cheap, no-zoning rural area. They sold new members lots at a reasonable rate with down payments of only $5,000 and owner-financed the rest, thus making it easy for new members to buy in while simultaneously giving themselves an income and enough time to develop the community. Not surprisingly this community has already sold most of their 42 home sites. In another community, members and close friends raised more than $200,000 to pay off the owner-financers, and now all the other community members are paying these members back rather than paying a bank or outside mortgage holder.

One last thing. Community founders could let go the idea of being in locations with mild winters near a major cultural center, where property tends to be more expensive. We've found beautiful places in the Adirondacks, for instance, where land still sold (at that time) for $400 an acre and there was little zoning. Yet across the border in Vermont, where so many people think they would like to start communities (including us at first), land prices were three and four times that and the zoning super-strict.

Sometimes when I start feeling gloomy over taking so long to think through this process, I realize how un-fun it would be to settle too quickly into a place that wouldn't fit us a few years down the line. We want joining a community to be a life decision, not just an experiment. Not rushing our search has allowed us the time to become clearer about our life directions and priorities and that will affect our choice.

So we're still dreaming about that little, mortgage-free, off-grid eco-house we'll build ourselves, about that tribe of good-hearted people, about those common meals out of the community garden, about the bartering of labor and expertise, and the sharing of cars, band saws, and bathrooms. Will we make it a reality? Seems like seeking community is a calling and, as the nuns told me years ago, there's no denying a calling. We have decided to go on trying.

A published novelist, Patricia Greene coordinates advertising for Communities magazine and runs the North Country Sustainable Energy Fair in Canton, New York. Her and John's community search continues.

Reprinted from *Communities* magazine,
Summer, 2001, and Fall, 2001.

Patricia and John faced hard choices when they evaluated the communities they visited. You will too. We'll take that up next.

Chapter 20

Evaluating Your Visits (and Debunking Some Assumptions and Expectations)

LET'S SAY THAT, like Patricia and John, you're dreaming about "a tribe of good-hearted people." What do you make of each group you visit? How do you interpret what you see, feel, and hear? Which ones do you want to return to for a second look?

Signs of Health, Signs of Distress

You'll need to discern what you're really seeing when you visit communities, distinguishing between what's meaningful and what's not. You'll need to look below the surface and understand what a community would really be like if you lived there. Here are some indicators of a healthy community:

- Community members generally seem upbeat and glad to be living there.
- People seem to like each other and enjoy one another's company. They're warm and friendly with one another. They seem to care about one another.
- They enjoy their meals together and they often linger in conversation after dinner.
- The children seem well-cared for, happy, and confident. They appear to have trusting, friendly relationships with other community adults besides their parents. You see kids of different ages playing together.
- The community has work days or work parties. People seem to enjoy working together. They seem pleased by a sense of accomplish-

ment. The group as a whole seems proud of their community.
- In community meetings people mostly listen respectfully to each other's views, even when they disagree or when dealing with controversial or highly charged issues.
- People seem generous: they loan tools and equipment to one another and help one another's work projects.
- People laugh openly. They seem affectionate with one another: a hand on someone's arm, an arm around someone's shoulder. They hug one another.
- In some communities, people tell each other how they're feeling emotionally; it's a natural part of their conversations. (However, this may be less likely in some cohousing communities, senior housing communities, and Christian communities which are nevertheless perfectly healthy.)
- The community buildings and common spaces are relatively clean and well-organized.
- Music and art are part of community life, perhaps with people getting together in the evenings to jam, or do drumming circles. They have art on the walls, vases of flowers, flowers planted here and there outside.
- A good sign — they sing together.

Some signs of distress or challenge in community can include:

+ Many people seem low-energy or emotionally flat, uninspired.

+ Many seem neutral or indifferent towards one another. Some seem to avoid or resent other members. You hear about cliques, feuds, and people who don't speak to one another.

+ People eat a meal, then leave; they don't seem to put much energy into making eating together a convivial social time.

+ Children often seem bored or dispirited. You see snotty noses and dirty faces; you hear more whining and crying than you normally find in groups of children.

+ The community has few work days. You don't

get much sense that people are proud of their place.

+ Community meetings are characterized by low energy, poor attendance, or bickering.

+ People seem serious. You don't hear much delighted laughter; when people laugh it's mostly nervous or scornful laughter. You see relatively few hugs.

+ The community buildings and common spaces seem neglected. Not much attention has been put to cleanliness or aesthetics. (Please note, though, that cleanliness standards are pretty subjective and variable, and communities in rural settings often deal with mud, mice, and other challenges.)

ASSESSING COMMUNITY WELL-BEING   By Larry Kaplowitz

Symptoms of Being Out of Relationship, Disconnected

To support our intention to keep our relationships clear and flowing, Lost Valley Educational Center brainstormed this list of symptoms of eroding relationships in our community — indicators that trust and compassion are waning and defenses are going up.

Arguing
Avoidance
Backbiting/gossiping
Bingeing (sugar, drugs, videos)
Blame
Chaos at mealtimes
Chronic lateness
Cliques/factionalism
Competitiveness
Defensiveness
Depression
Difficulty coming to agreements
Drama and struggle
Eating standing up or in a hurry
Feeling alone/unappreciated in work
Feeling of "not enough time"

Feeling unsafe to express feelings/thoughts
Going through the motions
Uncompleted projects/lack of follow through
Injuries
Isolation/separation
Kitchen a mess
Lack of physical touching
Non-accountability for decisions/passing the buck
Over committing
Overwhelm/burnout
Prolonged worrying
Qualifying our contributions
Resistance/resentment to service
Restlessness
Rushing or hurrying
Sarcasm/fractiousness/hurtful speech
Secrecy/covertness
Sickness
Sluggishness/heaviness in work
Speaking over each other
Superficial interactions
Suppression of enthusiasm
Territoriality
Unclear communication

While a community may be in distress or "have the flu" when you visit, this doesn't mean it would not be a good community to join at some time in the future. Communities are like people: they can get depressed, go through hard times and steep learning curves, and come out the other side wiser, kinder, and with a deeper sense of community. However, you may want to join a community *now*, and not wait for the months or years it might take a community to get it together.

Furthermore, finding signs of health or of community distress is not the whole story. Sometimes what may look like a sign of a problem may not be a problem at all; it may be only a sign of the visitor's unrealistic expectations about community. Many of us involved in the communities movement have noticed an interesting phenomenon — oftentimes people who don't live in community and don't know much about intentional communities nevertheless have rather strong views about what a community should and shouldn't be. This tells me the subject is really important to people at a deep emotional level; so much so that people often have an emotional charge around the idea of community and *expectations* about it. So before looking at the qualities that might draw you to various groups for longer visits, and some of the crucial questions to get answered, let's look at some of the common unrealistic expectations and false assumptions

Indicators of Being in Relationship, Feeling Connected

We also brainstormed this list of behaviors that are natural expressions of relationships in which intimacy, trust, love, and respect are flourishing.

Activities are exciting/stimulating/important

Adults and children have important and recognized roles to play in the community

Appreciation is given more often than blame

Attractive, competent, healthy people are drawn to us

Awareness and enjoyment of and interaction with our land

Beauty is valued

Calm in the face of crisis or emergency

Ceremony/ritual/practices that are reflective of individual passions/growth

Children embraced and included

Committees meet regularly

Coordination between areas of activity

Eagerness to participate

Emotions are visible/acknowledged/supported

Freely admitting mistakes

Generosity

Gratitude is regularly expressed

Joyful sharing of resources

Laughter

Listening before speaking/leaving a moment of silence after someone

Lots of touching/physical affection

Manifesting easily what we want and need

People freely saying in the moment what they feel/see/need

People working together without resentment

Playing music together

Reaching out to include others' perspectives

Responsibilities are fulfilled

Singing, skipping, breathing, whistling

Socializing freely and regularly

Spaces are kept clean and orderly

Spontaneously and easily asking for help

Spontaneously volunteering service to others

Taking care of our physical needs (exercise, good food)

Taking responsibility for our own emotions (not dumping or blaming, being vulnerable, seeing others as allies)

Visitors/guests feel welcome and comfortable/it's easy for them to fit in

Larry Kaplowitz

Reprinted from *Communities* magazine, Fall 1999.

community seekers can have. I'd like you to look at the communities you visit through the eyes of an experienced communitarian, to the extent that's possible. What would any long-time communitarian see if they visited the same communities you visit?

Assumptions and Expectations: What's Realistic?

1. **You will feel included in the group right away — experiencing that wonderful "sense of community."** As mentioned earlier, feeling included and feeling a "sense of community" between a newcomer and existing community members takes time, getting to know one another, and shared experiences — particularly shared experiences of working together and of emotional processing and truth-telling. You need to be there long enough to establish bonds of friendship. It will happen, though it takes patience. The larger the community and the more members it has, the longer it may take. Also, as noted previously, it's more difficult for people who tend to feel shy, timid, or socially awkward. People "expect to be included and loved fairly soon after arrival, because of an idea that all the people in a true community love one another," notes Twin Oaks co-founder Kat Kinkade. "It is a serious disappointment when they realize that this kind of love only grows after time and mutual commitment, and cannot be grasped quickly." (*Communities Directory*, 1995.)

Tip for seekers: Don't expect too much on the first date.

2. **The community should be ecologically, spiritually, and/or politically correct.** As mentioned in Chapter 18 on how to be a great guest, it's unrealistic to expect the community to live up to presumed idealistic standards of sustainability — that they'll simultaneously be wholly organic, en-

tirely off the grid, and entirely food self-sufficient, with every home natural-built by hand, and every fuel tank filled with biodiesel. It takes time and money to use sustainable alternatives; most communities don't have enough time in the day or cash flow to do all that, or to do it all just yet. Please don't expect community members to be exemplary parents who only homeschool, never raise their voices in frustration at their kids, or let a grain of sugar pass their lips. These parents are busy trying to live in community, make a living, and raise their children as best they can; they don't have time or energy to be perfect. Please don't expect the community to buy only locally grown, dolphin-free, union-label or fair-trade products, or those made by non-sexist companies which don't exploit their workers. On some days community members are so busy or hassled or in a rush that they just buy what they can find at the nearest store. Please don't expect every member to rise at 5:00 a.m. to meditate, then do an hour of yoga or tai chi before going off to their job (where they cultivate an attitude of *ahimsa* throughout the workday), eat a vegan dinner, and end the day reading the Bible or Bhagavad Gita. Just because people live in community doesn't make them saints.

"A viable community adapts to the needs and desires of its own community members much more than it conforms to abstract ideals," notes Kat Kinkade. "The probability is high that it will not, if successful, be very fanatical in its ideals. There will be some determined core idealism, but otherwise compromises will prevail. Doubtless some communities don't compromise. Some don't last either. I suspect a connection." (*Communities Directory*, 1995.)

Tip for seekers: Cut them some slack. While they may not be doing all of the above worthy practices yet, they're still living out their values better than most. Give 'em time.

3. The community should be well-established and its physical infrastructure built. How far along the community is in its physical development — finished or in an early phase and still under construction — can affect what you experience during your visit, and your expectation of what it will be like once you move there. In 1996, for example, my community had a road and a few footpaths and rudimentary huts. A decade later it had roads, bridges, community buildings, homes, on-site businesses, off-grid power, and agriculture. Kids grow up; so do communities.

Tip for seekers: Communities, like people, go through developmental stages. Don't expect too much of them when they're still toddlers.

4. Communities are frozen in time; what they're like when you visit is what they'll always be like. I have a friend who visited a rural community and felt sorry for the place. He saw a few funky buildings, and a few members supervising young, indigent, dreadlocked folks who lived in tents. The community was like a campground, he thought, not a place anyone could live comfortably, nor was it attracting solid, responsible members. But stopping by a few years later, he was wowed by its beautiful new buildings. Not only that, some of the young dreadlocked people with no assets had become some of the community's most "solid and responsible" members, who facilitated meetings, headed up committees, and led the construction crews that had built the impressive buildings. This visitor had seen the community in an earlier, less-developed stage, and couldn't imagine what the community would (and did) become.

Tip for seekers: Don't judge a book by its cover, or a community by its primitive conditions (or dreadlocks).

5. What you see is what you get. Visiting a community once, briefly, gives you a quick snapshot, but the reality is more like a video. "The community you see during any one visit is not the whole community," cautions Kat Kinkade. "It is almost impossible for visitors to understand this, but it is profoundly true. A little slice of time cannot give a deep understanding of the nature of an intentional community. Your visit is influenced by many factors that are trivial in relation to the entire community experience." ("How to Visit a Community," *Communities Directory*, 1995.) Here are examples of circumstances that can profoundly influence your visit and skew your perceptions:

+ *The season.* In winter, the place may seem quiet, inactive, and focused indoors. Many members may be off traveling or visiting family. In the warmer months the same place may seem like a hubbub of activity, with lots more people and outside work tasks.

+ *Who's there.* It's a small community, and an influential member is away from the community during your visit. The whole soup will have a completely different flavor without that particular strongly flavored ingredient.

+ *Current events.* The group may be responding to a high-energy event or an emergency: harvest time in a rural farming community; a member giving birth; a longtime ill member slowly dying; a member leaving the group in anger; or the whole group dealing with a serious problem one member might be having, such as fending off an abusive former partner, a child custody battle, or a profound loss.

Chris McClellan recalls his experience:

When we arrived one small rural community for a weekend open house, it was pretty obvious there was something wrong. From what we'd read and heard, the 20-year-old community of a dozen or so members seemed to have their act together, so the odd "vibe" was confusing.

The weekend was a well-planned event in a carefully thought-out community plan. Everybody was cordial, but stand-offish, maybe a bit defensive, and there was an overwhelming sense of loss.

It was none of our business, and we didn't want to pry, but to come into this sort of a situation without any warning is quite disturbing. A kind soul saw our discomfort and quietly told us that one of the core members had left the community and her husband to pursue other interests. Everyone seemed shaken. Her husband — we'll call him Mark — a normally vibrant, outgoing man, looked for all the world like a cancer patient, with a pain frozen deep inside him. We were at a loss as to what to do or say ourselves, but in this time of grief we saw something special happening. The community really was bearing him up emotionally. Most of it was subtle — a hand on his shoulder or an arm around him, a gentle back rub, taking up a conversation when he lost the thread, pointing out something to do when he looked like he was fading. Mark's community "family" was doing their job as well as I have ever seen; validating him, soothing him, needing him. I remember thinking "This is what community can be."

Mark seemed to know what he still had despite his loss. He was also reaching out to his community, letting the healing happen, because they needed it too. Late one night, a toddler and her mother were having the customary argument about bedtime. Both mom and girl were angry and beyond tired. There was no way mom was getting those pajamas on the little girl without a fight. Fortunately the little one knew what she wanted. She wrenched the pajamas out of mom's hand and made her way determinedly across the room. With a satisfied grunt she handed the pajamas to Mark and climbed up in

his lap for him to put them on her. As he started to laugh something cold in him that was melting seemed to melt a little faster. Soon almost everyone was laughing. Mom even managed a smile. I was reminded what a blessing it is to live in a community that cherishes you. (*Communities*, Spring 2007.)

- *Tip for seekers:* What you see is *not* necessarily what you get, so take this into account when you consider adding a community to your list of "possibles."

6. Communities are either healthy and functioning, or not. And if they're not, that's their normal state.

Communities not only have developmental stages, they can also have periods of dysfunction and demoralization, which I think of as like having a flu. If you visit a community while it's "having a flu" you'll surely be turned off, but if you visit again a few years later it could be quite a different place. I know of one community that had the flu for almost two years. Different groups of members resented one another for various reasons, including socio-economic ones. Some parents felt the community's overall energy and policies were unfriendly and unsympathetic to families with children. The people heading up the committees for maintenance and development of the community's physical infrastructure felt so overworked and underappreciated they quit in disgust. These committees stopped meeting altogether, bringing community functioning effectively to a halt. Many younger people were considering leaving, and one of the founders felt so much grief that the community had not become the spiritual place he'd envisioned that he withdrew from all community involvement. The group was disorganized, demoralized, barely limping along. But several new members who had lived in other communities before understood what they were seeing. They did some mediation work between the two groups and promoted new agreements to help parents and children. Some of the members joined emotional support groups and ended up seeking reconciliation with the other members, and going out of their way to help them financially. The community passed the child-friendly proposals, the defunct committees revived themselves and started meeting again, and new families with small children joined the group. Today the place is thriving.

Tip for seekers: If you like everything about a community's mission and purpose, lifestyle, and people, but it seems to be suffering from a flu when you get there, consider visiting again at a later time. It could make a full recovery. (For more on this, see "Community on a Bad Day," in Chapter 25.)

7. The views of a departing member with grievances against the community gives the visitor an inside scoop. Take the disillusioned member's views with a grain of salt. This member's story can make you think you're getting the low-down on the group, but be aware there's another side to it. If you become privy to a member's major grievances against the community, make a point to ask about the same issues with a member who feels good about the place.

Once two friends and I paid a short visit to a longtime rural income-sharing community in an exceptionally beautiful mountain setting. We heard primarily from two members. One, a middle-aged former corporate executive who had been there a few months, loved the community's principles, philosophy, and lifestyle so much he told us he intended to make it his permanent home. Our other informant was a man in his early 30s who had been there slightly over a year, and who would be leaving soon because, he said, he was disgusted with the community's poor process, power im-

balances among residents, and dysfunctional economic system. "The new guy won't last long," he predicted. "He'll leave soon; they always do."

Tip for seekers: A disillusioned member is not an objective information source. No community is perfect, but it's probably not as bad as the departing member makes it out to be.

8. If you don't see many people or community-like activities, the place hasn't got much going on. "There's no 'community' here," a frustrated visitor to Earthaven once told me. "Where is it? I haven't met hardly anyone on the roads or seen anyone around their huts, and there's no central place where people seem to eat together or do things together. There's nothing going on!" *Au contraire.* There may be plenty of "community" going on in a rural group whose homes are widely spread out on a large parcel of land, but it may be hard to see it from any one location or at any given time. I don't know where everyone was the day this visitor was here, but it's not uncommon for many people to be off the property at the same time, or off in some far neighborhoods doing projects.

Tip for seekers: If you don't see many people in a community with a large property, don't assume you can assess its degree of "community spirit" and connection.

9. A project or business run by one or more community members reflects the community's values. Not distinguishing between an individual community members' business venture and the community itself can tilt your evaluation too.

"What are your standards for cleanliness in community kitchens?" a visitor to a small community in the Northeast once asked its members. She was staying in a youth hostel facility on the property which was privately owned and managed by two young men who had recently joined the community. The visitor had mistaken the hostel for the community's own facilities. She had eaten only snacks she'd kept in her car for the last three days, she told the group, because their kitchen (that is, the kitchen in the hostel) was so grungy she was afraid she'd get sick if she ate any meals there. Other members told me tales of the hostel losing reservations when guests had showed up on time expecting a room, cobwebs over the top bunk bed a few inches from a guest's face, sour-smelling and mildewed sheets and towels, and dust bunnies rolling under the beds. I was told the community didn't require its young entrepreneurs to clean the place or manage things better because they didn't want to discourage or hurt the feelings of these good-hearted new members, they knew the men had little time and less money, and anyway the community was hoping things would somehow get better. Also the hostel offered visitors indoor lodging and three meals a day. The community didn't have the funds to build lodging facilities itself, so their visitors' only other option would be to sleep in a tent. The community wanted to be able to offer lodging and didn't know how to deal with this Catch-22, even with the potential impact on its reputation.

Of course, member-owned businesses can reflect well on a community too. Visitors to The Farm community in Tennessee, for example, can buy organic food and snacks, batteries, and other sundries in The Farm Store, an attractive, well-run onsite retail store. Although it's owned and managed by a Farm member, not the community itself, The Farm still gets the credit for having this cool place onsite.

If you have a less-than-delightful experience with a service during your community visit, before you judge the community too harshly, find out if it's a project of the community as a whole or a few of its members. While determining this may not matter to your psychological experience of your visit (since "yuck" is still "yuck") you can assess the community more objectively if you know who's responsible.

Tip for seekers: Cut the community some slack if you can; they may be confronting a similar Catch-22.

10. Community culture should be like mainstream culture; I'll be as comfortable there as I am in my own house. This is likely if you joined a cohousing community or housing co-op, but in many non-cohousing communities, especially rural ones, standards of order, comfort and cleanliness may be less than what you're used to. Some visitors to my community, usually people familiar with intentional communities who are seeking a refuge of ecological sustainability, ooh and ahh over the small apricot-colored earth-plastered dwellings and all the low-tech sustainability systems. For them it's a kind of eco-paradise. Others, usually more mainstream folks who are less familiar with ecovillages, look at the same huts and systems, and say, "You know, I could never live here myself. I mean, this is fine for young people, but it's really like *camping*, isn't it?" Some visitors who come for our Saturday morning tour take one look at one of our tiny wooden composting toilet structures with their 55-gallon barrels under the toilet seats, and get right back in their cars and drive out again, never to return.

Tip for seekers: If comfort, normal standards of cleanliness, and peeing indoors are part of your non-negotiables — and you certainly have every right to them — consider cohousing, housing co-ops, and other urban or suburban communities with normal amenities.

∽SECTION 4∽

Joining

☙ Chapter 21 ☙

Taking a Second Look

ONE WAY TO organize your community-search process is to arrange additional longer visits at the places that you liked the best so you can better imagine living there. If visiting communities is a bit like dating and joining a community is analogous to getting married, going back for a second visit is like dating more seriously — like going steady for awhile.

Or you may conduct your search with much longer initial visits, or a combination of both. Any way you do it, once you're close to deciding, what basic criteria should you use to select the community, or several communities, that you will consider joining?

I suggest you first look for resonance in the following areas.

Values

The community has the same values as you do. You can tell what their values are partly by the mission and purpose statements on their website or in their literature and from descriptions of their goals and lifestyle. But mostly you can tell what their values are by what they did and said. Did they seem to actually live their values? Did they seem resonant and congruous with what they say about themselves? And were you there long enough to really get a good sense of this?

A caveat: as mentioned in the last chapter, if the community is new, or intends to grow into a village-scale community, and it's still under construction (which it may be for many years), please don't assume the group is out of integrity with their values if they don't have important features in place yet. Visitors will ask questions like: "You say you care about the environment, but why are you driving through your creeks?" Or, "You say you're a community, but why don't you all eat together in one place?" Or, "You say you're an ecovillage, so why aren't you growing your own food?" Questions like these are similar to wondering why the nine-year-old you just met doesn't have a college degree. Keep in mind, too, the difference between most cohousing communities, which build all their physical infrastructure all at once (with construction loans and individual mortgages), and most non-cohousing communities, which develop their roads, bridges, community buildings, individual homes, gardens, and agricultural fields slowly over the years as they can afford it.

Mission and Purpose

The community's mission and purpose is what you want for yourself too, and you understand and fully support it. A group's vision is usually how they want the world to be a better, different place than it is now. Their mission and purpose is generally what *their* group specifically plans to do to help bring about that better world.

In my opinion, the group's mission and purpose is the single most important factor when it comes to selecting the community you want to live in. A group's mission and purpose need to match your own, or it's the wrong community for you. Let me emphasize this again — if you really like the people and how the community looks, and it's in the right part of the country for you, but they have a different mission and purpose than you want to live out, please don't join them. Doing so will only wear down your energy and theirs as well. It can be disconcerting when your actual, onsite experiences don't match the noble sentiments expressed on the group's website, but it would be a mistake to ignore what the group *intends* to do.

Twin Oaks co-founder Kat Kinkade writes in her article, "How to Visit an Intentional Community":

Years ago I knew a couple who read the philosophical material of a certain community and were appalled by it. They didn't agree with the published community tenets and didn't like the tone of the material either. However, they happened to meet someone from the group who was highly personable. So, they visited and found the entire group to be friendly, charming, and warm. My friends figured actions speak louder than words. They decided to ignore the declared goals of the community, believing instead the day-to-day behavior of the people they were getting to know and enjoy. They joined up.

But as the months of their membership progressed, my friends found themselves more and more at odds with the founding members of the community. Everybody was warm and courteous, but their goals weren't compatible. Serious internal dissension grew, which saw my friends in conflict with the original leaders over issues of community direction. Eventually the new couple left, and so did some other members, who were disillusioned by the bad feelings generated by the philosophical struggle.

This left the group weak, angry, and exhausted. It as a community tragedy, and not an uncommon one. I say, before joining an intentional community, read and believe the community documents. The chances are good that the published goals and values of every community are deeply respected by many community members, even though the behavior of some members may give consistent impressions of the contrary. (*Communities Directory*, 1995 Edition.)

An even more basic question is: does the group even have a shared mission and purpose? I know a community where the founder believes there is a common mission and purpose and believes everyone lives according to it. However, many of the other community members have told me they didn't know there was a common mission and purpose, never saw or read one or heard anything about it when they joined, and certainly wouldn't buy into it, whatever it was. If a community doesn't have a common mission and purpose, or most members don't support it, or agree on it, this can cause a particular kind of conflict. Some people want to put their time, energy, and the community's funds into one kind of project and others do not — and the group has no common touchstone to return to. Those on one side of the issue may be operating on the mistaken assumption that they're all in the community to do X, with others equally certain that they're all there to do Y. This is a common and often seemingly irresolvable source of conflict in groups whose members aren't all on the same page. And this inevitable, recurring kind of conflict will affect *you* if you join a group with no common mission and purpose.

If you want something very different than

what others want in the community, either because you don't support the group's stated mission and purpose (or you interpret it differently than its members), please don't join them. Wait and join a community that's a much better fit. You'll be happier, and so will they.

Overall Friendliness

On the whole, the people you met were open and friendly. That is, most community members were welcoming and interested in you most of the time. You were able to distinguish between the behavior of actual community members, whom you'd be living with as neighbors, and that of temporary residents such as interns and work exchangers, most of whom would be gone by the time you were to live there. If one or more temporary people were distant or uninterested, please don't assume the community itself is unfriendly. (Also, as noted in the last chapter, keep in mind that something really anomalous might be going on, such as someone in deep grief, or that the community might be in a temporary funk.)

Lifestyle

Was their daily way of life one you could live with? Were they smoking and drinking carousers while you're looking for organic and spiritual? Were they vegans who wear white muslin and speak softly, while you'd prefer folks who drum and dance and whoop it up? Did they drive an excavator, pour foundations, and bring in the harvest, while you prefer people who also talk about what they're feeling and hug each other a lot? Did they cook gourmet meals and arrange theater parties, while you like simple vegetarian fare and long bike rides? Were they middle-class, suburban-bred, college-educated, well-meaning liberals, but you found them behaving too hopelessly, too cluelessly like, er, white people?

Values are important, mission and purpose is crucial, friendliness feels good, but a community's day-to-day lifestyle — ah, that's where the rubber meets the road.

Aesthetics

The place looks good to you. On the whole it was clean enough, orderly enough, and attractive enough that you could live there and feel pleased and delighted. Or, if it is a newer community and much of it is still under construction, you could live with that all-too-common community feature — multiple stacks of salvaged items (also known as unsightly piles of junk). And if you really liked the community and would enjoy living there otherwise, don't scratch it off your list. If you joined it you could always start a project to help clean up and beautify the place.

Your Children's Needs

Your children would be happy in the community: there are other children close to their age and plenty of great places to play. You have a good sense that they'd be safe and healthy in this community, with plenty of other adults to look out for them. There are good schools nearby, or close enough, anyway. (As you may recall from Chapter 1, children tend to love living in community.)

Potential Friends

Did you especially connect with one or more community members who seemed like people you could become good friends with? Did you get that "my kind of person" feeling from some of them? If you made good connections with work exchangers, interns, or other visitors it will have helped contribute to the pleasure of your visit, but keep in mind that they most likely won't still be there if you returned; you'd interact with the full community members over the long term.

Housing

If you're considering a rural community, what kind of housing would you live in? If you expect to live in community accommodations or your own temporary housing before you build your own dwelling, or if you were to rent housing from the community, could you live with those housing standards? Would they be snug cabins or cozy apartments? Tipis or canvas domes? Moldy yurts or hard-to-heat camper shells? Year-round camping?

And while we're on the subject of physical amenities, if it's a rural community could you live with the group's method of heating homes (chopping firewood and woodstoves), storing food (insulated low-watt chest refrigerators; insulated picnic coolers with ice; root cellars), or dealing with human waste (indoor composting toilets with fans; five-gallon plastic buckets and sawdust; outhouses).

Financing

As you may recall, if the community is one in which members purchase and hold title to their own housing unit, lot, or house and lot, you may be able to get conventional financing from a bank, just as you might if you were buying conventional housing outside of a community. But if all the members own all the property (or all the property and all the dwellings) what would your financing options be? Would you need to purchase or build a dwelling with on-hand cash? Borrow money with no collateral from friends or family members? Buy from a departing member who owner-finances your purchase? Get a loan from a community member? Rent from the community?

It is also crucial for you to know and understand who owns the land. What are the financial ramifications when incoming members have to pay back the founders? (This doesn't apply to co-housing communities, and usually not to income-sharing communities either).

How the community makes decisions, who has decision-making rights and at what point in time they have them, are also hugely important. And of course, in a rural, independent-income community, the issue of how you would make a living would be hugely significant in your community-choosing process. We'll consider these issues, and many others, in Chapter 22, "Choosing Your Community."

You also may be considering how life could be during the Peak Oil period of energy decline and ever-escalating costs of fuel, food, and everything else. Maybe you're thinking a community would be a good place to live during hard times. For a consideration of the pros and cons of living in community relative to self-reliance and safety, see Appendix B, "Can Living in Community Make a Difference in an Age of Peak Oil?"

Let's assume you've considered these self-reliance issues, and you're satisfied with your course of action. Let's say that in the communities you've visited and are considering further, you resonate with their values and mission and purpose, the people seemed friendly enough, you liked their lifestyle, the place met your aesthetic standards, there were several people you thought you could become good friends with, and you could live with these communities' housing options, both physically and financially. (And you're going to find out about land ownership, decision-making, and how you'd make a living.)

What else should you look for? What are the crucial financial, legal, or other issues experienced communitarians would absolutely want to know about before taking the leap? We'll look at these next.

Chapter 22

Choosing Your Community:
The "Insider's Guide"

THIS CHAPTER discusses some of the most important things I've learned about how the organization of a community — its financial and legal structures and its decision-making and membership processes — can affect the daily lives of its members. This is especially true when people buy into the community and have independent incomes. Most of the following issues don't usually apply to cohousing (which in most cases have a cohousing-specific set of financing options), or to income-sharing communes or urban communities in which you pay rent. The information comes from researching what makes new community start-ups succeed or fail (see my book *Creating a Life Together*, New Society Publishers, 2003), because what makes a new community succeed or fail also influences how it functions over time, which would totally affect your experience living there. It also comes from living in a large, well-organized community in which I daily experience the interrelationships between a community's finances, legal structure, decision-making, and membership processes. With the benefit of my community research and this inside view, I would like to offer cause-and-effect information that the average newcomer to communities may not consider.

Who Owns the Land?

If the whole community owns the land, that's good. This helps create a much stronger sense of community and much less potential for conflict than in a landlord and tenant situation. All members owning all the land, or all owning individual plots and sharing ownership in the rest is how most communities own their property.

If just one person or one couple owns the land, however, this can be fine if the owner or owners are serving as kind of a private bank, owner-financing the sale of the property to all the other members, so everyone will end up having contributed roughly the same amount (or different amounts over time, but with the same relative value-to-joining-fee ratio).

But if the property owner has not arranged a way for people to buy into property ownership over time, the community is vulnerable to a particular kind of resentment and conflict that I call the "feudal lord and serfs" syndrome. I'd be cautious in joining a community with this situation given the inequities of power when someone owns the land and everyone else doesn't. The property owner can be oblivious to power imbalances, because, as studies on racism will tell you, people who have privileges are pretty much unaware of them, but those without the same privileges are acutely aware of them. A landowner can legally invite people to live on the property or leave it, raise or lower people's rents, lock up buildings or open up buildings and make them available, sell off parts of the land, mortgage the property, fell trees, plant orchards, build or raze buildings — all without the other residents having any say about it. Landowners can feel resentment towards tenants too, if the tenants don't keep their agreements or don't seem to understand or appreciate what the landowner may (generously) have made available to them. In any case, power imbalances often create resentment and conflict. I strongly recommend either finding a community in which all members own the land (or in an urban area, own the house), or else everyone is completely fine with being tenants, and the group has exceptionally clear and unequivocal agreements about the rights and privileges of both landlords and the tenants.

Clear agreements might include, for example, that the landlord has the responsibility to pay property taxes and insurance, and the sole right to make decisions about anything that affects property value, although with input and suggestions from the group, and that the group as a whole has decision-making rights, perhaps with 90 percent voting, about specific issues, such as a chore schedule, that both landlord and tenants might agree on. They could also state that tenants have the right to live there as long as they keep their agreements with the landlord and with each other, and they have the right to compel the landlord to evict a tenant if they don't want that person living in their midst anymore.

Sometimes you'll find a community where one person or a couple owns the property, others live there too, and they're all in the process of figuring out how the group might have equity ownership for everyone. New members join a community in this situation with the hopes that the group will figure this out fairly and reasonably. If, however, the group has been in this "figuring-it-out" stage for several years and it has *still* not arranged how people can buy in, there may be resistance in the owner, either from a subconscious (or conscious) desire to retain control over everything — which is

not uncommon — or because everyone is confused or intimidated about the process of figuring out common ownership of the property. I'd be cautious in joining a community in this situation, for all the same reasons.

Financial Information

This question is not only about what the community's financial information is, but whether community members will tell you about it. Once a young brand-new member to Earthaven pointed out, with good humor, in a community business meeting that it had been like pulling teeth to get anyone to admit that we had a way in which new people could purchase a site lease without paying a chunk of cash down, by just making monthly payments. "What is it, top-secret information?" he asked. "Are you afraid if you told new members about it you'd never get any full site lease fees again?" We all laughed, partly because it was funny, and partly from embarrassment — why *hadn't* we been more up front in telling new people about this? We now disclose everything: on our website, in handouts any visitor can pick up, and in our member handbook.

I think it's perfectly reasonable, if you're considering membership in a community, to find out:

+ If the property's not paid off, how much more is owed on it? What's the pay-back plan and interest rate? Are one or more large balloon payments coming up anytime soon? Is the community in arrears with the payments? If the property is being owner-financed by the former owners, what are the terms? What kind of relationship does the community have with the owner-financer?
+ What are the annual property taxes and, if the group has it, property insurance, and what portion of these does each member pay?
+ Do zoning regulations in the area allow the

number of members the community needs to attract to pay off the property in a reasonable amount of time? Or will too few members be expected to pay off too large an amount? Do the member joining fees and/or site lease fees or other fees add up to the amount needed to pay off the property and develop its planned infrastructure over time? (Has the community even thought about this?) If not, will all members suddenly get the unwelcome news someday that they'll need to raise a whole lot more money themselves, quickly, for unexpected community assessments?

- Is the community's physical infrastructure well-managed? Does the community repair and maintain its buildings, roads, bridges, fences, parking lots, water lines, and electrical systems? If not, the cost of later repairs can impact its members financially.

- How is the community's financial health? Stable, just OK, or precarious and on the brink? This is a serious question about whether the community has enough cash flow to continue on without being in danger of having mechanic's liens being placed on its title or having its property foreclosed on and sold. This is important information for you to have, of course, since if you join, the group's financial issues will affect *your* finances. You wouldn't want to pour your life savings into a place you saw as your community dream, only to discover the group was seriously in arrears with their owner-financer or other creditors. Even if your infusion of cash from a joining fee or buy-in fee helped the group pay off some of its debt, this might only delay matters. If the creditors foreclosed and forced a sale, everything you invested in your new community — savings, home, and your very faith in the whole concept of community — could vanish overnight.

If the group won't answer your questions about its financial health, or is vague, shifty, or cagey about the answers, something isn't right. You might be inadvertently sticking the finger of your inquiry into the tender wound of their painful financial secret. They may desperately need new members and their money to help stem the tide of their imminent financial disaster. If so, they owe you absolutely straightforward, accurate information. If your incoming member's joining fee could save them (and you think they're worth saving) and you'd really like to join this community, you've got a significant decision to make. Please ask to see their books. If finances is not your forté, get an independent bookkeeper or accountant to assess their situation, so you can see if your infusion of cash would really help, or if it would merely stave off the inevitable for awhile, at your considerable financial risk.

Do You Get Your Money Back If You Leave?

Some communities refund all or a portion of the joining fees or buy-in fees of a departing member; others do not. Some groups offer to buy your house or housing unit if you leave, or allow you to sell it to another community member or to an incoming member. Some communities will refund a portion of a departing member's buy-in or site lease fees, but slowly, with payments over time. In cohousing, of course, you sell your housing unit directly to the new buyer; however, the group may want to talk with potential buyers and invite them to orientation sessions about community membership first.

What Are Grounds For Asking People to Leave?

Most communities require that to remain a member of the community one must abide by its agreements, pay its fees, and contribute the required amount of labor. Violating the law, breaches of good conduct, or acts of violence or abuse towards other community members or one's own family may result in censure by the group and a request to leave. Please ask about this early on, when you are asking other important questions about the community.

What Legal Entity Does the Group Use to Own Property?

You'll find that most independent-income communities in the US own their land through LLCs

(Limited Liability Companies) or, in states like Vermont which have them, LLPs (Limited Liability Partnerships). Cohousing residents (who own, rather than rent) own their own homes with individual deeds. In most cohousing communities the group owns their shared property through a homeowners association or a condominium association, and in some states and provinces, through cooperative housing associations. Housing co-ops, depending on the state or province, may own their property through a corporation, a nonprofit corporation, or, in states and provinces which have

RED FLAGS AND COLD CHILLS

Are some communities known for financial misdeeds, other misdeeds, or lawsuits? If so, how can you spot such a place in advance, and not risk your money or waste your time?

I do know of a few communities with reputations like these. One was a rural project offering lots for sale. Various members claimed they had been hoodwinked by the landowner/founder, whom they claimed was charming but unscrupulous, and lawsuits followed. Another is a rural retreat center with cabins for guests. Its founder advertises the center as an intentional community, but it appears to have no members, and has an increasingly poor reputation among the work exchangers who leave the place in droves, disgusted, they say, by how they were misled by false advertising and the disrespectful, sometimes abusive, way the founder treated them.

I know of several different spiritual communities in which the spiritual teacher was accused of power-over sexual abuse with admiring devotees or students. Over the years the women reporting the abuse were vilified and cast out of these communities. In one case the teacher left on his own after being confronted by one of his students. In another, the group finally realized what their teacher was doing; they asked him to step down and he did. The community publicly apologized to their students,

friends, and supporters, and told the press what they had discovered and what they had done about it. In a third case, many women brought a class-action lawsuit against the teacher and the community, and won a large judgment against it, although the community and the teacher never admitted any wrongdoing.

You can find out if a community has had any lawsuits by Googling the name of the community and "lawsuit" or "class-action lawsuit," and seeing if any news stories come up, or as mentioned earlier, seeing whether former members have created their own "buyer beware" websites. Organic Volunteers has a website (*organicvolunteers.org*), where work exchangers rate the places where they lived and worked. It includes intentional communities. You can also ask the Fellowship for Intentional Community (FIC) if they've received any letters of complaint about a given community, and if so, ask if they would share those letters with you. Lastly, you can ask anyone you might know in the communities movement what kind of reputation the community may have. Granted, lawsuits can be spurious, newspaper accounts can be sensationalized, and unhappy ex-members can distort. But at least you can learn whether the community has generated controversy, and what kind.

this specialized legal entity, a housing co-operative association. All these legal entities for owning property seem to work well.

In Chapter 14 we looked at the sometimes unlooked-for consequences, including the potential for high member turnover, of owning property through a 501(c)3 nonprofit corporation in the US, or through a nonprofit cooperative or nonprofit society in Canada. (Note: In the US there are many IRS tax designations for nonprofits, and we're only talking about the 501(c)3 designation here.) I'm not suggesting that you not join a community which owns its land this way: many fine communities do. Rather, you need to know how this might affect your community experience.

I highly recommend that you be cautious before joining a community which owns its land as either a partnership, Tenants in Common, or Joint Tenants. Partnerships are vulnerable to one or more community members or the whole group being sued by creditors or by people seeking punitive damages in lawsuits, since simple partnerships, unlike most other legal entities, don't offer limited liability protection. Communities owning their property as Tenants in Common are vulnerable because any member could sell their ownership interest to someone whom the others didn't want as a community member, or worse, any disgruntled member could force the sale of the property to get their money out. Communities owning their property as Joint Tenants are vulnerable because if one member goes into debt, the creditor seeking collection could force the sale of the property to get the cash value of that member's share of the property. Any member could also sell or give away their interest without the approval of the rest of the group.

None of these difficulties apply if the community owns its shared property as a corporation or nonprofit corporation (which includes homeowners associations, condominium associations, and in some states, housing cooperatives), LLC, or LLP. All of these offer limited liability protection for community members and, depending on the group's agreements in their operating agreements or bylaws, most likely require agreement of all full community members to allow new members as fellow property owners, or to sell the property. Communities founded in the US since the late 1990s often use an LLC to own their shared property.

How Does the Group Make Decisions?

Many communities use consensus decision making. In most groups this means that people make proposals to the community, discuss the proposals over several different meetings, modify the proposal to meet concerns expressed by members of the group (or to incorporate good ideas to improve the proposal), and pass the proposal only if everyone in the group can live with it. People can either support its passing, "stand aside" from the proposal (which means it can still pass), or stand in the way of or "block" the proposal. If one person blocks a proposal, the proposal doesn't pass.

Many consensus facilitators teach that for consensus to work well the group must have three prerequisites: a common mission and purpose, equal access to power (not tenants and a landlord or employees and an employer), and taking a workshop in consensus.

In your community visits you'll find groups who seem to practice consensus decision-making quite well, and whose meetings are characterized by respectful treatment of one another, even when people disagree on an issue. This usually means they have experienced facilitators and skilled agenda planners and often that the group has a common mission and purpose, equal access to power, and training in the consensus process.

You'll probably be impressed with these meetings. You may also visit groups who practice consensus in ways that don't seem to be working well for them. You may find their meetings low-energy, meandering, interminable, or contentious. *How* a group uses consensus, and if they have the prerequisites to do so, could totally affect your experience if you joined that community.

Communities can also make decisions in other ways, and they can use more than one decision-making method. For example, they can employ the basic approach of consensus — including refining and modifying the proposal until, hopefully, it meets the concerns of everyone in the group — but not use consensus itself when they make the decision. They might instead use super-majority voting, requiring 90 percent or 80 percent of people in the meeting to agree to support the proposal before it would pass. Or they might use consensus-minus-one or consensus-minus-two (in which case it would take two or three people blocking, respectively, to stop a proposal). They might use consensus-with-voting-fallback, which means that if they can't reach agreement by consensus, they use some kind of super-majority voting. They might use sociocracy, developed in the Netherlands in the 1940s, which is similar to consensus and includes various other managerial aspects of democratic self-governance. Or for some kinds of decisions, such as deciding among many different options when allocating financial or labor resources, they might use multi-winner voting (as in the European parliamentary voting system), wherein the most number of people get the most of what they most want. A few communities use majority-rule voting, familiar to most of us, in which 51 percent must support a proposal before it is adopted. The trouble with majority-rule voting is that up to 49 percent of the group can be really unhappy with an agreement, and drag their feet and subconsciously sabotage a proposal's implementation.

The point for you as a community seeker is to know what kind of decision-making method the group uses. Do they seem to like it? Does it seem to work well for them? And if it is consensus, does the group have a common mission and purpose; do they have equal access to power; do they require that at some point people get trained in consensus? If not, it certainly doesn't mean this would not be a good community to join. It just means, in my opinion, that meetings in this community might be a bit more tedious or contentious than they might otherwise be, and sometimes you might run into large community conflicts that could be less onerous and time-consuming if the group's decision-making method was organized differently.

Who Has Decision-Making Rights and When Do They Have Them?

I suggest also finding out what the criteria are for having decision-making rights. Most communities require that one must be a full member of the group before having decision-making rights. Some communities that use consensus require a period of sitting in on meetings, or taking consensus training, or both, before having full decision-making rights. Some communities may have more than one decision-making group, one for everyone and another, smaller group with just the longer-term or more experienced members — sometimes called a "core group" — that makes more significant decisions. My point here is to find out in advance when you, as a new member, would have decision-making rights in the group.

I'd like to caution against joining a group that grants decision-making rights to newcomers right off the bat, without their first going through some kind of membership process or new member orientation. If a community allows newcomers to join easily and quickly, and then immediately grants them the same decision-making rights as members who have been there a long time, this tells me that the group is likely to have a lot of conflict (when newcomers want different things than the group as a whole wants), and that the community hasn't yet realized that this is a *set-up* for conflict. If you were drawn to a community with this situation, and equally drawn to one with a longer, more careful, and more rigorous membership process, that did not allow new members decision-making rights until they were oriented to the community, I'd highly recommend the latter. The community, and you as a new member, would be much less likely to experience the kind of conflicts that often arise when new people, with no context for an issue or skill in the decision-making process, leap into the debate and drive everyone else crazy.

The Membership Process: Organized or Laissez Faire? "Narrow Door" or "Ya'll Come"?

I consider it a good sign if a group has criteria for new members and a well-organized membership process. Criteria for new members means the group knows what kinds of people they're seeking in those who will join them. A well-organized membership process means they have certain steps people take and requirements they fulfill as they enter the community, such as filling out a questionnaire, being interviewed by the group, paying fees, and living onsite or visiting periodically for a six-month to a year-long "exploring member" or "provisional member" period. These steps help show the community that the new person understands and supports its mission and purpose, self-governance structure, financial obligations, and labor requirements, and that the new person is willing to abide by the group's agreements. It will also tend to attract a larger percent-

age of confident, well-functioning members and tend to repel people who resent or cannot comply with membership requirements and procedures.

It will be much easier and more fulfilling to join a community with membership criteria and a rigorous, clear and unambiguous process for accepting and integrating new members and screening out those who don't resonate with the group. Since community living involves getting along well with others, the community needs to select for people whose lives demonstrate they can function well there. Ideally, the community would select for emotional maturity and self-esteem. If, however, through a disorganized membership process, a community accepts new people who are not aligned with their vision, values, mission, and purpose, or won't follow their agreements, or who trigger strong reservations among members, it can lead to the group spending hours of meeting time on exhausting conflicts that leave everyone drained.

"If your community front door is difficult to enter, healthy people will strive to get in," says Irwin Wolfe Zucker, a psychiatric social worker and member of Findhorn community in Scotland. "If the community is wide open, you'll tend to attract unhealthy people, well-versed in resentful silences, subterfuge, manipulation, and guilt trips." (*Communities*, Fall, 1997.) Once these people become members of the group, he warns, everyone's energy may later be tied up in getting them out again.

If a community has an essentially open-door membership policy — "Ya'll come!" — this means that as well as wonderful people you'd enjoy having as fellow community members, troubled people who frequently upset others or might actually harm the community or its members can also join. I know of a large, long-lived community with relatively high member turnover that has no internal agreements to prevent or discourage surly behavior, verbal abuse, or drunkenness. The group's membership criteria and new-member orientation process do not screen out these behaviors either, so the group tends to repel potential members who dislike surliness, verbal abuse, or drunkenness, and attract new members who accept this. Hence, the group tends to perpetuate these as acceptable, and over time has developed a reputation for such behavior.

If you'd like to join a community with a disorganized membership policy, it may not at all mean the place wouldn't be good to live in, but it could make it harder on you during your provisional membership period, and you should know this in advance.

How Could You Make a Living, *Really?*

Hopefully you will have considered how you might make a living as you were visiting each community, especially the rural, independent-income ones. If you didn't, you'll surely need to think about this when you're considering which community to join. Are there jobs available in the local area? Do they pay enough to allow you to meet your expenses? Could you work one or more part-time jobs in the community, and would they be adequate for your expenses? If you telecommute, are the available Internet options acceptable to you? If you have a mail order business, are nationwide or international truck delivery services readily available in the area? If you're a traveling consultant, is an adequate airport within a reasonable driving distance? (And if you need to leave the community for weeks or months at a time to earn income elsewhere, is being away that long OK with the community?) If you're thinking, "Well, I can always offer X service or Y product to other community members and neighbors in this rural area," is there enough of a market for that service or product to

MEMBERSHIP PROCESS, SHARED MISSION AND PURPOSE, AND DECISION-MAKING

The relationship between these three aspects of community can affect the amount of conflict in a community, which, if you joined, would affect you also.

If a community has membership criteria and a well-organized incoming membership process, a shared mission and purpose, and makes decisions by consensus, it can work well. New people are oriented to the mission and purpose and agree to support it or they don't join. Making decisions by consensus works relatively well because everyone, existing members and newcomers, support the group's common mission and purpose.

But it does not work as well if a group has a common mission and purpose but a poorly organized incoming-member process, and makes decisions by consensus. Some incoming members may not learn or support the mission and purpose before getting full decision-making rights. This sets up the community for potential conflict later on, because if one or more members doesn't know or support the mission and purpose, they can block decisions that everyone else wants.

It also doesn't work well if a group has a well-organized incoming member process but no shared mission and purpose (or a poorly understood or difficult-to-interpret one) and makes decisions by consensus. This sets up the community for the same kind of potential conflict later on, since having no common ground as a group is in itself a conflict ready to happen.

make it worth your while? And would your income source be adequate for long-term or unexpected expenses such as children's needs, college tuition, or medical bills not covered by insurance?

How do you learn about all these issues ahead of time? You ask. Ideally, the community would provide much of this information in handouts or by email to those more seriously considering joining.

What Else Should You Consider?

By the time you have visited many communities, perhaps in "information-gathering mode," and considered all the factors in these chapters and factors of your own, you should have a pretty good idea of communities you'd like to consider more seriously, or visit again.

If you have been keeping a list of your must-have community attributes, strong preferences, and community attributes which would be nice but not required, you may have a pretty full list by now. If you sometimes changed your list when you got new information, that's good. Using a list like this is more of a planning tool than a plan.

Another way to approach communities you're considering is to compare the rights and responsibilities of membership in each of them. Some communities make this obvious in handouts for new members; in other communities you'll need to figure it out by reading the group's literature and asking questions.

- **Should you ask for references?** What if a community draws you, but you don't feel ready to decide; you'd like more information about what it's like to live there. Consider asking former members who might live nearby what their experience was like: what they liked best, what they didn't like, and why they left. You can also ask neighbors and community activists in various community networking or-

ganizations what kind of reputation the group has in the communities movement. Some communities ask incoming members for references; you can too.

- **Could you live with the community's idiosyncrasies, inconsistencies, and foibles?** If it's an urban collective household next to the railroad tracks, could you live with that overwhelming roaring rumble several times a day and night? If it's a suburban community with five friendly German shepherds with the run of the kitchen, could you get used to being hip-deep in panting, fur-smelling, tail-wagging doggy pals while you make your breakfast smoothie? If it's an urban cohousing community with fairly neat and orderly fellow community members, could you stand your burly neighbor directly across the path whose porch is redolent of motor oil and strewn with tools, toolboxes, and motorcycle parts? Or, in a semi-rural community, could you ever get used to the outdoor composting toilets and those, er...multiple stacks of highly useful salvaged items?

- **Should you compromise?** Let's say the community has everything you want — except one attribute that's really important to you. You haven't found any other communities that even come close — even if they *do* have the one thing you want. Should you compromise? Perhaps a longer visit could help you answer this. You also might check with everyone you know with any community experience — what do they advise?

- **Should you "go out on more dates?"** Because people project so much idealism onto community they tend to make the same kinds of mistakes in choosing communities as people do in choosing lovers — leaping before they look, projecting idealized archetypes onto ordinary folks, and refusing to pay attention to telltale signs. The community can be on its best behavior when you're visiting, and so can you, each of you hiding your more undesirable aspects from the other in hopes it might become a good relationship. Or you can see obvious down sides, but you like other things about the group so much that you turn a blind eye to reasonable concerns and just don't let your mind go there. They haven't figured out their decision-making method yet? "No matter, I really like the people and the land is *beautiful.*" It's not clear whether the joining fee can be returned if you later leave? "Oh, why think about that now? I love their vision of a better world, their social activism. And the *food* — it's so delicious." Fortunately, in dating, and in choosing a community, there's a cure for denial and dewy-eyed infatuation — time. Spend more time with the group before you decide anything. Pure, sheer, daily living in community can help you get the stars out of your eyes and show you a more balanced view of the pleasures and pitfalls of the place. Plus you can talk with lots of people: current members, former members, work exchangers, neighbors, and activists in the communities movement.

Which communities you've visited feel the best to you intuitively? Which ones touch you, warm your heart? Some communities might have seemed just right when you read about them; they had all the right stuff. But if they don't also feel intuitively good when you visit, maybe you need more information or a second visit before deciding to reject or to seriously consider them. Or maybe you wouldn't want to spend any more time on them at all.

If No Community Appeals...

If no community draws you and you can't imagine living in any that you've checked out so far, it could mean you haven't visited enough communities, or the right kinds of communities. So maybe you need to go back to square one, do more Internet research, choose more communities to visit, and try

RESOURCES FOR FOUNDING YOUR OWN

In addition to your basic education with the *Communities Directory,* Online Directory, *Communities* magazine, Geoph Kozeny's *Visions of Utopia* video, here are recommended resources for founding new communities:

Books
- *Creating a Life Together: Practical Tools to Grow Ecovillages and Intentional Communities,* Diana Leafe Christian, New Society Publishers, 2003. *newsociety.com* or *store.ic.org*
- *EcoVillage At Ithaca: Pioneering a Sustainable Culture,* Liz Walker, New Society Publishers, 2005. *newsociety.com* or *store.ic.org*

- *The Cohousing Handbook,* second edition, Chris and Kelly ScottHanson, New Society Publishers, 2004. *newsociety.com* or *store.ic.org*

Workshops
- Starting and Sustaining Intentional Communities. Occidental Arts & Ecology Center (OAEC), Occidental, California. Sowing Circle community and OAEC co-founders Dave Henson and Adam Wolpert. *oaec.org*
- Starting Successful Ecovillages and Intentional Communities, led by the author, at various venues around the US and Canada. *DianaLeafeChristian.org*

again. Or maybe you have unrealistic expectations (this happens) and, given such expectations, you may not ever find the place that fits all of your current criteria.

I personally don't think there are enough intentional communities and ecovillages in the world yet to make it easy to get everything one wants, in the most desirable area of the country, with the most desirable kind of climate, with just the right values and lifestyle, affordability, people, aesthetics, and so on. So, if you're running into the dilemma of "nothing seems exactly right," you may need to choose between living in an "almost" community, and taking the delightful with the not-so-ideal (as in love relationships); waiting awhile and trying again; starting your own community (see page 192); or not living in community after all.

The cure for this dilemma is also time: after all this visiting and further learning about various communities, you'll have a pretty good idea about what is and what is not reasonable to expect. Can you lower your original expectations and raise your sense of what's more likely?

Let's say, however, that no matter how much research, visiting, expectation-lowering, and soul-searching you do, nothing is just quite…right. Ah, you may be that rare breed, that unsung hero, that person cut out for a high-risk, high-reward job — the community founder. It may not be in the cards for you to join a group at all; you may be destined to found your own. Whew! Founding a successful new community can be done, and many fine people have done it and are doing it still. If this is your destiny, all your community researching and visiting puts you in a really good place to know what you want and don't want in the community you

want to start. The bad news: founding a new community is expensive and a whole lot of work, almost like a full-time job. The good news: you can craft your community pretty much the way you want, or rather, the way you and your co-founders, whomever they may be, will want. Good luck!

Don't Marry the First Community that Asks You

Because researching, visiting, and evaluating communities is so similar to dating, you could also fall in love with the very first community you visit because of the high contrast with your ordinary daily life. If, for example, you're used to a suburbs-and-mall existence and don't know many neighbors, or many people who enjoy their lives, visiting a community where people feel connected with one another and seem fulfilled can seem like paradise. Although it's not guaranteed you will experience a "sense of community" there, you might, and this can make the place seem all that much more desirable. And if the group shows its interest in you as a potential member, wow: what a wonderfully appealing combination.

But please don't marry the first community that asks you! Or at least, not yet. Rather, visit a number of communities before making such a big decision. Our parents tend to advise us to get some perspective and date many people before getting engaged or married, and the same applies to communities. Date a few first, OK?

Let's assume you've found the community you want to join. We'll next examine how to understand and succeed in the group's membership process and enter your new community with pleasure and grace.

Chapter 23

The Membership Process

Like your experiences visiting communities, the process of actually joining one is *also* a fertile, cross-pollination point, where your needs and those of the community come together, only this time the stakes are higher.

Most communities set up a period of time, sometimes called an "exploring member" or provisional member" period, when it's as if you and the community are engaged, but you're not married yet — you can still get out of it, and so can they. This is the time when you're looking at the group even more closely; they're looking at you; and you're both deciding whether or not to tie the knot. It's also a time when the community is orienting you to its culture, agreements, processes, expectations, and traditions.

While *you* want to find a community home and begin your adventure of living in community, what does the community want? Most groups want more members in order to help deepen and strengthen what they've already got, help build physical infrastructure, contribute needed funds through joining fees, add more insight and experience to the decision-making process, and help the group accomplish their mission and goals. So you represent an opportunity and a benefit for these folks, just as they represent opportunity and benefit to you. You might see a gleam in their eyes: "Are you potentially one of us?"

As mentioned earlier, visiting communities is like going on a blind date, applying for a job, or being the new kid on the block. While entering a community's provisional or exploring member process ends up feeling a lot like courtship, it can start out feeling similar to the early phase of dating someone new, entering a job's probationary period, or furtively sizing up the other kids while they size you up too. There can be some anxiety and ambivalence on both sides. Sometimes, the new person and the community fall in love with each other early on, and there's no *question* but that the new person will become a member. Then it's just a matter of fulfilling the membership requirements and walking through the steps while you romance each other. Other times, the community members aren't sure of the new person, and have to sniff at 'em for a while before they get used to and then finally accept the new scent, so to speak.

Courting and Assessing the Community While They're Courting and Assessing You

The official steps to joining a community vary from group to group. Larger and older communities, and especially communities where you buy into shared property ownership, tend to have longer membership processes, often from six months to a year, and usually require more interim steps. Smaller and newer communities, and those like cohousing communities in which you get title to your own lot or housing unit and the group has less control over its choice of members, tend to have simpler and more informal membership processes. Appendix A includes a wide range of sample community membership documents you can consult.

During a typical provisional or exploring membership period the community screens incoming members while the new people seek to be accepted and are, at the same time, evaluating the community. This period can last from several months to a year or more. Some communities require that the provisional or exploring member live onsite. In other communities, if the person lives elsewhere, they visit frequently, or visit less often but for longer periods. In my community, one incoming member lived in Texas most of the year and had extended visits with us every summer and fall, for several years. Two provisional members who lived a three-hour drive away alternated living in their home and living in our community every other week for a year. Another provisional member who lived an hour away lived half the week with us and half the week at her home.

The provisional or exploring member period is not only about mutual screening, but also so you can learn the community's culture, policies and agreements, and ways of doing things. Some of this may be transmitted by observing and talking with community members over time. Sometimes communities also offer this education through member handbooks and/or new-member orientation sessions.

Many communities require that the person begin with a supportive role, such as first becoming a "supporting member" or "associate member." This allows people to offer financial and other kinds of support as well as to stay in closer touch by being included in work days, social events, and meetings, and being allowed to read meeting minutes and documents. As a supporting or associate membership, you're still just looking, but looking more closely.

Some communities require that new people live in the community for awhile before they begin a more official membership process. This status is often called "resident," "exploring member," "supporting member," "associate member," and so on. If it's an income-sharing community, the new person would plug into the work scene and probably be assigned living quarters. In an independent-income community, they would probably rent a place to live. Another first-step way to enter a community is as an intern or work exchanger.

Many communities require that interested people fill out application forms, or be interviewed by the community's membership committee, prior to living onsite. (See "Application Forms and Interview Questions" in Appendix A.) Sometimes an application form to apply for residency will be online at the community's website. In some communities, the topics in a questionnaire or interview with community members can be quite personal, for example, touching on your finances, physical health, mental health, eating habits, drug or alcohol consumption, brushes with the law, family issues, childrearing philosophy, relationships, or your love life. This is because new members will be metaphorically in bed together, financially, legally, and in terms of the group's reputation with neighbors and others. Communities want to know who they're getting!

Some communities have a relatively simple process for allowing people to get to know the community by beginning as non-members or work exchangers, and screen people more rigorously only if they later indicate an interest in joining the community. Some communities ask for and check references, particularly if they host the public, such as conference and retreat center communities. The Farm, and Abode of the Message, two large rural spiritual communities, as well as Mariposa Grove, a small urban community, all ask for references. Some, like The Farm, also require a credit check. One community, which asked not to be identified, also reserves the right to do a criminal background check if they think they need to.

Are these communities uptight, paranoid, or exceptionally controlling? Or brand-new and so uncertain that they're not yet comfortable trusting people? Or so spiritually undeveloped they don't know they should "let go and let God?" Oddly enough, the reverse is true. This level of carefulness tends to occur more often in large, well-established communities, including large, well-established spiritual ones. Here's why. The newer the community, the more idealistic and visionary it may be; the older a community, the more its idealism has most likely been tempered by painful real-life experiences. New communities can start out with a three-week provisional member period, for example, then after encountering that time-consuming and draining new member, X, increase their provisional period to three months. And after experiencing that super-challenging new member Y, they extend it to six months. And after enduring that downright destructive new member, Z — they make it a whole year.

Two friends of mine started a rural community in the Northeast with a community-owned business to help their members earn a living on-site. But the member who managed their community business mismanaged it so badly it failed, and then the community failed, filled with conflict and dissension. Turns out the man had a history of embezzling from employers, was fleeing court-ordered judgments for punitive damages, and had been "hiding out" in intentional communities!

Another community, a large rural group, was plagued by a new member who not only violated their agreements, but wouldn't leave the community when they asked him to. He then blackmailed the group. Several community members had married Latin American political refugees who had entered the US illegally, to keep the refugees safe from deportation back to countries where they'd most likely be tortured or killed. This is illegal in the US, and this new member threatened to turn over to the Immigration Service the community members and their in-name-only immigrant spouses unless the community paid him hush money. These people rushed off all over the country to move in with their immigrant spouses, so no one would be arrested or deported. As soon as no one was vulnerable, the community kicked the guy out. But he still took off with two of its credit cards and ran up huge debts before the community could stop him. Is it any wonder experienced communities are so thorough in screening new members?

If you're joining a community that checks you out thoroughly, this is good. It means the members aren't naive; they care about their financial, legal, and emotional well-being; and they understand the sensitive process of adding new people to an existing group. If you become a member there, their prudence will protect you too.

Before you pay any joining or new-member fees, find out whether or not the community refunds these fees if they decline your membership during your provisional membership period, or if you decide not to pursue membership during this time. Is their refund policy acceptable to you?

I've Got Major Challenges — Should I Tell Them?

Yes, you should, and depending on the community, it may not make any difference. Some communities regularly say yes to people who've had addictions and have joined twelve-step programs. Communities don't necessarily want new members to have led an exemplary life before coming to community (since who has?), but they do want people to be transparent and honest in telling the group their situation. Some friends of mine welcomed into their community a man who had periodic panic attacks, which he told them about before joining. He became a leader in their community, focalizing various committees and co-founding a community-based cooperative business. When he'd have a few days or weeks of panic attacks, his community mates would talk with him on the phone, come over and visit, sleep over at his house, or accompany him on errands, which they were all happy to do. At least two new members entered my community with a history of serious drug and alcohol use and brushes with the law, which they each told us about when they told their life stories to the group. Both had shifted their attitudes and their habits by the time they got here, and both became so inspired by the opportunities for living an ecologically sustainable life that they became exceptionally valuable members: one in growing food for the group, and the other in construction, maintenance, and committee leadership.

I know of an experienced carpenter and fine woodworker, whom I'll call Ned, who presented a fairly serious "red flag" for the group he wanted to join. He'd experienced major trauma as a small child, involving violence in his family. He'd had a history of depression and the periodic need to take medication, he'd had a problem with alcohol and had broken the law in various ways. Ned was completely up front about this when he was interviewed by the community. When asked what he would need to stay on top of his tendency to get depressed, he said what would help was being with people who knew, liked, and understood him well, who he could work with on a daily basis for something greater than themselves, and who would point it out if they saw him getting depressed so he could start taking medication. While some in the community were a bit nervous about his situation, Ned did three things as a provisional member that won him wide respect and mitigated people's concerns. First, he learned as much as he could about the community and participated actively in committees. Second, he contributed his considerable skills in physical labor, construction, and supervising community work days. Third, he demonstrated a lot of self-awareness about his emotional and psychological situation, which itself tends to create safety in a group. He had put his issues "on the table," and so they were legitimate to talk about, and people could easily approach him about them. Community members said yes to his membership, because by the end of his provisional membership period he was a valued contributor who offered leadership in many ways, from committees to work crews to creating more opportunities for music and theater.

I also know of people with chronic illnesses of various kinds or physical disabilities who have entered community and done quite well.

If you've got a disability, or are in recovery from an addiction, or have a family situation that's difficult, by all means tell the community. As you may discover, it can be a whole lot easier to manage ongoing difficulties when living in the good company of friends, as compared to living in mainstream culture.

Taking an Even Closer Look

Everything mentioned so far about signs of a healthy community and your compatibility with the group still apply. When you become a provisional member you'll still be learning about the community's values, and if and how they seem to fulfill their stated mission and purpose. You'll be learning more about their general tone towards one another and towards you, and how they live on a daily basis. If you have children, you'll be getting a better idea of whether the community will be good for them, and you and your children will be making friends with various community members. You'll be getting a much better idea of the available housing options, and gaining a deeper understanding of the group's ownership, financial, legal, decision-making, and other interconnected organizational matters.

If you still aren't sure about the financial details of your membership and potential housing arrangements, find this out now.

Does anything raise red flags for you? If the community has what seems a high turnover or unhappy work exchangers, this might be something to pay attention to. If you see signs that some members have quite a bit more power than others, and the less powerful resent it, this could be something to be cautious about as well. Perhaps the community only "has the flu," but that may not be easy to determine, and you may not want to wait out the illness and recovery. If you see what seems like an unusually high number of members leaving the group, particularly in a smaller community, is this a sign that something's wrong in the group? It could be, or it could merely mean more people than usual are leaving for the typical, quite legitimate reasons people leave communities. If you can talk with the people who are leaving, or who already moved away, that could give you valuable insights into the community. Or, it could skew your perceptions falsely, depending on whether the person left under unhappy circumstances and is taking full responsibility for their part in the conflict, or is blaming the community. You'll need to use good judgment and discernment here.

Stranger in a Strange Land?

Some things about the community may seem odd or unusual. There may simply be cultural differences between yourself and the community, particularly if you've lived a fairly mainstream-style life until now. Here are examples of some typical cultural differences found in many intentional communities.

Self-revealing emotional honesty. In some community cultures (though usually not in cohousing communities or senior housing co-ops), it's considered normal and desirable for people to willingly and openly express anger, elation, sadness, grief, and so on, to engage in honest, self-revealing truth-telling, and to say what's going on with them in the moment. The idea is that when what's hidden under the surface is revealed, everyone can breathe easier and understand why people feel as they do. In any interaction, whether discussing a proposal in a business meeting, or a personal interaction between two friends, more of the pieces — the logical, intuitive, and emotional — are taken into account.

A few communities may expect and encourage people to be in "emotional processing" mode much of the time. This can be off-putting, to say the least, especially when it seems lugubrious or forced.

"A week after my arrival I was hermetically sealing myself into my camper," writes Frank Beaty about the time he apprenticed at one particularly process-oriented community. "I was struggling hard with something I could only identify as 'spiritual correctness,' a somewhat stifling community rectitude — and I took the only refuge I knew, solitude. The apprenticeship program called for extraordinary immersion in personal-growth practices of all kinds, and that alone would have tested me. But then, even the everyday protocols in the community, like greetings in passing, seemed suffused with an odd, reflective hyper-awareness, a heaviness I could hardly pinpoint, much less address." (*Communities* magazine, Fall 2006.)

Most communities aren't as focused on process as this particular group, and some communities do it better than others, but even a slightly greater practice of emotional honesty in a group can be unsettling for some folks. This characteristic, however, is related to....

Noticeably respectful treatment of one another in meetings, even where there's strong disagreement on issues. One of the things visitors most often say they're impressed with when they sit in my community's meetings is how well people treat each other, even when they disagree 100 percent about some proposal or issue. Because communities tend to put so much attention on practicing good process and communication skills, and people want to still feel connected with one another despite strong differences in strategies or priorities, meetings are often more harmonious than new people are used to. Typical behaviors of experienced communitarians in a meeting include speaking with neutral, rather than shaming or blaming language; focusing on issues rather than on positions or on someone's character; and finding ways to modify a proposal to come up with a mutually agreeable solution rather than attempting to tear the idea down.

Giving critical feedback, talking about "taboo" subjects openly and directly. In mainstream culture when someone doesn't like another person's behavior or attitude, the usual recourse is to avoid that person, and/or to resent them, and complain about or berate them to others. Community culture encourages people to speak directly to the person with whom they have a problem, and tell them, perhaps one-on-one, or with a mediator, how his or her behavior, language, attitude, etc. may be affecting them or affecting the community, and perhaps ask the person to consider modi-

fying them. This can take some getting used to! It takes skill to speak in non-shaming, non-blaming language, and willingness to do what's uncomfortable — and it may take awhile living in community before one is willing to develop these new skills.

The need to get approval first before taking action. Sometimes new people see an obvious task or project they can do to improve the place, and don't realize that they need to get an OK from a particular committee or the whole group first. The community might have plans afoot for that area already; there may be background about it the new person doesn't know; or other factors might be present the new person isn't yet privy to. Stopping to ask permission first can be mighty annoying, especially to self-starters and people used to running things. Yes, assertiveness *is* a desirable trait in community members, but this doesn't mean leaping in before looking. In a smaller community, this might mean asking about something informally over dinner. In a larger one it might mean submitting a request or drafting a proposal to a committee or to the whole community.

Slowness in decision-making. It often takes longer to accomplish something in community than people are used to, especially in larger ones. In a larger community, for example, it can take time to get a proposal or request onto the agenda of an upcoming committee or whole-group meeting. Even then it may be placed at the end of a stack of many other proposals or requests awaiting time in meetings. Unless the issue is urgent or time-sensitive, this proposal will have to wait until the committee or community works its way through the stack.

Then there's the time it takes to decide things, particularly if the group uses consensus decision-making. The consensus process takes longer to consider and approve decisions than, say, majority-rule voting. But with everyone approving a decision, it takes a lot less time to implement a proposal since, theoretically, everyone's behind it. However, because the consensus process is by necessity deliberative, and seeks input from many people in order to draw on the wisdom of the group, it often takes more than one meeting to introduce, discuss, and agree on a proposal. Getting permission to do some simple thing or start some obviously needed project can seem glacially slow to a business manager or self-reliant homesteader used to getting an idea and then — bang! — doing it. While the whole process can take less time in a smaller community, the principle is the same. Because every community member is simultaneously upstream and downstream of everyone else — with each person's actions often affecting and being affected by other people's actions — the group looks at ideas from many angles before proceeding. Beneficial for the community; crazy-making for the go-getter.

Slowness in completing community projects. In large, rural, or newer communities you'll often find projects and buildings in various stages of completion seeming to progress at only a snail-like pace. This can irritate the hell out of new people who like to get things done and then move on to the next project. The community as a whole may be disorganized, or it may not have members yet who are experienced in project management. It may not have enough people, or people with enough spare time, to work on all these projects.

Once when I visited a fairly new rural community it was like touring a veritable Museum of the Unfinished — half-built buildings, partially completed roads, partially created garden beds — with mounds of gravel and stacks of construction materials strewn everywhere. The community was too new, and had too few members, to move forward at a normal pace, not to mention that everyone was busy just taking care of daily life while living in tents, and trying to build their own small dwellings in the hours before and after going to work. I visited again a few years later and it was a completely different place, with people living in real homes, the community buildings finished, the roads built, the gardens growing.

If the community you're joining is new, large, or rural, you may run into this. There's nothing wrong with the community, and nothing wrong with you for feeling discomfort about it. It's a developmental phase, and the group will most likely move beyond it.

Nudity or partial nudity, men wearing skirts, etc. No doubt you will choose a community whose values and lifestyle matches your own. You would already know if members of the community you're joining go nude at the swimming hole, or even around the kitchen, or if women sometimes go topless or small children are naked much of the time, or if people wear unusual clothing by mainstream standards, such as men wearing skirts in hot weather. While unlikely in cohousing communities, senior housing co-ops, spiritual communities, or Christian communities, you may find nudity or partial nudity in political activist communities, rural communities, and income-sharing communities. But if you visited in winter when people were bundled up, seeing a lot of bare skin in summer can be disconcerting. Either you'll get used to it or you won't, and if not, you can always not continue the membership process.

This is partly what provisional and exploring membership periods are for, so incoming members and the community can get to know each other better, and in that process learn any aspects of values, lifestyle, or behaviors that either might not like in the other.

"Poly" relationships. "Polyamorous" means taking one or more other lovers when one is partnered or married, with full knowledge of and permission of all parties. "Polyfidelitous" means several people having a committed, exclusive romantic relationship with one another. In the former, one or all parties may take on other lovers; in the latter, people are fidelitous within the group. Again, one is less likely to find poly relationships in cohousing, Christian communities, and so on, but may often find them in activist, rural, or income-sharing communities. The same dynamics apply: if you're not used to poly relationships, it can take some adjusting of expectations. It won't affect you much as an incoming member, unless you get involved in a poly liaison, but, as you'll see in the next chapter, it's not recommended to get involved in any kind of romantic relationship while you're still a provisional member.

Sustainable living practices you may not have considered. The community may car pool, car-share, take public transportation, and/or use bio-fuels instead of gasoline. They may use less light, heat, electricity and/or water than you're used to. They may use composting toilets and/or deal with humanure, or use only biodegradable soaps so as not to harm graywater recycling pits or constructed wetlands. Presumably you learned in your first visit what the community practices, so it's probably not a surprise. You may have chosen this community partly because of its ecologically sustainable practices. But sometimes a person has only a partially informed idea of what they want and doesn't realize what they might be getting into.

I was struck by the poignant situation of a young father who wanted to get his family to a rural, food-growing, off-grid community because of concerns about economic collapse and other issues surrounding Peak Oil. He and his wife were excited about what he saw on Earthaven's website and wanted to visit and consider joining. He had

WHY PEOPLE LEAVE COMMUNITY

Major life change. The person may want to go back to school, deal with a family situation elsewhere, travel to a place that interests them, or earn more money than if they remained in community. They may have begun a love relationship with someone who lives elsewhere and doesn't want to live in community, or have a failed romance with someone in the community and want to get away.

Impatience. They may feel annoyed or impatient because of slow decision-making and/or the need to get community permission before moving ahead on projects.

Emotional pain. They may be smarting from too much critical feedback too often, or from being in conflict with too many people seeking mediations.

The community doesn't meet their needs. For whatever reason, living in this particular community may not be ideal for their children, for example, with no nearby acceptable schools, or not enough similar-age children to play with. It may not be ideal as they grow older, perhaps with too many stairs to climb, or no wheelchair accessibility. Or maybe the community doesn't meet their needs for sufficient income, or onsite sustainable agriculture, or social justice or environmental activism, or spiritual practice.

questions, however. His wife was from a northern country with long, cold winters, and she had grown up in a small village. In her country, villages were embarrassing, low-status ghettos for poor, uneducated people which one did one's best to escape. Since our community was intending to be a village, he asked, did we have to walk through chickens and cows and such? And he had been awakened by crowing roosters when he visited another country once, and it was distressing because he needed his sleep; did we have roosters? And since his wife didn't ever want to live in snow again, did it snow here? As I was explaining that it snows a little, we have roosters, and we feel blessed to be creating a village and working with livestock, he realized I'd mentioned we use composting toilets, the home-made outdoor kind. He was stunned. While I told him people here could certainly use the indoor, manufactured version with electric fans in their vent stacks, the idea of composting toilets was nevertheless too much of for him to bear. He wanted to get his family in a more sustainable situation, and quickly, but hadn't bargained on what this would actually mean in terms of day-to-day living.

Even as you're "trying on" the community, the community is screening you as a potential new member. Is there anything you can do to make this process easier and more comfortable for yourself? There is! We'll look at this next.

≈ Chapter 24 ≈

Entering Community Gracefully

To join a community with comfort and ease and to make the fewest missteps, it's helpful to cultivate the same qualities that work well in living in community: confidence, assertiveness, humility, and a willingness to work and contribute.

While communities tend to like members who are confident and assertive these qualities really help you too — especially when dealing with a community's foibles and undeveloped areas. For example, several years ago a young man joined Earthaven who intended to raise food as his primary livelihood. Unfortunately, we hadn't yet made any of the necessary agreements about what constituted sustainable agriculture or how we'd lease agricultural fields or reimburse lessees their physical infrastructure costs, and without these agreements, no one could lease large enough fields to grow food as a business. So this new member joined the appropriate committee and helped lead the way in a year-long process to draft and get the whole group's agreement on these needed documents. His confidence and assertiveness got him what he wanted and needed in his new community.

The other two qualities that work well for entering a community gracefully — humility and willingness to contribute — benefit the community itself, and also benefit you. When new people operate in listen-and-learn mode and are willing to work and help out, the community tends to like them better and accept them faster than those who seem arrogant, critical, or not focused on what they might contribute.

How to Win Community Friends and Influence People

Entering gracefully also requires the same behaviors and attitudes as needed to be a "great guest" — follow the rules; be socially sensitive; work.

"You're joining us; we're not joining you." Following the rules means not only abiding by the group's agreements and following its policies for day-to-day living, but also meeting its membership requirements with good grace, whether filling out a questionnaire, getting interviewed by the membership committee, meeting with the whole group to answer questions, working a certain number of hours, or attending a certain number of meetings. To see examples of membership criteria, interview and application questions, and membership processes, see Appendix A, "Sample Membership Documents."

When an incoming member *doesn't* follow the rules it can be frustrating and time-consuming for the community, not to mention reducing the chances of the new person getting accepted. Once a community applicant with many skills and gifts, whom I'll call Sonya, wanted to join a large community, but balked at keeping a written record of her required labor hours. She had done her community labor hours, she said, but had not recorded them for several months. Various community members tried to encourage, counsel, and cajole her into fulfilling this requirement, but she resisted mightily. She said it was difficult for her to deal with left-brained processes such as keeping track of time and quantifying data. She was almost wholly right-brained, she said, and when she worked she entered a kind of all-pervasive "no time" zone. She wanted the community to honor that characteristic and not require her to do something so onerous and distasteful as to break into the zone to stop and quantify data. Didn't the group see how much she would contribute, and already had contributed to the community? Why would they impose a left-brained, mainstream corporate-style task on her when the group was trying to create a whole new culture, wasn't it? Weren't they creating an alternative to the punch-the-clock, rat-race world?

People pointed out that Sonya paid her car payments and rent payments on time every month, and *did* fill out her labor-hour sheet for her part-time job working for the community. She said this was true, but it was difficult and she paid attention to time and wrote down these hours only under duress of the negative consequences that would follow if she didn't. But for joining a community, she said, it should be different. The community should honor and respect her "disability," as she jokingly called it.

The community explained that no matter their brain hemisphere dominance, new people still needed to train themselves to follow the group's requirements, because the kind of people they were seeking would consider the group's needs more important than the convenience or even self-indulgence of continuing their idiosyncrasies. "Please get over it," they said. "You're joining us; we're not joining you."

(Sonya later got some professional counseling about this issue, began recording her labor hours, and eventually was accepted into the community.)

Energy Etiquette. All the same recommendations for interacting with community members as a "great guest" also still apply. These include being sensitive to other people's needs for privacy and quiet time. Instead of assuming people are necessarily available for conversation when you'd like to talk, feel it out first. (Of course when you have questions about how the community operates, your community sponsor or the membership committee are the best ones to answer questions, rather than people you might meet around the community.)

And it's still a good idea to pay attention to what kind of energy you may be putting out. If you're feeling anxious, impatient, or critical, please downshift these energies to low gear, and continue to watch, listen, and learn. If you are sensitive to your own and other people's energies you'll be more likely to make good personal connections — which is exactly what you'll need to become a new member. If a new person comes across as needy or anxious, people could tend to avoid them and lose interest in their membership.

A former computer programmer I'll call Stan moved to a community to begin his incoming membership process. He was smart and friendly, followed the group's agreements, and was always willing to work. But he didn't appear to have much awareness of his energy presence and managed to turn off a number of members in subtle ways. He stood too close to people, and asked questions in a tense manner. He often seemed ill at ease and confused, with a hesitant half-smile, which seemed to make others feel ill at ease too. He didn't seem to understand the nuances of meeting behavior, asking abrupt questions at the wrong times. Common terms applied to Stan were "spacey" and "clueless." Many people in the community had little enthusiasm for his potential membership, but didn't have a real good reason to say no either. Others took the time to get to know Stan. They found he had a good heart and he did understand things if one explained them patiently. They explained that he was merely shy and socially awkward, kind of nerdy but also rather dear, and people should give him a chance. The dilemma Stan presented the community was that few people had the patience, or the time, to look beneath the surface and get to know his fine qualities well enough to generate more patience for him. The dilemma he created for himself was that he didn't seem to understand the feedback he was given or take it well, saying things like: "But why should I change?" and "This community is uncompassionate; it judges people too harshly!" The last I heard the situation was unresolved; Stan took a leave of absence and left the community for a few months.

But don't despair. If you don't feel confident, rarely feel assertive, and don't often take the initiative, you can certainly still live in community. Not everyone is a Type A, super-star go-getter. Regular folks deserve community too, and can contribute much to the group. If you're shy, or unconfident, or often feel uncertain, that's OK. People with characteristics like Stan, in my opinion, can win wide support by being willing to respond well to feedback, and assume a less "in your face" demeanor. If, like Stan, you get feedback that you seem ill at ease or socially awkward, you can put people at ease by saying relatively little but simply working and contributing. When community members see you quietly doing the dishes, weeding the garden, hauling out the trash, volunteering to take notes, consistently showing up for work parties, even though you don't say much in meetings, they'll notice.

They'll be especially impressed if you listen to and respond well to feedback, even if you just listen and say a few words, like "I'll think about that," or "Thanks for telling me." You'll get a reputation as a quiet, hardworking, open, and responsible person, someone the group can count on. A quiet, hardworking, responsible, good-hearted new member who listens to feedback, a solid contributor who doesn't demand a lot of community energy, is like gold.

It demonstrates that you respect other people's time and energy, and gives you a reputation as considerate and respectful. To repeat Geoph Kozeny's great advice: "The real secret is to make personal connections. Let people see that you're an interesting person who is sensitive to their needs: someone who wants to contribute and help but who isn't pushy about it."

Another aspect of energy awareness has to do with your motive for entering the community. If, for example, you have long been interested in intentional community but have only recently thought, "It's time," motivated by concerns about Peak Oil or global climate change, please lead with your interest in community itself. These folks want new members whose attitudes, words, and deeds show that they want to support the community's values and purpose, not just flee the suburbs or find a safer place to live. If they perceive that you're scared or desperate (no matter how well founded your concerns), rather than genuinely interested in the community, they'll sense it and be turned off.

If energy awareness isn't your strong suit and you believe you might blunder here and there, that's OK too; you can always learn. Most community members will cut you lots of slack and allow you time to learn their community etiquette. Most likely they still remember what it was like being newcomers themselves.

Duct Tape and Work Gloves. Being willing to work and contribute to the community in myriad ways counts hugely in a new member's favor, as you are well aware by now. This was brought home to me when a friend described a man I'll call Randy, who at first seemed like an ideal member to my friend's community, since Randy was an entrepreneur who owned his own business, which he would relocate to the community. Randy could not only make a living for himself there but could offer his heavy equipment services to people doing construction onsite, as well as employ a few community members part time. It looked like a membership made in heaven. Randy was smart, seemed kindly disposed towards others, and, he said, was always willing to work. But it didn't quite turn out that way. The man loved to talk, and talked a blue streak about what he wanted and needed from my friend's community to move his business there, including special permission to store equipment on the property ahead of time, a special business plot in a special location, and a leave of absence so he could work out of town for several months before resuming his membership process. He also had lots of advice for the builders in the community on how they could do things better. He had so many needs to work out ahead of time for his business that he'd occasionally put his foot in it and take action without getting permission first, or think he had permission when he really didn't. Then he'd call up a member to talk a lot about what happened, and say that "So and so said I could do it," then call another member and tell them what the first member had said, and so on. But when people compared notes, they realized he'd been saying things that weren't true about what each one had supposedly said. Soon Randy had a fairly negative reputation, with many viewing him as "a politician," always trying to curry favor and shore up his reputation with community members. As tiresome as this was, people were still willing to give him time to get used to community culture, quit politicking, and start being more straightforward, until people began to realize that he hadn't actually worked very much. He'd participated in work projects sometimes, but at an hourly rate for the use of his truck. He had a lot to say about the work he would one day do, but by the third month of his incoming membership process, he still hadn't done much actual work. When this realization made its way throughout the community, few people had enthusiasm for him anymore, and several said they could no longer agree to his membership.

Could Randy have turned this around? If he was interested in my community, at this point I'd probably bring him a roll of duct tape and a pair of work gloves. "Randy, your membership here is hanging from a thread right now," I'd say. "You need to shut your mouth and just work." I'd hold up the tape. "See this duct tape?" I'd say. "Imagine it taping your mouth shut. You've alienated people here by talking too much. Now, stop! — don't say anything right now, either. Just imagine yourself wearing this tape from now on and be quiet." I'd hold up the work gloves. " See these gloves? Imagine yourself wearing them, and being willing to work long hours in the community to get yourself back in the group's good graces. Go to each member you've alienated and ask if you can help them with a project. And then work your butt off and *don't say much*. Just work. Maybe, if you work hard and keep your mouth shut, you'll be able to turn things around and people will reconsider and say yes to you." In my imagination, because of the duct-tape-and-work-gloves therapy Randy would totally get it, change his ways, work hard, be quiet, and enter the community as a valued new member.

I don't know how Randy's story will turn out, but I sure do think this is good advice. Low on mouth; high on labor: it's a great formula for winning friends in community. Randy was neither demonstrating humility nor fulfilling the community's new-member requirements. He also wasn't putting the community's needs first, which brings us to the next point.

"Ask Not What your Community Can Do for You…"

"Ask not what your ecovillage can do for you, but what you can do for your ecovillage," we sometimes say at Earthaven, to paraphrase John Kennedy's famous line.

Sue Stone, whom you met in Chapter 17, joined Earthaven after her long community-visiting journey. She and her husband Geoff immediately began finding ways to serve the community: Geoff on the finance and documents committees and Sue in the membership committee as well as taking on other leadership roles. After Sue had been here several years, our membership committee was considering a new member's request that he be exempted from one of our membership requirements. After we talked about it awhile, vaguely expressing our discomfort, Sue thoughtfully put the whole thing in perspective for us all. "We don't ask very much of people," she said. "It's not a lot of trouble to do what we ask. So I don't want to hear a provisional member say, 'I don't want to do that.' I want to hear a provisional member say, 'Of course I'll do what the community asks. And *what else* can I do?'" We all sort of sat back and thought, that's it; that's exactly. Most communities are looking for members who are looking not so much at what they can get, but at what they can give. A community, especially a new one, offers people a huge opportunity to demonstrate that they're willing to give to the community as well as to receive from it. But incoming members seem to sometimes get the balance wrong.

Randy, for example, obviously had the balance reversed in terms of meeting his needs compared to the community's. He was not thinking, "Ask not what the community can do for you" — but was insisting it first meet his requirements and his good ideas on his terms.

The Surprising Power of Humility.

Sonya and Randy each demonstrate a kind of innocent arrogance. Innocent, because they didn't intend to be arrogant; arrogant, because they were not considering the effects of their behavior on others. It was as if they were shouting from the rooftops, "I don't care much about *you*; I mostly care about *me!*"

As mentioned earlier, what I mean by humility is not self-deprecation but the assumption that one still has things to learn, and may not know much about the community yet. It has a gentle and respectful energy.

A new member doesn't demonstrate humility when they're bristling with impatience, barely concealing criticisms, or broaching all their ideas for improving the place too soon after entering the membership process. "Tell them to practice some humility!" several friends have told me after they've read these last few chapters. I really can't stress this enough.

One new member to Earthaven managed to drive away her community sponsor and annoy several others by her insistence that we were not doing certain things well and should do them a different way. Regardless of the merit of her ideas, her observations weren't made in a thoughtful or "what if" manner, but with an attitude of impatient superiority. Please don't fall into this all-too-appealing trap. An attitude of knowing what's best for the community, or how they might do things better, no matter how well-meaning, tends to annoy the hell out of community members — and when the community is evaluating you as a new member is *not* the time to annoy people with criticisms and helpful suggestions. (You can always annoy them later, once you're a fully invested member.)

Even if you feel superior or you're bursting with community-improvement tips, please *act as if* you're patient and grateful. If you see all kinds of ways the community could improve itself, hold off on saying so until you've become a well-liked, trusted part of the group. If you feel annoyed by the parts of the community that may be disorganized, don't set the group straight just yet. If they're doing things you believe they could do a whole lot better, save your advice till later, when you're unquestionably "one of us." If you see these people as well-meaning but incompetent, wait at least a year before commencing a 12-Point Program to straighten them out. And, last but not least, if you think you know better than they do about things, consider yourself *still* on an information-gathering mission and don't judge too quickly. Wait until you have more data. You'll be amazed at the different perspective you might have in a year or two. Chances are high that the group knows more than you do about their available options, what hap-

SEXUAL ETIQUETTE FOR NEW MEMBERS

The period of your incoming-member process is *still* not a good time to enter into a romantic liaison with a community member, another provisional member, or a visitor. There are reasons for this. One is that most communities want to get to know you, and for this you need to be fully present, and not dreamy-eyed and distracted with a new romance. Another is that you need to approach the community as yourself rather than as a particular community member's partner or lover. Getting together romantically with an existing member can sometimes work against you, particularly if the community member has a poor reputation in the group. Is this the group's loneliest or most desperate member who goes after all incoming men? Or the community's most on-the-prowl guy who hits on all the women of a certain age? What does this tell the community about your self-esteem or judgment? (And doesn't it make sense to find out the person's reputation in the community before leaping into bed with them?) Or, the community member could influence you in ways that don't help your chances for membership, for example, by espousing an unpopular viewpoint in the community, or telling you, "Aw, you don't need to attend those meetings. I never do."

"Entering into a relationship right away often adds more complexity to the process for both the incoming member as well as the rest of the community," notes Earthaven member Lee Warren, who prepared an "About Sexuality in the Community" document for new members. "It might serve everyone if a love affair were to be postponed until more settling in has happened."

Another reason to postpone romance for later is to not step on the toes of an existing member by taking up with her or his recent ex-lover; this is considered really bad form in most communities. While it's almost unheard of in mainstream culture, in much of community culture one asks the former partner how they'd feel if one were to get together with their ex. If it's "No, please not yet," ideally the new person holds off on pursuing the romance. Lee Warren puts this very well:

If you are in a particularly sexually active time in your life, please know that your entrance can send ripples through the community. It can do so in several ways. It can manifest as attractions to and interest in you by single or available members. It can also manifest as jealousy or feeling threatened in partners of attracted members or anyone that might be envious of your beauty,

pened in the past, and what the relevant pressures, opportunities, and the nuances of their current situation are.

"Come Here, Go Away" — Take Two

"Who *is* this person?" asks a community member in some part of his or her mind. "Who do they think they *are* that they presume to think they could join us?" In their conscious minds, of course, they know very well the community needs new members. "Is this new person arrogant?" they ask. "Full of themselves? Critical of us? Trying to take over? Trying to tell us what to do? Who the hell *is* this guy or gal?"

This "come here, go away" attitude towards incoming members is subtle, and few communitarians would admit to having such thoughts deep in their psyches, but if you thought you saw some of this energy when you visited communities, please know that it can come up again when you go to join. A community can be a tight, bonded entity. The group's current member configuration is a known quantity. It's familiar; it's safe. You, as a new member, might change everything. Also, the group

youth, or sexuality. Although it may be appealing and certainly natural to go towards the attraction and away from the jealousy, it isn't advisable. We strongly encourage you, when entering the community, to *first and foremost forge friendships with the folks of your own gender*. This choice infinitely strengthens bonds of trust, and allows us to all heal from the competition and distrust that have been conditioned in us. Even if you think you are not moving in on someone else's mate or love, please check it out thoroughly. Having a conversation with the former lover can go miles in saving everyone heartache and bad feelings.

Sexuality is a powerful force. When a new person comes into a group, an unconscious process of evaluation often occurs. In the reptilian part of our brains we often unconsciously ask questions such as: "Is this someone for me to fight, run from, nurture, get nurtured by, or have sex with?" A new person entering into any fairly stable community group will be checked out. When entering a new community, please be conscious about how much sexual energy you put out at first. Connecting heart and sexuality, especially at this point, goes a long way to helping folks feel safe with you as a new person."

Here are more sexual etiquette tips for later, when you're a full member and may choose to have a romance in the community. First, if you want to get involved with someone who says they and their partner are in an open relationship or are polyamorous, make sure to check it out with the person's current partner or partners first. If you don't, and the person is mistaken, or worse, lying, the resulting misunderstanding can negatively impact on the entire community — and *you'll* look bad. Second, unless you and your new partner intend to settle into shared domestic life and raise children, by all means use responsible birth control. Unplanned pregnancies put an undue burden on the group and annoy and disappoint many people beyond yourselves. "As a new member," writes Lee Warren, "you have many challenging tasks ahead of you: finding your place, settling in, generating income, participating socially, and contributing to the whole in many ways. A pregnancy at this time can be difficult indeed. Please be conscious with your birth control methods; men as well as women. As a temporary resident, please take extra care to make sure a pregnancy doesn't happen during your time here. As an incoming member, please be careful to plan your family in a way that assists the integration of your family into the community."

may have grown cautious from too many recent experiences with clueless new members with critical or know-it-all attitudes, which can be tiresome at best. Your presence represents the unknown for the group. They want new members, and yet… they might feel ambivalent as well.

This is not true of all or most community members, nor true most of the time. It just comes out now and then, and in subtle ways. The group needs new members and you've got a lot to offer, so why is so-and-so subtly challenging you? Why do you detect among some a "This is our in-crowd; don't think you can just waltz in and join us" energy?

Fortunately, there's a certain cure for this kind of mixed message: time and familiarity. Ignore this behavior; they'll get over it. Let these folks get to know you while you follow the rules, meet their requirements, show sensitivity, pay attention to the kind of energy you're putting out and to what's going on with the other community members, and contribute to the group as best you can. The old "come here, go away" syndrome, if it arises, will pass.

However, cultivating an attitude of humility as a balance to any inadvertent arrogance and to counteract any "come here, go away" energy goes a long way in winning people over.

Like a Wolf Entering a Wolf Pack

You can enter a community awkwardly, stumbling around a bit first before getting the hang of the place, or you can enter gracefully and easily from the beginning, triggering the least amount of subtle defensiveness in existing community members. I want it to be easy for you to enter, so I suggest you enter your new community, with the attitude of a wolf joining a wolf pack.

A lone wolf can't just waltz up to a tightly cohesive wolf pack and say, in wolf body-language,

"Howdy, I think I'll just join ya'll tonight and howl along." The other wolves would instinctively perceive this as a serious breach of species etiquette and drive the intruder away with growls and snarls.

So wolves who want to join a pack have to ease into the situation gradually, gracefully — and they've got a ritual for doing this. Lone wolves first let the wolves in the pack hear them howl from some distance away. The others know the new wolf is in the area, but he is not a threat; he's just announcing his presence in the general area. After awhile the lone wolf also gets upwind of the pack and lets them get a whiff of him. Now they've heard him and smelled him. Gradually, oh-so-gradually, he comes closer, and at some point in his courtship, and believe me, he's courting them just like you and I would court a community we want to join, he lets the pack see him, but from a ways off. By this time they know who he is: he's that new guy in the neighborhood. He's not so alarming and potentially dangerous, because he's a known entity. Not "one of *us*," to be sure, but at least no longer a strange phenomenon instinctively responded to as a threat. At last comes the day the wolf asks if he can join their pack. He approaches them gradually; they know he's coming. He enters their space crouching low, his tail down, his ears laid back in submissive, non-threatening body language. Then he flops down, legs curled up in that "I'm harmless" position, revealing his vulnerable belly and throat. While ripping out throats and bellies is what wolves *do* when they kill prey, for some reason when a wolf bares its vulnerable underside to other wolves, they usually do not attack; some wolf instinct stops them.

In growl 'n snarl language the wolves say, essentially, "You don't know anything yet. We're the ones with status here. You've got no rank and no privileges and if you ever did you'd have to earn them first. So there!" And the new wolf lying there is essentially saying in wolf body language, "I know I don't know anything yet. You're the ones with status. I've got no rank and I don't presume anything. Looky here, you've got me, here's my throat." The pack finishes up their dominance message, the new wolf rolls over and, he and the others make each other's acquaintance more thoroughly through sniffs and licks, now that pack rank order is established and everyone feels safe.

Et tu, Lupus. We'd do well to consider wolf packs when entering a community, because the same kinds of issues are at stake in our species. You're new and unknown. What kind of subtle, barely conscious threat might you represent? What kind of change to the group might you bring them? Are you someone who will be dominant and pushy? Will you be submissive and needy? Might you become a good pal? Might you be someone to mate with? If you're thinking, "Oh, this is stupid," that's OK too. But please know that these subtle kinds of dynamics can and often do take place when a new person joins a group, and any confident-but-humble behavior you show to your new pack can make a difference in your favor. I'd like you to *not* come across like Sonya or Randy; I'd like your experience of joining your new community to be easy and pleasant for you all. So please take a tip from the Wolf Book of Etiquette and, in human style, enter your community mildly, courteously, and yes, humbly.

Developmental Stages of the New-Member Process

Just as in romance, there are phases of the relationship with your new community — and they're not dissimilar to the phases of a new love relationship.

The Honeymoon. You're smitten by this community, which seems so wonderful — the warm laughter and camaraderie around the dining room table; hot bowls of delicious soup and warm, fresh-baked bread; people circling up to hold hands before well-organized, productive meetings; children gamboling happily in sunny wildflower meadows — the fabled "sense of community." And the community is smitten by you: you're so personable, so likeable, so willing to help, so eager to learn more about the community, so impressed with their accomplishments, so grateful to be there.

The Honeymoon's Over. But after awhile you grow increasingly weary. You're disappointed with the community. They don't always live up to their mission and purpose; they sometimes trip and stumble all over their supposed values. (The place is *not* like what it said on their website!) Sometimes meetings can be tiresome and so disorganized nothing gets done — a colossal waste of time. And the unfinished projects — why don't they clean *up* this place?! Some people really grate on your nerves; you feel so impatient you can barely treat them courteously. If this were "real life" you'd simply avoid such idiots. And community members begin to notice a few of your less likeable characteristics too, and tell you so. Some of these people who want to do that damn *processing* all the time: what's their problem? Get a life! And then there are those noxious community members who want to have *mediations* with you; who want to give you *feedback*; who have the gall to ask you to please behave more consciously or say things differently.

People take you aside and explain the Magnifying Mirror Effect: living in community often evokes people's most destructive or alienating attitudes and behaviors; it tends to magnify these attitudes and behaviors and reflect them back to us, painful though it is. "We're magnifying mirrors for each other," you're told. "The more intensely you dislike certain attitudes and behaviors in other people here the more likely you have the same things yourself, though you probably don't know it yet."

You'll discover the famed Rock Polisher Effect. Like rocks in a rock tumbler which first abrade and then polish each other, the rough edges of people living in community are worn smoother by frequent contact with everyone else's rough edges. Getting your rough edges polished can be hard to take. But, you're told, through good communication and process skills people can make the rock-polisher effect more conscious. "Community living can be a powerful opportunity for personal growth," these know-it-alls will tell you. No one can get away with their usual behaviors — living in community can be a wake-up call to the soul. We have an opportunity to finish our perhaps-stopped-in-its-tracks growing up process.

Aieeeee! Let me *outta* here!

Acceptance and Understanding. And finally, later, it begins to get easier again. You feel like you're starting to get the hang of community culture. You learn to say less in meetings and listen more. You get used to the slower pace of decision-making; you begin to see that the group wants to gather many viewpoints in order to make a better decision over the long run. You see that the group values depth and breadth of inquiry over efficiency.

You begin to understand this thing called "process and communication skills." You begin to see that in mainstream culture there's always a winner and a loser; but in community people want to invest the time to find out, if possible, what solutions might work for everyone. You understand that it's not acceptable to dismiss someone as a jerk and simply avoid them, that you need to take the time, getting help from others if needed, to work things out. You see that people *invest* in each other. They're not passing strangers on a suburban street; they function more like siblings and cousins who take the time to understand and find ways to work things out with each other, because they're all in something important together.

You begin to get a sense that you're growing emotionally larger, more patient, more tolerant. You're learning to accept the pleasant and unpleasant aspects of each person in the community; you begin to value the well-being and harmony of the whole group more than the need to set someone straight or ignore them. You begin to tolerate other people's odd and unique foibles. You even begin to accept them.

You begin to accept the slow pace of accomplishing tasks; you get used to the partially completed projects. (And wonder of wonders, what formerly looked like sloppy piles of junk begin to transform before your very eyes into valuable stacks of salvaged materials.)

You start feeling an appreciation for how hard it was for the founders to create the community in the first place; you start to feel proud of the place. You begin to feel grateful for being there in spite of its many flaws.

Finally, you no longer think of the community as "they." You think of it as "we."

These stages are not really sequential, since the second two actually alternate and blend into one another, but you get the picture. What this really describes is the process of *self-adjustment* — learning what you need to do to make community work for you. It means joining committees and having a say in community issues, learning to speak up for yourself, learning to look at your less pleasant qualities and perhaps make adjustments, protecting your private time, guarding against burn-out.

What If I Don't Like It?

It sometimes happens, however, that newcomers to a community don't like the place once they get to know it, and no amount of additional time, deeper understanding, or long conversations with members makes any difference. It may be that the most reasonable option is to leave. It may be that you chose too quickly, or you needed more information before deciding to go for membership. Or it may be that the community has two personas: their public face and what they are like when you actually live there. No matter the reason, you're not obligated to stay.

If you paid a joining fee and it's refundable, that's great. If it's not refundable, or only partially refundable if you don't continue your membership, you would have paid this fee knowing that you'd forfeit it if things didn't work out. Knowing this ahead of time means that if they later said no at least not getting all your money back wouldn't be an awful surprise and you wouldn't feel ripped off. Consider the fee a donation to a good cause and move on. You can consider joining your second-favorite option, or even go back to the *Communities Directory* and online directories and try again.

What If They Say "No"?

It also could happen that the community declines your membership. This can be painful and emotionally devastating, and I won't pretend it isn't. You'll need to be prepared for this possibility, of course, even as you meet the group's requirements, pay attention to your energy, show your willingness to work and contribute, and so on. If the group says "No," consider it a blessing. This is far, far better than this group having whatever concerns they may have about you but saying yes, and your confidence being undermined because they treat you for years in a way that is less than welcoming. It's far better than if you uprooted your life to move there and then later were asked to leave.

Why might a community decline your membership and say "No thanks," "Not at this time," or "Please wait and perhaps try again later?" It could be that it isn't a good fit between you and the community, and they see it before you do. It could be that they believe you're not at a place in your life to join a group with their particular lifestyle, agreements, or financial requirements. Or it could be that they're not drawn to you, for whatever reason. I know of one community that hadn't said "No thanks" to anyone, but finally did to a young woman who was energetic, strong, willing to work and contribute, talented musically, and who clearly had a big heart. She raised red flags in several areas, however, including her tendency to fly into rages, a sometimes scornful attitude towards the community, and an apparent difficulty in following instructions or planning ahead. Rejecting her membership was a painful, difficult, and controversial experience for the community, since some were fiercely loyal to her and others felt sad and yet duty-bound to say no. I know of a rural, ecologically sustainable community that declined the membership of a woman who bred small show dogs for a living. The group couldn't see how her career choice might contribute to ecological sustainability in their community (and no one wanted to live near small barking dogs). She also had a tendency to criticize the community for not being spiritual enough. It was not a good fit for the community and they saw it sooner than she did, but it was still hard for the group to tell her this.

In any case, please know that saying "No" is not that common, and can be difficult for the community as well as for the new person they decline.

If you've paid a joining fee, usually a group will refund it in full if they say "No thanks" to your membership. Again, take the time to find this out at the beginning.

If a group says "No thanks," and you had put all

your hopes and dreams into joining that community, what then? It may take a period of time before you feel like trying again. It may be emotionally difficult to even consider this, but please know that you're now in an excellent position to choose a second community. You know so much more about communities, and probably about yourself, than you did when you first started.

What if you tried to join several communities and were turned down each time? This does happen sometimes. A series of "No thank you's" can be extremely painful and exhausting, and might put you off ever wanting to try again. As difficult as it may be, one way to respond to this repeated response is to interpret it as a message. Is there something you might learn from this rejection? Is it possible you may have some particular behavior, attitude, or energy which generally puts people off? I say this in all respect. If this happens to you, again, it may be a blessing in disguise; it may be a way a kindly universe is trying to give you important, helpful information. If you have physical challenges that may affect your demeanor, such as multiple chemical sensitivities, chronic fatigue syndrome, or liver ailments, or an addiction, if you resolved these issues and tried community again, you might find yourself warmly welcomed. Similarly, if you have long-standing issues of emotional distress that trigger attitudes and behaviors that you haven't been aware of, this can be a painful though important wake-up call to perhaps seek some outside help. Humans can change and heal and grow. People who wouldn't have been accepted into a community in an earlier part of their life can do physical or emotional healing work and become perfectly acceptable new members at a later part of their life. If you think back on your own life, most likely you weren't at all the same person when you first got out of school as you are now.

My guess though, is that if you've read this far, you've got the stuff that communities want, and you'll enjoy your period of provisional membership, stumble relatively infrequently, and enter into your new life in community with grace and delight.

Chapter 25

"The longest, most expensive, personal growth workshop you will ever take!"

OF COURSE your journey to find community doesn't end when you join. As you've probably realized by now, it's only just beginning.

"Community — the longest, most expensive, personal growth workshop you will ever take!" is the oft-repeated phrase coined by cohousing activist Zev Paiss. And it's true. Living in community will most likely change you profoundly. You'll not only live a more sustainable lifestyle, save on expenses, and learn new skills, but you'll shift internally too, in ways you can probably barely guess at now.

You'll experience other people doing and saying things you really enjoy, and cherish. And… you'll find other people doing and saying things that drive you crazy! You may find yourself developing a great aversion to community, or developing increasing reserves of patience and compassion for others. (Or maybe aversion at first, then learning patience, and eventually feeling compassion and connection regardless of other's idiosyncrasies.)

You'll also get feedback yourself, both positive and negative. You'll learn new and wonderful things about yourself, you'll deepen capacities and spread your wings and fly higher. From time to time you'll get critical feedback. It may be delivered gently, by someone with good communication skills, or it may be delivered awkwardly or harshly. If you listen and consider it — regardless of how it's delivered — the feedback may shed light on

and help you face and deal with some of your darkest corners.

My first years of living in community were challenging for all these reasons, and it often still is, but living at Earthaven is now the most joyous and rewarding thing I've ever done. I wouldn't trade it for anything.

As David Franklin writes of his experiences living at Walnut Street Co-op in Eugene, Oregon:

> Maybe the experience of actually getting to be close to people (or even the possibility of being close), of sharing our lives together, overrides any other obstacle that might arise. Maybe our need for connection, family, and tribe is so deep and primal that it makes everything worth it. Instead of living our lives through televisions or computers, we desire real, face-to-face conversations. Rather than living vicariously through fictitious characters or silently stewing in cynicism, we choose to attempt to resolve our difficulties and work together. We choose not to play it safe, to find a way to not be ignorant *and* to be blissful, and to meet basic human needs that are seldom met in our culture."
>
> "Why Does Anyone *Do* This?,"
> *Communities* magazine, Winter, 2004.

As you go forward to join the sustainable community of your dreams, I'd like to share two more short tales of life in community. Each illustrates what I'd like to leave you with — you'll struggle sometimes in your new community, yet you may discover that living in community is one of the most valuable ways you can spend your energy and time. I wish you every good fortune in this wonderful new life.

Community on a Bad Day

By Larry Kaplowitz

On my good days I can often be found waxing poetic about our idyllic life here at Lost Valley Educational Center, our 87-acre community of 20-some people in Dexter, Oregon. I also have my bad days. Sometimes I have a whole string of them. What does a bad day look like for me?

It's been raining non-stop for a week in a month that has seen only three dry days. My wife and children are all irritable and edgy from having spent the whole weekend cooped up in our one-room house. I am frustrated because my "variety in work" has left me with uncompleted projects wherever I look, and my backlog of phone messages and correspondence waiting to be answered has grown to an absurd level, causing me a continual, low-grade sense of guilt. The food orderer has been on vacation and we're out of fruit, vegetables, and bread. Our recent deep freeze, in addition to bursting many pipes, killed most of our over-wintering crops in the gardens. Several community members are sick, in the throes of yet another microbial onslaught, delivered by one of our continual stream of visitors, apprentices, and conference guests who have partaken in our touchy-feely lifestyle. Consequently, every pre-meal circle now ends with a frenzied flight to the washrooms, where we queue up for the anti-bacterial soap to disinfect ourselves from our hygienically corrupt hand-holding. The phones are malfunctioning, causing every other incoming call to get cut off, and our computers all have viruses.

At our morning circle in the kitchen, everyone is soggy and puffy-eyed and the energy is grim. Someone is heating up week-old rice, which is burning in the pan, and another is looking forlornly at the barren toaster. During Lost Valley winters, our primary diversion and comfort is toast, and the empty breadbox is a cruel insult. We circle, and after a long silence during which everyone looks at the floor, someone finally begins a song. Several of us join in despondently, with dirge-like effect, until the song raggedly peters out.

I sometimes think of Lost Valley as a whirling centrifuge, where all our impurities are pushed to the surface at an accelerated pace.

It is Monday morning and on the plate for today are the cheery tasks of trying to figure out why our sewage system, water system, and phone system are all malfunctioning. We also have to work on next year's budget to find a way to recover from our deficit last year, and to once more redesign our organizational structure so we don't end yet another conference season burned out, frustrated, and broke. Several of us are beginning to feel desperate because it seems like it will never get done, should have been completed a month ago, and probably won't work anyway. Add to this mix relationship blowouts, existential crises, automobile breakdowns, lice, pinworms, mysterious rashes, and seemingly irreconcilable philosophical differences, and I begin counting the hours to bedtime.

I sometimes think of Lost Valley as a whirling centrifuge, where all our impurities, both individual and cultural, are pushed to the surface at an accelerated pace, continually erupting to the surface like boils. While this affords tremendous opportunities for growth, self-discovery, and healing, it also makes for an unrelenting intensity, particularly in the summer, when dozens of new people are thrown into the hopper every week. Depending on my mood and frame of mind, this can make for abject agony or blissful ecstasy. And I can switch from one to the other without warning. The community way of life is not for the faint of heart nor the weak of spirit. It is a warrior's path, for those whose vision (or bullheaded stubbornness) is stronger than their desire for comfort. Comfort, however, can be a good thing, and in my weaker moments I have succumbed to thoughts of returning to the good life, from which I bid a hasty retreat five years ago. Then I remember. "Wherever I go, there I am." This is as good as it gets.

Community is not for the faint of heart.

Yet Lost Valley is a functioning, nourishing community. Something is working. Perhaps all this is what it takes to create the space in which our love and compassion can grow. Welcome to community. Applications now being accepted. And don't forget to wash your hands before dinner.

Excerpted with permission from The Permaculture Activist *magazine 1999.*

We Set Out to Change Our World...

by Roberta Wilson

As fate would have it, Winslow Cohousing on Bainbridge Island near Seattle, formed in 1988, ended up being the first owner-developed cohousing community in the U.S. We certainly didn't have much experience to go on. Only one of us had lived in an intentional community, and only a few had even visited any intentional communities. None of us had seen cohousing in Denmark, and of course there were no models of it close to home.

What we had was McCamant and Durrett's *Co-housing* book and an incredible amount of energy.

As with all communities, we made some wise choices and some poor ones. We met every weekend for over two years, with many of us meeting in committees during the week. This vigorous schedule allowed us to buy land, get through the construction process, and move into our 30 duplexes and flats by Spring 1992, but it cost us potential members who couldn't devote such time to development. Finding loans for what looked to financial institutions like some kind of middle-income commune was difficult and may have cost one credit union representative his job. The stress resulting from engaging some of our own members to work for us hurt the group and hurt some of these members as well. Our original group was deeply bonded by the sheer effort of the project. Yet, after move-in we retreated to our individual homes to recuperate. While our idealism had carried us through the forming stages, we weren't quite prepared for the reality of living cooperatively — so many of us were used to having our own way in the world.

We also had the inevitable turnover. We had problems with new residents who either had their own heroic notions, or who soared and then dove as the honeymoon phase ended. We had kids who couldn't get along, a dog that bit, divorces and deaths, births and celebrations. For the most part, our surrounding neighbors were friendly. We figured out a work system, each serving on clusters — Administration, Process and Communication, Grounds, and Common Facilities. We figured out a meal system, with dinners five nights a week. We figured out how to work with consensus. We learned to keep good track of our finances, and we continued to work towards emotional literacy. We still struggle with issues such as member participation and how to make capital improvements, yet our meetings are now civil, efficient, and more emotionally honest. Folks have found their own level after the first years of feeling overwhelmed. Some of them have been disappointed with the lack of emotional intimacy, while others, especially teens, have felt uncomfortable living in a fishbowl.

At times, most of us have probably asked ourselves, "What am I *doing* here?" — a question, I believe, that arises from a complex calculation of time and energy spent and one's tolerance for conflict. Sometimes I've asked myself, after a difficult confrontation, why I should put so much of my life energy into something that seems, at the time, to give back little. Yet I'm sure that at other times each of us has surely declared: "I can't *imagine* living anywhere else!" — a response to the very personal exchanges that make living in community so rewarding. I can call my neighbor and ask her to turn off the coffee pot that I forgot. Chil-

We set out to change our world, and now community is changing us.

dren come to visit and play with my dog. A neighbor pauses from her chores a moment and tells me about her life. In the forest, we scatter the ashes of a member who died; in our orchard, we bury the family dog. A neighbor's sister comes to stay and offers massages. The children are delivered to school by adults who share the duty. Our community feels safe.

The idealism, dreams, and devotion, while still here, have given ground to the practical and the real experience of living in community — the good, the bad, and the ugly. Community is seeping into our cells, I believe, so that even the challenges become just part of who we each are. Cooperative culture is gaining ground over our individual upbringing in competition; slowly, we are giving up the need for absolute control. We set out to change our world, and now community is changing us.

Excerpted with permission from Communities *magazine, Spring 2000.*

Appendix A

Community Membership Documents

These sample community membership documents are offered to give you an idea of what various communities seek in new members, and how they've organized their membership process. These include:

- **New-Member Criteria:** what kind of people and qualities the community is looking for.
- **Rights and Responsibilities of Community Membership:** what you get as a member; what you do in return.
- **Application Forms and Interview Questions:** the questions communities ask to learn more about you and see if you might be a good fit.
- **Membership Processes:** steps you must take to join the community.
- **Membership Agreements:** what a community expects you to abide by once you join.

You'll find differences between urban communities like Mariposa Grove and Walnut Street Co-op and rural communities. Also note that the membership processes of some communities are relatively simple and others are more elaborate.

New-Member Criteria

Red Earth Farms Membership Criteria
(*Red Earth Farms is 4 members on 76 acres of clustered homesteads and farms bordering Dancing Rabbit Ecovillage in rural Northeastern Missouri.*)

Red Earth Farms is still in its youth and the land is raw, so individuals or groups wanting to join Red Earth Farms need initiative, abundant energy, homesteading skills and knowledge, and at least some independent financial resources.

You may be a good fit for our community if you want to be accountable for your impact on the earth, reduce your ecological footprint, or make progress toward a more ecologically sustainable life. You will need to be willing to engage in open, nonviolent communication and conflict resolution. Since we are still in our formative stages, we also would welcome any energy you may have for helping set up our formal systems and structures.

It would be helpful (but not absolutely necessary) for you to already have experience living in community before planning to move here. Also, you should be aware that Red Earth Farms will require a lease payment for the land you live on and caretake, whether up front or over time, so you will need to have financial resources. We are located in a rural area, so you will need to take that into account when planning your source(s) of income.

Mariposa Grove Membership Criteria
(*Mariposa Grove is an urban community of 11 political activists and artists living in 7 housing units and sharing common kitchen/dining and other facilities on 2 adjacent lots in Oakland, California.*)

Mariposa Grove selects people to join our community based on the following criteria. We fully acknowledge that human beings are not creatures of perfection, but we seek people who fulfill many/most of these criteria. Future Mariposa Grove members:

+ Are enthusiastic about living collectively with a diverse group of people.
+ Have collective living experience and/or a strong desire to live collectively.
+ Have other skills and/or experience with collective, cooperative, or consensus-based groups.
+ Have the ability and willingness to commit time for and share equally in household activities: house meetings, chores, shared meals, maintenance/renovations/repair of the land and houses, creation of new legal and organizational systems *and* fun/social time with members.
+ Have the initiative to add beauty and inspiration to the community.
+ Are dedicated to a socially and environmentally responsible lifestyle.
+ Contribute to the diversity of our community.
+ Are kid-friendly and supportive of all types of families.
+ Are able to communicate openly and honestly on a one-to-one basis as well as within a group setting.
+ Are capable of participating in and contributing to consensus decision-making.
+ Respect personal boundaries and those defined by the group as a whole.
+ Have skills in dealing with conflict.
+ Have an interest in and/or talent for vegan and vegetarian cooking.
+ Have an enthusiasm for good food, shared meals, and a vegetarian lifestyle.
+ Are able to make a commitment to the financial responsibilities of living at Mariposa Grove.
+ Are willing and able to comply with community rules, including no smoking in indoor common areas.

+ Are truthful in their public and personal affairs.
+ Have a commitment to nonviolence.
+ Have good communication skills.
+ Have the ability and willingness to remain free of addictive/destructive behaviors.
+ Have an enthusiasm for life and a good sense of humor.
+ Know themselves well enough to communicate effectively about their impact on others.
+ Have an intention to build and experience a growing, learning, supportive, challenging, and spiritually thoughtful community.
+ Are supportive of and comfortable in an environment of people with diverse sexual orientations.
+ Are willing and able to contribute to the long-term sustainability of Mariposa Grove, recognizing that the decisions and actions made by current members may well affect the lives of people living here 5, 25, or 50 years from now.
+ Are compatible with our community's income requirements and have positive credit histories and glowing (good) references.
+ Have involvement in social justice/social change activism.
+ Have skills and/or experience with arts and creativity.
+ Are open to having pets in the community.
+ Have the ability and commitment to become a member of our development corporation, which includes an investment of $5,000.

Rights and Responsibilities of Community Membership

Abundant Dawn Members' Rights and Responsibilities

(Abundant Dawn is a rural community of 6 members on 90 acres near Floyd, in rural southeastern Virginia. The community has several sub-communities, called "pods,"

and distinguishes between consensus group members, who must live on the land at least nine months a year, and members who don't have decision-making rights, because, for example, they might live in the community fewer than nine months a year.)

- Live on Abundant Dawn land and have access to community facilities (community house, pond, animal barn, to be woodshop, etc) and to the land and its resources (drinking water, firewood, garden produce, etc) in accordance with current policies.
- Behave off Abundant Dawn land as they choose unless they are representing Abundant Dawn or using its name.
- Generally attend community meetings and events and participate at the level specified in "Who Attends What" chart.
- Be considered for managerships in community endeavors.
- Participate in any cooperative/bulk food buying that exists.
- Have input into Abundant Dawn membership decisions.
- Have gone through the Abundant Dawn membership process and be a current member of a viable pod.
- Live on Abundant Dawn Land on a designated site in accord with their membership status.
- Have signed the membership contract acknowledging and agreeing to the rights and responsibilities of membership policies of Abundant Dawn.
- Make labor contributions to the Community under the current form(s) of accountability. Accountability may be held at the pod and/or individual level.
- Contribute financially to the Community mostly through their pods according to the Formula Policy and other financial policies.

Members are individually responsible for their $300 security deposit.

- Be willing to participate in conflict resolution, keeping the vision statement in mind. See discussion in Conflict paper for limits and guidelines.
- Generally attend community functions and participate at the level specified in the "Who Attends What" chart.
- Familiarize themselves with the agreements and policies in the policy notebook.
- Remain a member unless they voluntarily leave or are expelled by defined community or pod process, except for non-consensus group members if accepted for a time-limited period.
- Take sabbaticals as outlined later in this document.
- Have per person fees reduced because of Longevity.
- Accumulate and collect upon leaving from the Leaving Fund in accordance with current agreements.
- Consensus Group Members also have rights to participate in the activities of the Consensus Group including making decisions about community issues.

Application Forms and Interview Questions

Walnut Street Co-op: Questions for Prospective Housemates

(Walnut Street Co-op is an urban group household of nine members and housemates in a large house in Eugene, Oregon. Four members are co-op co-owners; others are tenants.)

- What calls to you about the idea of living here?
- What are your concerns about it?
- What is your previous group living experience?

- What is your relationship like with your family?
- What have you accomplished in your life that you feel proud of?
- What are your pet peeves, things around the house that might really annoy you?
- What do you think other people might find irritating or hard to live with about you?
- How is your financial situation? Do you have stable income? If you lost a job, how many months' worth of savings do you have on hand?
- What kinds of projects can you imagine getting excited about around the house?
- Are you willing to commit to not leaving dishes in the kitchen and other public spaces?
- Where are you on the neat and clean vs. cluttered scale?
- How do you feel about living with people who are queer or polyamorous?
- Do you have any experience with consensus decision-making process? (And how do you feel about it?)
- If you are feeling frustrated or upset with someone, how do you decide whether or not to bring it up with them?
- The house has a clear expectation of making efforts to resolve interpersonal conflicts. Are you willing to do that?
- Have you read the policy notebook? Are there any agreements that you have concerns about?
- What is your average video consumption? Are you ok confining video usage (including on computers) to private rooms? And closing the door to avoid impacting other housemates with the noise from it?
- Are you ok with monthly work parties, currently on Saturday mornings for 3 hours?
- How do you feel about committing to being at the house meeting every week (unless you on a trip out of town)?
- What kind of hours do you tend to keep?
- Where are you on the noise spectrum, both as a creator of noise and in terms of your personal sensitivity to noise? Are you a light or heavy sleeper?
- Do you have any food allergies, restrictions, or major sensibilities? Are you ok with cooking every week?
- We do not allow illegal drugs on our property, period. That means making sure that your friends don't bring any over either. How do you expect that would impact your life?
- Can you tell us some about your mental health history?
- What else do you want us to know about you?

Membership Processes

Procedure to Become a Resident at The Farm

(*The Farm is a rural spiritual community of 175 members on 1,750 acres in central Tennessee. Full members must first get permission to live onsite as residents, and the process below is for that first step.*)

1. Visit The Farm several times in order to become acquainted with the community and individual members within the community.
2. Arrange a personal interview with a Membership Committee member stating their desire to move to the community. Following consultation with the rest of the committee, this request is encouraged or denied.
3. Write a letter of introduction and intent to the community. This letter includes a biographical sketch, method of livelihood, and their vision of what they hope to contribute to the community. Upon receipt of this letter, a file will be started on the applicant. Copies of this letter will be posted by the secretary at the Farm Post Office for one month and published in the community's Free Press newsletter for two weeks.

4. Following the publication of the introduction notice, the applicant continues to visit the community and attend community functions. At this time they need to find a sponsor who will vouch for their character and help integrate them into the community.

5. The applicant and their sponsor formally meets with the Membership Committee and applies for residency.

6. The Membership Committee votes on whether or not to continue the application process. If approved, the applicant is sent a residency packet to be completed, which contains: Application Form, Financial Disclosure Form, TRW information for a credit check, Medical History sheet, sample Residency Contract, notice of $25 processing fee. The application should be returned within one month.

7. Upon receipt of completed forms and the application fee, applicant will be given: Letter of Acknowledgement from the secretary, original of the residency papers filed in the applicant's folder, financial forms given to the Finance Committee for review and clarification.

8. Upon return of financial forms from the Finance Committee, the application is reviewed. The applicant meets with the Committee or has a telephone conference with Community members to answer any unresolved questions. When all issues are resolved, the applicant will be approved for residency.

9. Prior to moving to The Farm the Residency Contract should be signed and sent to the Membership Committee along with the first and twelfth month's rent.

Extended-stay visitors and Provisional Members are asked to find a member of the community to be their Sponsor. A sponsor must be a resident Full Member. Responsibilities of Sponsorship: (1) Will take an active role in notifying new resident(s) of all community meetings and gathering, and facilitate participation. (2) Will act as an interface with the community or individual members, should the need arise. (3) Will take an active role in seeing that the resident is gainfully employed and paying their community dues.

Whole Village Membership Process
(Whole Village is a rural ecovillage of 28 people on 200 acres near Caledon, Ontario, Canada.)

Members have fulfilled all obligations for membership and have purchased a share of Whole Village Property Co-operative Ltd. Provisional members are essentially potential members who wish to be on a waiting list.

In order for a person or family to become a Full Member of the Whole Village, they must fulfill the following conditions:

A. Attend an Orientation Session and be assigned a mentor from the current membership.

B. Attend at least six meetings in not less than three months.

C. Fill out a New Member's questionnaire, including an up to date biography.

D. Have their personal portion of the questionnaire distributed to current members.

E. Be accepted as a member by the Round (whole group).

F. Purchase a share in Whole Village Ltd. ($10,000), pay a catch up amount of $2,000 for back dues, and pay dues and make loans to Whole Village Ltd. as required.

G. Be inducted into Whole Village at a welcoming ceremony, signing the Founders' Document.

H. Take a seat on the Board of Directors of the co-operative.

Provisional members (those on a waiting list to be members), will fulfill (A) to (D) above, be accepted as a Subscriber by the Round (whole group), pay a refundable deposit ($1,000), non-refundable monthly dues ($50), and be officially welcomed by the Round. They will then be able to attend all meetings and participate in discussions but will not be able to vote or block consensus.

Becoming a Member at EcoVillage at Ithaca

(*EcoVillage at Ithaca is a semi-rural community comprised of 162 members in 2 clustered 30-unit cohousing communities on 175 acres just outside Ithaca, New York. Because this community offers cohousing units on the open market the process is much less elaborate than in communities who have more rights in choosing or rejecting potential members.*)

Prospective residents, both buyers and renters, participate in a structured learning process before deciding to live at EcoVillage at Ithaca. The goal of the process is to provide prospective residents with enough personalized information to decide for themselves whether the community is the right place for them. The first steps in the learning process are:

+ Learning about our mission and principles by reading this website thoroughly.
+ Taking a tour of EcoVillage at Ithaca.
+ Visiting overnight and participating in community activities.

Each cohousing neighborhood has additional requirements, and additional steps may be required for prospective buyers.

Lost Valley Educational Center's Membership Process

(*Lost Valley Educational Center is a rural conference and retreat center community valuing ecological sustainability and good group process, with 24 members on 87 acres located near Eugene, Oregon.*)

Bringing new people into our community is a serious commitment on both sides and we try to do our best in inviting people into our extended family who are likely to be successful. By design, our process is comprised of gradual steps to bring new people into greater knowledge of themselves and of our community while we also get to know them as individuals.

The process often begins with a call, letter, or email in which a person expresses an interest. People then sometimes come for a tour or short visit or a weekend workshop. Then they typically attend a Community Experience Week, occasionally followed by one or two additional weeks to experience living in community. This is followed by an application for our Prospective Membership Months. If invited, prospective members live with us for three months before seeking acceptance into our year-long Exploring Membership process. At the end of this year the person may become a full Long Term Member. At the beginning of the Exploring Member and Long-Term Member steps, there is an in-depth review with the entire community, and acceptance into either of these membership categories requires the full consensus of all current Long Term Members.

Membership Agreements

Dancing Rabbit Membership Agreement

(*Dancing Rabbit Ecovillage is a rural ecovillage of 25 people on 280 acres in Northeastern Missouri. One needs to first become a resident on the land before applying for full membership.*)

As a member of Dancing Rabbit, Inc.:

+ I agree to help Dancing Rabbit achieve its stated goals and mission.
+ I agree to pay dues (money and time) as set by the membership, in a timely manner.

- I will participate in an inclusive democratic decision making structure of Dancing Rabbit government (or consciously waive my right to express my opinions) and abide by the decisions made, including those made before my membership in Dancing Rabbit. I understand that a democratic government depends on the integrity of its participants and their commitment to the ideals of trust, respect, self-empowerment, cooperation, equal access to power, and non-violence.
- I agree to give up my membership upon request of the members and according to the process outlined in Dancing Rabbit's Bylaws.
- I agree to resolve conflict peacefully and be open to the use of mediation.
- I am committed to pioneering a lifestyle that will serve as an example of ecological sustainability, as explained in the Sustainability Guidelines. I will weigh the implications of my actions, continually striving to minimize my negative impact and increase my positive impact on the Earth. I will participate in the creation of a physical and social structure and culture that will move us towards long term sustainability.
- I am committed to the vision of diverse membership of Dancing Rabbit and will not discriminate against any person on the basis of race, ethnicity, religion, sex, sexual orientation, creed, age, ability, educational level, or economic background. I will attempt to minimize barriers to members of minority groups wishing to participate.
- I understand that part of the Dancing Rabbit mission is to serve as an example of sustainable living through outreach and education. I understand that Dancing Rabbit will continually pursue this goal by being open to new members (as resources allow), guests, and visitors and by publicizing the actions and activities of our community.

CONTACTS FOR COMMUNITIES CITED IN APPENDIX A

- Red Earth Farms, Rutledge, Missouri. *redearthfarms.org*
- Mariposa Grove, Oakland, California. *healthyarts.com/mariposagrove*
- Abundant Dawn, Floyd, Virginia. *abundantdawn.org*
- Walnut Street Co-op, Eugene, Oregon. *icetree.com/walnut*
- The Farm, Summertown, Tennessee. *www.thefarmcommunity.com*

- Whole Village, Caledon, Ontario. *wholevillage.org*
- EcoVillage at Ithaca, New York. *ecovillage.ithaca.ny.us*
- Lost Valley Educational Center, Dexter, Oregon. *lostvalley.org*
- Dancing Rabbit Ecovillage, Rutledge, Missouri. *dancingrabbit.org*

Appendix B

Can Living in Community Make a Difference in an Age of Peak Oil?

Can it make a difference to the planet, and to energy usage overall, that some of us living in communities conserve energy, share resources, grow food, and employ other ecologically sustainable practices to create a smaller ecological footprint? I think so. But because there are relatively few communities at present, it probably doesn't make much difference overall, at least not yet. At the same time, no great historical movements ever started without *some* people getting the ball rolling, so it might as well be us. I like to think that we who live in communities and might be living more lightly on the Earth, might be part of a grassroots movement that ultimately makes a huge difference. At least, it's heartening to proceed as if this were so.

Another question is, can living in community make a difference in terms of how comfortable or safe one might feel during increasingly tough economic times stemming from dwindling supplies of oil? Here's what Richard Heinberg says in *The Party's Over: Oil, War, and the Fate of Industrial Societies.* "Life in an intentional community could offer many advantages... Association with like-minded people in a context of mutual aid could help overcome many of the challenges that will arise as the larger society undergoes turmoil and reorganization. Moreover, new cooperative, low-energy ways of living can be implemented now, without having to wait for a majority of people in the larger society to awaken to the necessity for

change." He goes on to recommend ecovillages, including Findhorn, Mitraniketan in India, EcoVillage at Ithaca, The Farm, Earthaven, and Dancing Rabbit.

In *Powerdown: Options and Actions for a Post-Carbon World*, Heinberg mentions friends of his in various intentional communities and ecovillages worldwide who are pursuing "Powerdown" and "Building Lifeboat" strategies simultaneously. "While they engage in activism on many fronts," he writes, "participating vigorously in the anti-globalization, peace, and environmental movements — they also have established rural bases where they save heirloom seeds, build their own homes from natural and locally available materials, and hone other life-support skills that they and future generations will need. I admire those people unreservedly: if there is a sane path from where we are to a truly sustainable future, these folks have surely found it."

I frankly don't know if people living in ecovillages or intentional communities will be any better off during energy decline than people living in mainstream culture, or if so, to what extent, and for how long. My friend Jan Steinman and I considered the pros and cons of these issues in our editorial, "Community Survival During the Coming Energy Decline," in the Spring 2006 Peak Oil issue of *Communities* magazine. Essentially, Jan and I do think communitarians will be better off than many others on the planet, but perhaps not as well off as communities — or people who want to join them — might think.

Community Survival During the Coming Energy Decline

"Well, we've got off-grid power from solar panels and wind power," a community might say, "and we've got wood stoves, too. No matter how high the price of gas goes, we'll be fine."

Perhaps, but does the community buy any food items they don't grow themselves? While its members can certainly bicycle, car-pool, or use biodiesel to get to the local food co-op, are any of these food items grown, processed, or packaged in other regions? If so, they'll pay for the ever-increasing cost of transporting these items into their area. The same is true if the community uses local suppliers for seeds, soil amendments, fencing, hand tools, or other gardening supplies that originate elsewhere, or building supplies from other regions — from lumber to cement blocks to electrical supplies and PVC pipe.

But this is only considering the rising price of *gasoline*. It's harder to grasp, but equally true, that the cost of all manufactured goods *themselves* will steadily increase in price — because manufactured goods are tied to the price of oil. Why? First there's the electricity used in factories to manufacture things: the electric power in most regions of the world is generated in power plants fueled by non-renewable fossil fuel such as oil and coal. Second, there's the use of metal in manufactured items, which must be mined, smelted, and formed into parts — all of which requires electrical power. The same is true of rubber, machine oil, glass, and other materials used in manufactured goods — not to mention the silicon used in items from solar panels to computer chips. Third, there's the plastic used in manufactured items themselves and the plastic used in the packaging and shipping

of such items — since plastic itself is made from oil.

What happens when a community's wind turbine or inverter needs a new part? Most likely its members are used to clicking a mouse or picking up a phone, finding the part hundreds or thousands of miles away, performing an electronic transaction that depends on the fossil-fuel-powered infrastructures of electricity, telecommunications, and banking, and then a large brown truck — powered by fossil fuel — brings the part in a week or so. But with the coming energy decline it won't be so easy.

And even if the community did happen to have an "Off-Grid Power Parts 'R Us" franchise nearby, does that retail outlet actually mine the copper, aluminum, iron, tin, cobalt, antimony, beryllium, niobium, and various other metals that they smelt, forge, and extrude into wind turbine or inverter parts? Do they have equally basic methods for obtaining any rubber, plastic, glass, or silicon required for these parts? And if they do happen to have such parts on hand, their seeming availability just masks the dependence on fossil-fuel-driven infrastructure that goes to the very core of our civilization.

Well, you get the picture. But there's more. Many rural communities are already growing at least some of their own food, however, this is usually vegetables, and usually in the summer — few communities also have produce year-round, or grow or raise their own protein, fat, or grain-based carbohydrates. In mainstream culture, outside of the tiny percentage of food that's organically grown, the entire food industry (and thus, the world's burgeoning population) is totally dependent on fossil fuel. That's because most non-organic fertilizer is either made from the byproducts of refining oil or from natural gas. As a civilization, we are literally *eating* fossil fuel, from the natural gas that produces virtually all commercial fertilizer; to the diesel farm machinery that prepares the land, weeds the crops, and harvests and distributes the yield; to the energy-intensive processing, packaging, and distribution networks that get the food to us.

All told, about ten calories of fossil fuel goes into each single calorie of food we eat (not counting fuel used for cooking). And make that ratio at least 100:1 for heavily processed foods.

So agribiz-grown food (even though we communitarians don't eat it), heating oil for home furnaces (even though we choose renewable heating sources), manufactured goods (even though we eschew most of them), and transportation fuel (even though we car-pool or bicycle), all affect the greater economy. And most ecovillages and intentional communities are embedded to some degree in the greater economy — whether we intend it or not — and the greater economy is completely driven by fossil fuels. And it's not just the economy — it's almost everything we take for granted in our lives: modern medicine (antibiotics, anesthetics, insulin, glasses, hearing aids); holistic medicine (nutritional supplements, Chinese herbs); communications (telephone lines, electronic switching equipment, satellite dishes, satellites themselves, computers, networks, modems, servers); law and order (police cars, police communication systems, police officers' salaries), the ability to govern — these are but a few examples of non-obvious things we take for granted that are totally dependent on fossil fuels.

This means, of course, that as the supplies of fossil fuels become more scarce, and the price of oil and natural gas goes up, *everything* will become more expensive. As the economy worsens, many businesses will severely downsize or even shut down because they can no longer afford parts, repairs, or needed services. Thousands of people, then tens of thousands, then hundreds of thou-

sands, will lose their jobs. Thus while living in an ecovillage or other kind of intentional community may make us less reliant on the typical energy sources and commercial products of mainstream life, it is *not* automatic protection from the coming energy decline. The Great Depression of the 1930s and the gasoline shortages of the 1970s were just warm-up acts for what is coming — the permanent, irrevocable decline of fossil fuels.

And it will impact those of us living in intentional communities — whether or now we grow our own food or are off the grid.

"But at least we've got our wood heat," a community might say. "At least *that's* renewable!" Yes, but for how long, and at what cost? Throughout history, civilizations have gotten into deep trouble by "timber mining" at unsustainable levels. The Greeks, for example, once lived on fertile forested mountains and islands. After centuries of logging their forests for homes, ship-building, and firewood, they used up their timber resources, and the forests did not grow back and Greece became the relatively arid landscape it still is today. It is only since the availability of fossil fuels in the mid-1850s that the population on every inhabited continent has been able to grow much larger without disastrous timber harvests.

If the price of the natural gas that heats many of the homes in North America goes up by a factor of ten, how many trees are going to be left standing when people start burning every tree in sight just to stay warm? (And, in such a case, who will be able to breathe the air?) Keep in mind that there are about ten times the number of people on the planet now as there were when humanity last depended entirely on wood for energy!

Although things look bleak for current generations, Peak Oil offers humanity an opportunity to learn and prepare for the inevitable Peak Coal that will impact generations to come. It's too late to hope for a pleasant decline from Peak Oil, but if we pay attention, humanity may choose to plan for a long and orderly Peak Coal.

Is Intentional Community the Answer?
Julian Darley, author of *High Noon for Natural Gas* and founder of the Post Carbon Institute, believes civilization is necessarily headed down the path of "re-localization"; that is, reversing the energy-fed globalization trend that has wracked the Earth for the past century or so. Those who already enjoy a measure of self-sufficiency, such as ecovillages and other kinds of sustainable intentional communities as well as sustainably organized neighborhoods, will already have the skills and experience needed for re-localization.

"This is a time of tremendous challenge," says Richard Heinberg, author of *The Party's Over* and *Powerdown*, "but also a time of great opportunity." In *Powerdown*, Heinberg notes that small, self-sustaining communities may become cultural lifeboats in times to come. "Our society is going to change profoundly — those of us who understand this are in a position to steward that change. We are going to become popular, needed people in our communities." When asked at a Peak Oil conference in 2005 about what can be done, Heinberg replied, "Start an ecovillage!"

These changes are not going to happen overnight. James Howard Kunstler, author of *The Long Emergency*, calls the coming energy decline a "long emergency" because it is occurring almost too gradually for most of us to register. The energy decline is often compared to the metaphor about boiling frogs: if you want to cook frogs and you put them in boiling water, they will immediately hop out, but if you put frogs in room-temperature water and only gradually turn up the heat, the frogs will stay in the water — not noticing it's gradually getting warmer — and slowly cook to death.

We could say this is happening to our civilization at large. Most of us have a vague feeling that things in general are getting worse, but from minute-to-minute, day-to-day, and even year-to-year, the worsening is not enough to get us to change our energy-consuming ways.

The Trends Research Institute, a network of interdisciplinary experts who forecast developing trends, echoes Darley's prediction for "re-localization." One of the hottest trends they see is a "rapidly growing desire of more people to be self-empowered, non-reliant, and off the grid," in the broadest possible sense, as in "off the grid" of mainstream society. Such as, for example, ecovillages, sustainable intentional communities, and organized neighborhoods.

"It's time to return to the community," says Pat Murphy, executive director of The Community Solution, "to clean up the mess and get back on the right path." Murphy ended his organization's second annual conference on "Peak Oil and the Community Solution" by noting that the survivors of this crisis will be those who seek out a "low-energy, caring, community way of living."

Humanity faces its biggest challenge since at least World Wars I and II, or perhaps even since the great plagues of the Middle Ages, or perhaps ever. No matter how prepared an intentional community may be, it will be adversely impacted in some way.

Is Intentional Community Enough?
Experts suggest numerous scenarios for the coming energy decline. These range from a "magical elixir" scenario — a totally unexpected technological fix, to a "power-down soft landing" scenario of everyone cooperating to reduce energy use by perhaps 90 percent or more, to a "Mad Max" scenario of anarchy and insurrection. Some even whisper the possibility of human extinction, since by most

measures, we have overshot our resource base, a situation that ecologists believe is often a cause of extinction. But the point is, any of these scenarios will present significant challenges for intentional communities.

In the "soft landing" scenario, there will still be massive structural changes in society, with winners and losers. In this and other scenarios, being in debt may be the undoing of many. Let's say a community is deeply in debt, for example, and is still paying off its property purchase or one or more construction loans. Let's say the community loses its financial resource base — if many members lose their jobs, for example, or if a weak economy reduces the market for the goods and services the community produces — the group could default on its loan payments and may have its property seized by the bank or other creditors. Common advice among Peak Oil experts is to get out of debt! (Although a vocal minority say you should take on as much fixed-interest debt as possible, in the hope that escalating energy prices will inflate the debt away.)

A property-value crash may worsen the debt situation for intentional communities. During the last oil crisis, the market value of prime farmland fell by 30 percent or more. If a community's property value falls below their equity in the property, they won't be able to save themselves from defaulting on loans by selling off their land, which is typically the last resort of farmers in debt. (Again, a vocal minority claims that as energy prices escalate, fertile farmland will also increase in value.)

All the shortages and systems failures that can affect mainstream culture can affect intentional communities as well. Clearly just "living in community" will not confer any kind of immunity from this gradual but drastic change. A community in a mountain forest setting may have plenty of water and firewood, for example, but little flat, arable land for growing food. A community on the prairie may have plenty of fertile, arable land, but little firewood. A community in the Great Plains may have plenty of sunshine for passive solar heating and off-grid power from solar-panels, but not enough firewood or water for growing food. A rural community may have enough space to grow food but little help from local emergency food-distribution networks; an urban community or organized neighborhood may have little place to grow vegetables, but proximity to emergency food distribution networks and local government assistance. But any community may not have enough foresight, labor, tools, or funds to create alternatives to whatever their members use now for heating, lighting, cooking, refrigeration, water collection, water pumping, and disposing of graywater and human waste.

Then there's the matter of community security — a subject many find "politically incorrect" even to consider. Many communities that embrace nonviolence may find it difficult to nonviolently defend their community in the face of anarchy or insurrection in the society around them. If the local government fails or if a local law and order system falls apart, there can be various kinds of dangerous consequences. Desperate, hungry people can loot and steal and take what they want from others. Vigilante groups can form to either deal with the lawlessness, or take what they want themselves. State or national government can declare martial law, rescind constitutional liberties, send in troops, and restore order or take what they want from others. Having supportive neighbors and good networking in the greater community may help. But in the worst-case, "Mad Max" scenario, it may not help much.

Embracing weaponry for self-defense may not be useful, either, as the presence of weapons and ammunition may simply make one a more attractive target of people who want to get their hands on the community's weapons.

Another, much more basic and subtle challenge to preparing for the coming energy decline is even being able to, as Richard Heinberg advises, "start an ecovillage" in the first place! It's really hard to start a new community in today's political, cultural, and financial environment. Land prices are exorbitant and getting more so every day. Zoning restrictions, designed to protect homeowners' property values, can severely limit a group's ability to create the community they want with the numbers of people they need. Building codes, designed to protect a county from lawsuits from approving unsafe buildings, and county and state health codes, designed to keep people safe from biological and other health hazards, can stop a community's sustainability plans faster than you can say, "That's illegal!" And the all-too-human tendency to bring habitual reactive and destructive behaviors to community settings — making it hard to get along well and resolve inevitable conflicts — can make cooperating with friends or neighbors, especially in frightening and desperate times, even more challenging than it normally is.

It is also difficult to radically change one's energy-consuming lifestyle. It may be easy to think, "I'd like to join an ecovillage some day" or "I'll stop depending so much on fossil fuels and live a more sustainable lifestyle soon," yet it's easy to become inexorably distracted from that goal by the demands of jobs, family, and other responsibilities. Tearing oneself away from the status quo may be the most difficult thing we can ever do. Once we make the break, resisting the allure of today's cheap-energy lifestyle can be a constant effort.

Yet we must. The experts agree: the future will have more in common with the 18th century than it does with the 20th. Societal upheavals will favor those who have prepared over those who come to realization late, without building community and sustainability skills.

In just a century and a half, humanity has spent down about half of its "bank account" of formerly cheap energy that has taken millions of years to accumulate. This may be our species' greatest crisis ever, and there will be a very few winners, and possibly billions of losers over the rest of our lives and longer. The winners will be either those with the power to hoard much of the remaining fossil energy, or those with the foresight, knowledge, resources, and will to live within the Earth's sustainable energy budget.

We certainly have no answers, solutions, or magic bullets for this dilemma. We both believe it's better to live cooperatively and sustainably with others, but we don't know what else is needed to truly be prepared for the inevitable energy decline. Is it better to be widely connected with one's neighbors and bioregion, or isolated and inaccessible? Is it better to grow all of one's own food and generate all of one's own energy, or to create a tight web of trade and barter relationships with one's friends and neighbors, supplying some of what they need and vice-versa? We are sure of one thing though: people who understand what is happening, and act with others of like mind to build sustainable agriculture, culture, and energy systems — in right relationship with the Earth's finite energy resources — will have at least a chance to live fulfilling lives in these challenging times.

Excerpted with permission from Communities *magazine, Spring 2006, by Jan Steinman and Diana Leafe Christian. Jan Steinman is a founding member of EcoReality Co-op on Salt Spring Island, British Columbia: EcoReality.org*

Index

About the Author

Diana Leafe Christian, editor since 1993 of *Communities*, a magazine about intentional communities in North America, is also author of *Creating a Life Together: Practical Tools to Grow Ecovillages and Intentional Communities* (New Society Publishers, 2003). She gives presentations on ecovillages and offers workshops and consultations nationwide on the practical steps to start successful new ecovillages and intentional communities (including mission and purpose, decision-making, communication skills, legal structures, and finding and financing land) and on how to research, visit, evaluate, and join a community. Her articles on ecovillages and intentional communities have appeared in publications ranging from *Mother Earth News*, *Communities*, and *Earthlight* magazines to the Encyclopedia of Community. Her work has been cited in the *New York Times*, *Harper's*, *AARP* magazine, New Dimensions Radio, NPR, and the BBC. Diana lives in an off-grid homesite at Earthaven Ecovillage in the mountains near Asheville, North Carolina. DianaLeafeChristian.org.

If you have enjoyed *Finding Community*
you might also enjoy other

BOOKS TO BUILD A NEW SOCIETY

Our books provide positive solutions for people who want to
make a difference. We specialize in:

**Environment and Justice • Conscientious Commerce
Sustainable Living • Ecological Design and Planning
Natural Building & Appropriate Technology • New Forestry
Educational and Parenting Resources • Nonviolence
Progressive Leadership • Resistance and Community**

New Society Publishers

ENVIRONMENTAL BENEFITS STATEMENT

New Society Publishers has chosen to produce this book on Enviro 100, recycled paper made with **100% post consumer waste**, processed chlorine free, and old growth free.

For every 5,000 books printed, New Society saves the following resources:[1]

33	Trees
2,995	Pounds of Solid Waste
3,296	Gallons of Water
4,299	Kilowatt Hours of Electricity
5,445	Pounds of Greenhouse Gases
23	Pounds of HAPs, VOCs, and AOX Combined
8	Cubic Yards of Landfill Space

---

[1]Environmental benefits are calculated based on research done by the Environmental Defense Fund and other members of the Paper Task Force who study the environmental impacts of the paper industry.

For a full list of NSP's titles, please call **1-800-567-6772** *or check out our website at:*

www.newsociety.com

NEW SOCIETY PUBLISHERS